# The Morals of History

Tzvetan Todorov

*Translated by Alyson Waters*

University of Minnesota Press
Minneapolis
London

The University of Minnesota Press gratefully acknowledges assistance provided for the translation of this book by the French Ministry of Culture.

Originally published as *Les Morales de l'histoire* copyright 1991 by Editions Grasset & Fasquelle, Paris.

Published by the University of Minnesota Press
111 Third Avenue South, Suite 290, Minneapolis, MN 55401-2520
Printed in the United States of America on acid-free paper

Library of Congress Cataloging-in-Publication Data

Todorov, Tzvetan, 1939–
    [Morales de l'histoire. English]
    The morals of history / Tzvetan Todorov ; translated by Alyson Waters.
        p.    cm.
    Translation of: Les morales de l'histoire.
    Includes bibliographical references and index.
    ISBN 0-8166-2297-3 (hc.) — ISBN 0-8166-2298-1 (pbk.)
    1. History—Philosophy.   2. Comparative civilization.   I. Title.
D16.8.T5713   1995
909—dc20                                                    94-28977

# Contents

# Translator's Note

The original title of this work — *Les Morales de l'histoire* — is a play on the phrases "the moral of the story" and "the morals of history," that is, the moral lessons we can learn from the past. I have kept only the latter meaning in my translation, since it seems to be the dominant chord Todorov wishes to strike.

In the interest of obviating notes, titles and page numbers of works from which Tzvetan Todorov quotes appear in the text. Complete bibliographic information can be found in the Works Cited.

For quotations from works written in Russian, German, French, or Spanish, I have used a published English translation whenever possible. These books and articles are referred to in the text by their English titles, and page numbers given are those of the translations; the Works Cited lists these translations. When necessary, I have worked from the quotations in French that appeared in *Les Morales de l'histoire,* occasionally consulting the original-language text; these titles appear in the original language, with an English translation following in parentheses where appropriate.

I would like to thank Allison Tait for her research assistance and Roger Celestin and Gwenaël Kerlidou for their advice throughout.

# The Moral and Political Sciences

A slight change in terminology occurred precisely at the time of the French Revolution of 1789. It was then that the expressions "social sciences" and "human sciences" appeared for the first time, replacing the traditional "moral and political sciences." The revolutionary context is not called to mind arbitrarily: the new label could be found in the writings of some of the major philosophers and politicians of that time. The most important figure for our purposes is Condorcet, heir to the Encyclopedist spirit and theorist of the new state. The phrase "social sciences" is found in a letter written by Joseph Garat to Condorcet. (Garat later became part of the Ideologues circle, who were in turn close to Condorcet.) Condorcet himself adopted the phrase in *Esquisse d'un tableau historique des progrès de l'esprit humain* (Sketch for a historical picture of the progress of the human mind). It was then taken up by Auguste Comte, and from him was handed down to the scholars of the twentieth century.

It may be that the substitution in terminology had no particular significance for these authors. For us, however, it is difficult not to notice that it coincided with a growing tendency to free the study of man and society from any normative project. Although they may be purely descriptive, the terms *moral* and *political* generally imply a value judgment. Like the other sciences, the human sciences—those that would later be called psychology and sociology, anthropology, and history—were striving to free themselves from any ideological influence, whether religious or political; this is why a name that designates only the specificity of its object—the human, the social—was preferable to terms that were reminiscent of a particular discourse whose finality was prescriptive rather than simply descriptive.

In so doing, these disciplines were merely following—although somewhat belatedly—in the wake of all the other sciences; they were simply following the trail that had been blazed by the astonishing success of their elders. The stories are well known: Copernicus did not dare publish the results of his observations and calculations that advocated a heliocentric conception of the world for fear of offending the religious hierarchy; Giordano Bruno was burned at the stake for having declared that the universe was infinite and had no center; Galileo was forced to repudiate his findings even though he was certain of their truth. In each of these cases, ideological intervention (embodied by Catholic orthodoxy) was detrimental to the progress of knowledge; reciprocally, science advances all the more rapidly as it is freed from religious influence, relying solely on its own laws: empirical observation and logical reasoning.

Of course, such a powerful movement could not leave understanding of the human world unscathed. In Galileo's century, Spinoza brought the debate to the humanists and furthermore, onto the most perilous ground imaginable, the interpretation of the Bible. In contrast to traditional exegetical schools, which took it for granted that the Holy Book related official Christian doctrine in all instances, Spinoza called for a new method of investigation in this area also. Of what was this new method to consist? In his *Theological-Political Treatise,* Spinoza affirmed that the new method was to be similar to the one used for "interpreting nature." In other words, this interpretation relinquished explaining what the meaning of the biblical text *must* be; it relinquished, therefore, using a preestablished truth as a means of analysis, and contented itself with collecting impartial information about the meaning of words at the time of the Book's creation, about the historical circumstances in which this creation took place, and about the relations that existed between the different passages of the same book. Instead of *using* doctrinal "truth" to clarify the meaning of obscure passages and arrive at the edification of believers, Spinoza wanted to use the naturalists' methods — observation and reasoning — to *seek* the truth of the text; the edification of the faithful was no longer part of his ostensible concerns. The goal of knowledge was truth, not good.

With the exception of a few rare instances of militant obscurantism, the freedom of the natural sciences seems to have become, since Galileo's time, a generally accepted principle. The explanation is simple: this is how these sciences progress most rapidly and achieve the practical results that benefit the states in which the scientists live. Granted, the usefulness of the human sciences *is* less obvious; and it is not clear that this usefulness grows proportionately to freedom from ideological influence. Whether for this reason or another, the principle of autonomy from ideology, freedom from the world of values, still seems to meet with unforeseen obstacles here. In point of fact, the continued appeals for these human sciences to align themselves with the natural sciences attest to this. In the eighteenth century, Helvétius found it necessary to reiterate Spinoza's plea and did not understand why moral science — the study of customs (mores) — could not be included among the other sciences. "I imagined that morality should be treated like all other sciences, and founded on experiment" (*De l'esprit;* or, *Essays on the Mind and Its Several Faculties,* iii). A few decades later, Condorcet took up the cry once again: why, he wondered, should the study of man escape scientific understanding as it is applied in other areas? In both cases, findings could achieve the same certainty. In the middle of the nineteenth century, the idea was still expressed in the imperative: "History must be made to enter into the family of natural sciences," wrote Gobineau in his *Essai sur l'inégalité des races humaines* (1152). And his contemporary Hippolyte Taine offered this now famous comparison: "No matter if the facts be physical or moral, they all have their causes: there is a cause for ambition, for courage, for truth, as there is for digestion, for muscular movement, for animal heat. Vice and virtue are products like vitriol and sugar" (*Histoire de la littérature anglaise,* 1:xv).

In the twentieth century, the age of science triumphant, the appeals to order addressed to recalcitrant specialists in humanitarian disciplines are too numerous to count. One of these appeals—found in the last text by Marc Bloch, a father of the "new history" who became a victim of the fight against Hitlerism—must be mentioned here because of the dramatic circumstances surrounding its writing. From the start of his *Apologie pour l'histoire, ou Métier d'historien,* Bloch stigmatized what he called the "satanic enemy of true history: the mania of judgment" (7), and he brought it up again and again. "When the scientist has observed and explained, his task is ended" (69), he wrote. Further, "Robespierrists, anti-Robespierrists, we beg you for mercy: for pity's sake, tell us, simply, what Robespierre was" (70). Or again, he railed: "Were they [historical characters] right or wrong? What does the belated decision of a historian matter to me? . . . The lesson from the intellectual development of humanity is clear nonetheless: the sciences have always proved to be more fruitful—and, as a result, more obliging to practice in the end—the more deliberately they abandoned the old anthropocentrism of good and evil" (71).

The best minds appear unanimous, and yet the desired evolution of the human sciences is slow in coming. Before attempting to discover why it is so difficult to eliminate value judgments from the knowledge of man, however, and why one cannot manage to talk about vice and virtue with the requisite impartiality—the same impartiality of the chemist analyzing vitriol or sugar—it may be useful to ask oneself if the above representation of the relations between science and ideology (under any name: religion, moral, political) is, in fact, faithful to reality. Have science and ideology really become autonomous, each acting independently in its own domain? Or, rather, has a new situation arisen? Perhaps science, taking revenge on its old mistress, has not been content to act as it sees fit, but has usurped the master's place and forced its previous occupant into a new servitude. In short, has science simply ceased to be dominated, or has it, in addition, become dominant?

The question warrants asking when one reads the works of those who fought for the emancipation of science from religious influence. When Diderot and the other Encyclopedists rejected the claim of conventional ethics, they had no intention of leaving the ground unoccupied: according to them, human behavior is all the more worthy of praise as it conforms to the tendencies of nature. "The code of morality appropriate to men should rest on no other foundations than what makes man what he is" ("Supplement to Bougainville's 'Voyage,'" 228). And it is science that helps us discover who man is, science that reveals his nature to us. In a way that is certainly indirect, but no less constraining for all that, science thus decides what is good and what is evil. According to Condorcet, "Knowing the truth in order to make the order of society conform to it is the sole source of public happiness" ("Vie de Turgot," 203). Taine was even more explicit: "History... can, like [the natural sciences] ... govern the concepts and guide the efforts of men" (*Derniers essais de critique et d'histoire*, xxviii). If it is enough to know the truth (which is undoubtedly the work for which science is best equipped) in order to decide what the order of society must be, it is up to the human sciences, to history, psychology, and sociology, to define society's goals and to lead mankind toward them.

From reading Taine one could conclude that the relation between knowledge and ethics that prevailed in his time was merely an inversion of the one that characterized the world prior to the Enlightenment: "The right to govern human beliefs has shifted entirely to the side of experience, and ... precepts and doctrines, rather than authorizing observation, receive their entire credibility from it" (ibid., xxi). Previously, observation had obeyed doctrines; now, doctrines were subject to observation: the two domains had not really become autonomous. Ernest Renan, one of Taine's contemporaries, was of the same opinion. He believed that the metaphysics and the religion of old had to be replaced by science—natural or historical; it was the very knowledge of the world that would determine the choice of the correct route for each society: "Sense must govern the world," and the best incarnation of sense was science. France had already experienced this government: "Condorcet, Mirabeau, Robespierre are the first instances of theorists meddling with the direction of affairs and endeavouring to govern humanity in a reasonable and scientific manner" (*The Future of Science,* 19–20).

But was this situation—the governing of public affairs and the judging of private affairs placed in the hands of scientists—always positive, and must it necessarily be so? Renan was a representative of scientistic ideology, and directly following the Franco-Prussian war of 1870–71 he wrote a curious work, entitled *Philosophical Dialogues.* In this work, a character imagines the world of the future. This society, whose objective is not the personal happiness of each individual but rather the perfection of the universe, was obviously to be run in a way most in keeping with reason, by the most intelligent beings possible, that is, by scientists. At the head of the state there would be not the philosopher-king found in Plato's Republic but "positivist tyrants" (62). These tyrants would protect the scientists, because the latter would ensure the strength necessary for their rule.

How, exactly, was this to be accomplished? Renan predicted that scientists would make three major contributions. First, they would develop an institution that would take the place of hell and that would, in contrast to the hell of mythology, have the advantage of actually existing. This institution would act to put fear in the hearts of the country's inhabitants in order to make them submissive: "The being possessed of science would set up unlimited terror in the service of truth" (62–63). Any thought of rebellion would vanish. Terror would be instilled by a specially trained elite corps, janissaries of a new kind: "obedient machines, unencumbered by moral scruples and prepared for every sort of cruelty" (62).

Second, the scientists would develop a new, superior race of human beings who would replace the aristocracy, whose privileges were purely arbitrary. In order to accomplish this, the scientists could eliminate defective human specimens and facilitate the spreading of the most useful functions among the remaining individuals. Finally, scientists would develop a new weapon, capable of destroying any and all adversaries, thereby ensuring absolute mastery of the universe: "The day when a few persons favoured of reason shall really possess the means of destroying the planet, their supremacy will be established. These privileged persons will rule by means of absolute terror, because they shall have in their hands the life of all" (63).

The reign of scientists is thus possible. But is it really desirable as Renan depicts it? Do we want to submit to it? The hundred or so years that have elapsed since the publication of this text have in fact seen some of Renan's promises—which appear to us as just so many threats—become more concrete. Scientists have discovered nuclear energy, and states actually have at their disposal the absolute weapon, capable of destroying the planet. Has this brought the universe any closer to perfection? Terror and torture, even if they do not rule the world over, have in this century reached degrees of intensity previously unheard of.

The forging of a superior race, which could seem the most fanciful point of this program, deserves particular attention. Renan himself took the first steps toward its realization. Because he was profoundly convinced of the inequality of the races, he hoped to see the establishment of a world order that would sanction this state of affairs (knowledge again assigns goals to humanity), where Whites would be soldiers and masters, Asians would become workers, and Blacks would be content to work the earth. In other words, he advocated dividing the world among the European colonial powers. As far the white race itself was concerned, the Aryans—inventors of science—were to eliminate the Semitic peoples little by little because these latter had already accomplished their historical mission in having brought the world monotheism. At times these social changes seemed insufficient to Renan, and, in his utopia, he imagined a physiological intervention to improve the inferior races: "A very small quantity of noble blood put into the circulation of a people is enough to ennoble it" ("Lettre à Gobineau," 204).

It is pointless to dwell on Hitler's attempt some seventy years later to purify the human species by exterminating all groups that, in his opinion, were defective (Jews, Gypsies, homosexuals, the mentally ill), or on his attempt to improve the remaining populations through selective breeding. But one may recall that Renan's utopia had certain affinities with some present-day practices carried out in nontotalitarian states, namely, various scientific interventions in human reproduction—although it is true that these take place on the individual, rather than on the collective, level. Thanks, as they say, to progress in the field of genetics, it is possible to eliminate human embryos that do not have all the requisite traits. More daring projects that would allow parents to choose the sex of their child or, so they say, the degree of his or her intelligence are also in the works. Yet, once something is technically possible, does it necessarily follow that it must be carried out?

The attempt to make ethics dependent on the results of science thus raises many problems. This could already have been perceived in the Encyclopedists' time, had sufficient attention been paid to the reasoning of one of their marginal disciples, the Marquis de Sade. Taking literally the principle that everything found in nature is good, Sade had no difficulty justifying, and even glorifying, what societies normally considered a crime. "Cruelty, very far from being a vice, is the first sentiment Nature injects in us all"

(*Philosophy in the Bedroom,* 3:253). Certain contemporary biologists are doing no differently when they *affirm,* first of all, that aggressiveness is a characteristic of human nature (or possibly only of *male* nature, but that is enough); and who then, armed with this scientific certainty, *justify* aggressive or exclusionary behavior (territorial defense).

Having arrived at this point, however, we must ask ourselves not if science has the right to dictate the norms of our behavior, but rather if it is in fact a matter of *science* at all in the instances outlined. Even prior to the confusion about the relationship between science and ethics, isn't there a kind of preliminary confusion about the nature of scientific discourse? For it is obviously naive to imagine, as scientistic philosophy would have us do, that science produces truths: rather, it produces hypotheses about the workings of the world, constructs that are scientific only inasmuch as they are, as one says today, "falsifiable." And in practice scientific hypotheses are indeed falsified—proved false—one after the other, only to be replaced by others whose sole distinctive feature is that their "falseness" has not yet been proved. If a hypothesis is raised to the level of a truth, in other words, if it becomes dogma, and if we no longer have the right to criticize or question it, we have left the domain of science and entered that of some kind of ethics, whether religious, political, or other.

In addition, even supposing that a scientific statement were true, no ethical precept automatically ensues. For example, it is obvious that certain human beings are stronger than others; but from this true proposition one cannot deduce that one must therefore give the stronger the *right* to mistreat the weaker. On the contrary, laws exist in order to protect the weak from the despotism of the strong. Even supposing that Renan's science were correct, and that human races are unequal, it in no way follows that the superior race has the right to dominate the others; such a conclusion can only be the result of a position that—in spite of everything—is a moral one, and according to which the most intelligent people have the right to exploit those who are less intelligent. Taine wrote that "science leads to morality by seeking only truth" (*Derniers essais,* 110), but this is not so: science never leads to ethics, nor even to truth; all science can do is *seek* the truth with patience and humility.

It is not, therefore, physics and its discovery of the secrets of atomic fission that are to blame for the production of nuclear arms; it is a government, a political and not a scientific body, that must decide if it will devote its means (that is, the taxes levied on the entire population) to the production of arms and the construction of peaceful reactors (but which can kill when necessary), or if, facing the risks that both choices entail, it will forgo nuclear energy and assume the consequences: military dependency or economic impoverishment. It is not biology—which revealed the mystery of heredity—that must be held responsible for the aberrations of the manipulations of human embryos, but rather governments that, in the name of their political and ethical considerations, decide to devote their research budgets to experiments that allow, in the best of cases, the distress of a few sterile couples to be relieved, while the world is threatened with overpopulation and millions of children continue to die of disease and hunger (granted, the two series of events do not occur in the same countries).

Political and ethical decisions attributed to science have always been made in the name of political and ethical positions, even if these positions have never dared reveal their true nature and have hidden behind the authority of science. This is why it is excessive to forbid scientists to seek the truth, whatever its nature: truth in itself holds no dangers. When Alexis de Tocqueville learned of Gobineau's theories on the inequality of the races, he responded that these theories were most certainly false. In the event, however, that they were true, Tocqueville continued, one would have to conceal the conclusions, since they could only have a negative effect on the said races. Tocqueville believed that the idea of equality acts as a goad: one tries to equal the best by doing better than before. The idea of a natural inequality, on the other hand, anaesthetizes: if one is doomed to failure, why try? Gobineau believed that physical inequities justified political inequities: frightened by such a conclusion, Tocqueville preferred that one remain ignorant of the facts. But such a chain of events, as we have seen, is not automatic; and if the applications of science must be *controlled* by ethics and politics (or rather, if one must recognize that these applications are submitted to that control, and no other), scientific inquiry must on the contrary have one guiding principle only: the seeking of truth. Moreover, it is not because a jealous husband smashes his wife's skull with a hammer that the manufacture and the improvement of this kind of tool should be proscribed.

We can now return to the question of the lagging of the human sciences in relation to the natural sciences, due in particular to the inability of the former to eliminate value judgments from their discourse. When one realizes that the outcomes of the natural sciences must themselves be submitted to ethical and political control, one could be tempted to reverse the standard hierarchy, praising the social and human sciences precisely because they are never devoid of a relation to values. Somewhat like in the fable, the humanist tortoise would overtake the naturalist hare, since the starting point would itself have been declared the finish line. But here we would run the risk of following in the footsteps of those scientists who do not see any qualitative difference between human and natural sciences (even if, in the end, we go the opposite route).

These two forms of knowledge—human sciences and natural sciences—have much in common indeed. Both, in their approach, must follow only the laws of the search for truth and reject any dogmatic influence. And, in addition, to reach the conclusions that must be drawn from their discoveries, both rely on decisions whose moral and political character must be openly admitted. They cannot, as has been attempted at times in the past, be opposed on the one hand as the sciences of the particular and, on the other, as those of the general. Although history deals with particular realities, when the same realities are examined from the point of view of the economist, sociologist, psychologist, or linguist, they appear as the manifestation of general laws; reciprocally, biology and physics obviously establish general laws, but they depend just as much on the observation of specific cases. Finally, one cannot say that the one studies *things* whereas the other studies *signs,* since signs are also things and at the same time what one believed to be pure things prove in their turn to be signs. Don't we speak of a genetic *code* nowadays?

And yet a qualitative difference does exist, and Condorcet, who wanted to see that difference disappear, was one of the first to express it clearly: "By thinking about the nature of the moral sciences, one cannot, in effect, help seeing that, supported like the physical sciences by the observation of facts, they must follow the same methodology, acquire a language equally exact and precise, and attain the same degree of certainty. Everything would be equal between them for a being who, alien to our species, would study human society in the way that we study the society of beavers or bees. But in this instance the observer is himself a part of the society he is observing, and the truth cannot have judges who are either forewarned or seduced" (*Discours de réception,* 392). We are not, however, alien to our species and never will be. The defining characteristic of these sciences is thus the identity of subject and object—in other words, the fact that this object is a human being. Even when studying the human organism, the natural sciences study it in the same way they would study a bee or a beaver. The sciences of man, on the other hand, study what is particularly human about human beings. The major difference between the two is not, therefore, one of method (differences exist, but they are not decisive); it is in the nature of the object being studied.

The fact that it is human beings who are being studied has several consequences. One of the simplest is that, in order to understand them better, one cannot treat human beings like laboratory rats. Gérando, a founder of contemporary anthropology, remarked that it would be much more convenient if we could bring savages from distant countries to Paris in order to study them. He realized, however, that such a study would run the risk of neglecting the context in which they live and he therefore recommended reducing this inconvenience by bringing their families to Paris, too. He justified this as follows: "The naturalist is not content to bring back a branch, a flower that is soon withered; he tries to transplant the whole tree or plant to give it a second life on our soil" (*The Observation of Savage Peoples,* 101). Gérando forgot only one thing: unlike trees (not to mention branches), human beings are endowed with a will and, unlike sycamores, they can be consulted before being transplanted. Contemporary experts of human societies have not always taken this fact into account; I recall an incident where the inhabitants of a village in Brittany, enduring a "total" investigation by Parisian scientists, decided, when all else had failed, to abandon their village. The object of study in this case is capable of becoming our interlocutor, of speaking in its turn: such is the particularity of these sciences.

Something else occurs as a result of the fact that the object of inquiry is human beings. As the great humanists of the eighteenth century—Montesquieu, Rousseau—remarked, human beings do not obey their laws with the same regularity as other beings; they can even decide to transgress these laws precisely because they are aware of them, just as the "underground man" did when confronted with the psychologists and positivist ideologues of his time. In other words, although they are subject to various determinisms—historical, geographical, social, psychic—human beings are also characterized by an inalienable freedom. This does not mean that their behavior is sheer chaos, or that they escape all rational explanation; it means, rather, that a theory that on principle ignores all consideration of this freedom is doomed to fail.

Finally, we must recall that human existence is permeated throughout by values, and as a result, trying to eliminate all relation to values from the human sciences is an inhuman task. Can one ask, as did Marc Bloch, "What was Robespierre?" without bringing into play one's value judgment? Can one say anything sensible about him without having decided whether he was a bloody dictator or the liberator of a people? Can one dispose of the relation to good and evil with the excuse that it is an "old anthropocentrism," when it is in fact a matter of observing and understanding the *anthropos* in question? It is not *after* explanation that value judgment intervenes: it is in its very heart, in the identification of its object. One could say that the history of societies becomes something more than a mere collection of archaeological artifacts the moment we feel our common humanity with a distant people and when, as a result, we can include them in a circuit of values. Bloch said that the human sciences are more "obliging to practice" the more they are freed from their "judgment mania"; but what good is it to facilitate an inhuman practice?

The social and human sciences thus necessarily maintain a relation to ethics and politics (to notions of the good of the individual as well as that of the community) from which the natural sciences escape. And there is no reason to assume that things must change in this regard. The constituent interweaving of humanist disciplines with moral and political categories does not mean, however, that the two are identical. When Montesquieu used the opposition between despotism and moderation as the basis of his typology of political regimes, the terms are valorized, but there is no objection of principle to raise: since the matter closely concerns human interests, it would be absurd to attempt to reject this opposition. However, when he purposefully blackens the portrait of Oriental regimes the better to illustrate his ideal type of despotism, we feel that he has contravened the laws of science and find it necessary to correct him: this is an example of inappropriate ideological intervention. Moreover, one must not imagine that it is the task of these sciences to help us make human beings the way they should be, rather than showing us the way they are. Were this the case, they would no longer deserve to be called sciences, but would be transformed into sheer techniques of manipulation.

Once we have realized that the separation from the world of values is neither possible nor desirable, perhaps we will go back to using the previous name of these disciplines, calling them, once again, "moral and political sciences." This book was written in that spirit. The studies it comprises attempt to illustrate, as well as clarify, this relation between facts and values. They recall certain "(hi)stories" and, at the same time, are a questioning of their "ethics." Of course, these "(hi)stories" have been told by others, in much more detail. I am not attempting to compete with these scholars, for I believe I am addressing an audience more interested in the present than in the past. If there is anything new in my readings, it is perhaps simply the perspective from which I question the facts.

Although the book is not a systematic treatise, the order of the chapters is meant to be significant. The first section is devoted to the problems raised by the relations between different cultures. In this part I continue the reflection begun in my book *Nous et les autres* (1989) (*On Human Diversity*, 1993). I start with a specific instance: the image of Bulgaria in classical French literature; it is specific, but at the same time emblematic for me. Next I move to the conquest of America, an old "encounter" (to which I also devoted a book, *La Conquête de l'Amérique* [1982] [*The Conquest of America*, 1984]). I arrive progressively at the present by examining two forms of interaction: colonialism and travels. I then consider the domain of contacts among cultures in its entirety. In the second part, which I have called *Entre Nous* (At Home among Ourselves), I address two philosophico-political notions — truth and democracy — through the use of historical examples. The first three chapters of this section situate truth(s) in relation to fiction and lie, interpretation and eloquence. The remaining chapters discuss the two principal criticisms leveled against democracy, the one liberal, the other conservative, and in so doing attempt to determine certain boundaries. I conclude with a questioning of the present role of intellectuals.

# Part One

## Looking toward Others

# 1 / Bulgaria in France

In order to know a people better, must one look at them from the inside or from the outside? Whose view of a group is more perceptive, that of someone who belongs to it or that of someone who observes it from outside? As soon as we go beyond the innate egocentrism of each individual and each community, we see that the member of the group, although more familiar with its customs, is at a disadvantage. This is precisely because each group believes itself to be the best, if not the only, group in the world. In his *History*, Herodotus describes the Persians as follows: "They honor most of all those who dwell nearest them, next those who are next farthest removed, and so going ever onwards they assign honor by this rule; those who dwell farthest off they hold least honorable of all; for they deem themselves to be in all regards by far the best of all men, the rest to have but a proportionate claim to merit, till those who dwell farthest away have least merit of all" (Book One, 134, I, 175). In these terms, however, what group is *not* Persian? All peoples make judgments from their own backyard, and condemn foreigners in order to glorify themselves. Such a prejudice is certainly not a necessary condition for the best self-knowledge.

In modern times, times of a growing consciousness of the existence of *others,* an entire discipline — ethnology — has arisen whose first premise is that the outside gaze is more lucid and more penetrating than the indigenous.

In effect, the difference between ethnology and the other social sciences lies not in its object, for ethnology deals with the same economy, art, customs, and habits that are studied by experts in each of these areas. Its distinctive characteristic—which in its eyes is also an advantage—lies in the observing subject, not in the observed object. Situated outside the society he is studying, this subject is in a position not only *not* to be influenced by blinding egocentrism, but also to perceive what a member of the group—no matter how clear-sighted—fails to recognize: everything that the latter believes natural, self-evident, and which, as a result, remains invisible.

The ethnological stance was used primarily with respect to traditional societies. But voices have been raised in the recent past to affirm the fruitfulness, or even the necessity, of this approach regardless of the culture under study. Among those voices, one of the most important has been that of Mikhail Bakhtin, the great Russian thinker. Bakhtin coined a neologism, *vnenakhodimost,* which can be translated as "exotopy" and which designates this nonbelonging to a given culture. According to Bakhtin, not only is exotopy *not* an obstacle to thorough knowledge of this culture, it is the necessary condition of it. "The chief matter of understanding is the *exotopy* of the one who does the understanding—in time, space, and culture—in relation to that which he wants to understand creatively," writes Bakhtin. And he adds: "In the realm of culture, exotopy is the most powerful lever of understanding. It is only in the eyes of an *other* culture that the alien culture reveals itself more completely and more deeply" (cited in Todorov, *Mikhail Bakhtin: The Dialogical Principle,* 109–10).

It is thus with justified curiosity that when one wants to learn more about the Bulgarians and their culture, one turns to the foreign mirrors represented by the writings of scholars, travelers, and poets belonging to an *other* culture; that one turns—and why not?—to French culture. What image do the French have of the Bulgarians?

# I

The image is at first rather vague. In the Middle Ages, the reputation of the Bulgarians was the same as that of Attila's Huns, and their characteristics were in effect reduced to a single trait: ferociousness. A famous phrase from Cassiodorus confirms this: "Bulgari in omni orbe terribles" (Bulgarians spread terror everywhere). Only since the Renaissance and, in particular since the eighteenth century, have regular contacts allowed a more complex image to take shape.

For a Bulgarian, however (even one living in Paris), reading these texts — diligently collected by N. Mikhov — is disappointing. This is not because they are hostile to Bulgaria. In fact, quite the opposite is true: they are so well disposed toward Bulgaria (as are the abstracts annotated by G. Sergheraert in the three volumes of his *Presence de la Bulgarie*) that at times one wonders if the editors' preferences were not somehow responsible for this state of affairs, since all the French people in the collection believed that Macedonia belonged to Bulgaria. Nonetheless, the fact that they are well disposed toward Bulgaria does not carry over into any complex image of the Bulgarians, about whom, in the end, we learn almost nothing.

Specifically, these writings seem to be divided — in terms of values — into two groups, possibly corresponding to the ambiguity of Bulgaria's geographical location, which allows it to be perceived either as the last bastion of the West on the way to the Orient or, conversely, as the most advanced tip of the Orient on the way to the West. In the latter instance, it is the barbarian aspect that prevails: the Bulgarians were the first barbarians to have met the philosopher's gaze as it swept across the map of Europe. For Montesquieu, for example, they had lost even their name: "Once having established themselves, the barbarians who live along the Danube became less frightening and even served as a barrier against other barbarians" (*Considérations sur les causes de la grandeur des Romains,* chapter 23). Even once they had become sedentary, the barbarians remained barbarians. They were forced to play a strange role, serving as a "barrier" against wilder and, at the same time, less familiar barbarians. Montesquieu does not tell us what this barrier was protecting, but we can guess: it is civilization, it is the Roman Empire. It was as if Providence had provided a protection around the chosen people: the Bulgarians, although they were themselves barbarians, "served" a purpose, and the historical meaning of their fate was to prevent the invasion of peoples even more barbaric. Yet what would remain of this meaning and of this fate if one were to accept — following Las Casas and Montaigne, who both wrote in the sixteenth and not the eighteenth century — that "each person calls barbaric anything which is not familiar to him" (Montaigne, *Essais*)?

In the nineteenth century, one believed in the virtues of progress and in the advantages of civilization; but travelers in Bulgaria found neither. "Bulgaria's civilization is not very advanced," wrote Destrilhes in 1855. In 1869, Baradschka wrote that "the Bulgarians . . . are still located quite far down on the ladder of civilization, and they have much to do in order to acquire the intellectual and moral development that alone is necessary to make them into a nation living its own life" (both quoted in Mikhov, 54, 87). "Civilization" is always in the singular in the writings of this period, and preceded (in French) by the definite article; what is not said, but what is heavily implied, is that *our* civilization is *the* civilization, and that there is only one. Not to be like us is to not be civilized, to not *be* at all.

The flip side of this viewpoint is more positive, but hardly more trustworthy. When one author writes, "Crime is unknown among them, and the traveler who crosses their country is not only sheltered from the effects of vice but experiences all of the goodness that is the result of the most abundant virtues" (Walsh in 1843; quoted in Mikhov, 14), and when another affirms, "One thinks one is dreaming upon seeing for the first time those beauties of the barbarian world . . . one watches in amazement those virgins of the Balkans pass, as if one were seeing a desert gazelle run away, or a lake swan in Greece" (C. Robert in 1844; quoted in Mikhov, 44), it is clear that these travelers are describing their ideal — ethical and aesthetic — rather than the realities of the country they are crossing. Yes, the authors are well disposed, but are they really speaking about Bulgarians?

These two versions of a distant people — one rosy, the other dark; one idyllic, the other satirical — differ only superficially. In reality, they rely on one massive and common fact: the misunderstanding of these people, or rather, a lack of interest in them. For these travelers, the Bulgarians incarnate one variation of the image of the savage. According to one's attitude regarding the merits of the primitive age, either the purity of the Bulgarians' customs or the absence of civilization will be emphasized. Whether to praise or to denigrate, the painter always condescends to the image he paints: as soon as one posits that the others are *now* the way *we* were *before,* one denies them any independent identity; and the admiration that one has for them is in fact quite fragile, since one can generously attribute goodness to them, but never strength (otherwise the evolutionary schema collapses). This interdependence of two points of view that are, on the surface, conflicting is illustrated by the words of a French engineer, which begin in praise and end in barely disguised scorn: "Their customs, their character are so sweet that we call them sheep, and all the engineers who have known and studied them for a long time agree unanimously that to kill a Bulgarian is to kill a fly" (F. Bianconi in 1876; quoted in Mikhov, 99).

The opinions of the French travelers in Bulgaria reveal not only their ethnocentrism but also a particular conception of sociopsychological determinism. The writers of this period most often attributed two characteristics to the Bulgarians: they are hardworking and they are hospitable. Let us assume that their impression was correct. What is its value for understanding a people? Very little. To be hospitable, to be hardworking, cannot in themselves be attributes of a people, but only of a society in a particular stage of its evolution. The ideology of individualism that prevailed in western Europe at the time was hardly known in societies such as the Bulgarian one. The customs one observes belong to a stage of the society, and it is at that particular stage that they take on meaning: the hospitality of a desert dweller is in no way equivalent to the hospitality of a city dweller. The nineteenth century, rather than practicing a cultural determinism, practiced a determinism of races and people: the French were "light" and the Germans "heavy"; the Serbs were "proud" and the Bulgarians "hardworking." Possibly this was a way of dealing with egalitarian doctrine, that inseparable complement of individualism: equality must prevail, of course, but it must also be tempered, since races and peoples differ irreducibly. Equality must somehow be made proportionate to the merits of each people: this is how the generous principles of the French Revolution could coexist with the colonialist expansionism that would characterize the nineteenth century.

## II

Thus, the image is disappointing. Perhaps, however, the fault lies in my choice of sources. Until now, I have presented only second-class writers, forgotten by science and literature. In order to clear up the matter, let us turn to the greatest writers and first, to Voltaire, the one who did so much to popularize the very name of the Bulgarians:

> It was an Abare village, which the Bulgars had burned, in strict accordance with the laws of war. Here old men, stunned from beatings, watched the last agonies of their butchered wives, who still clutched their infants to their bleeding breasts; there, disemboweled girls, who had first satisfied the natural needs of various heroes, breathed their last; others, half-scorched in the flames, begged for their death stroke. Scattered brains and severed limbs littered the ground. (*Candide*, 5)

As for Cunégonde, the heroine of this tale, "she was disemboweled by the Bulgar soldiers, after having been raped to the absolute limit of human endurance; they smashed the Baron's head when he tried to defend her, cut the Baroness to bits..."(7).

What a horrifying picture one must have gotten from these descriptions! But we can rest assured: even the least informed reader of *Candide* is aware that it is not Bulgaria that is being described here. This "Bulgaria" is the neighbor of "Westphalia" and of Holland: it is reduced to being a mere signifier, since Voltaire was really taking aim at Prussia. The misdeeds attributed to the "Bulgars" and the "Abares" come straight out of the Seven Years' War. Using conventional misrepresentation, Voltaire was writing about what was familiar to him. Moreover, the Prussians themselves are, although in a different way, a means of speaking about France and its social and philosophical preoccupations. The technique was not unusual at the time. No one sought an exact description of the Persian empire in Montesquieu's *Lettres persanes.* If Bulgaria is indeed present in *Candide,* it is in an entirely different way, and one Voltaire perhaps did not intend: in the character of the old wise man Martin, who is at times Voltaire's own spokesman, and who claims to be a follower of Manichaeanism, a heresy that at the time was commonly associated with the influence of Bulgaria. The signifier and the signified "Bulgarian" never meet in this book.

What remains, therefore, is a use of the "Bulgarians" that has nothing to do with the inhabitants of the country Bulgaria. There seems to be a moment when Voltaire is in fact being ironic about this exploitation: a theater critic in a later chapter speaks indignantly to Candide about an author who does not know "a word of Arabic, though the action takes place in Arabia" (*Candide,* 49). But there is no irony. In fact, it is the critic who is supposedly making a fool of himself by holding forth in this way; under the transparent disguise of the critic is hiding one of Voltaire's worst enemies.

*Candide,* however, is a work of fiction, not of science; and it is certainly somewhat ungracious not to forgive a novelist for the use he makes of the world's populations. But Voltaire also devoted an article to the Bulgarians in the *Dictionnaire philosophique,* and it is here that one has a better chance of discovering his real position. Why does an article entitled "Bulgarians" appear in a philosophical work in the first place? Because in French the word "Bulgar" has provided *bougre,* which means heretic (Manichaean) or homosexual; the influence of the Bulgarian *bogomiles* on the French *cathares* is responsible for this shift in meaning. Voltaire who, as we know, sympathized with the Manichaeans and was ready to use their arguments to fight his enemy the Church, thus availed himself of an opportunity to write anticlerical propaganda; the Bulgarians are hardly more relevant here than they were in *Candide.* The history of Bulgaria is reduced to a few anecdotes: Krum drinking from the skull of his enemy Nicephorus, Boris converting the Bulgarians to Christianity, Kaloyan triumphing over Baldwin.

None of these Bulgarian kings, however, is given as much text as the Empress Theodora of Byzantium, because her behavior was better suited to Voltaire's anticlerical raillery.

As the context of publication shows, the Bulgarians are put to "philosophical" use here, which was typical of the spirit of the century. Rousseau used American Indians in much the same way, without worrying whether what he was saying about them was true or false. But by what strange shift did the word "philosophy" cease to designate a reflection that goes beyond observable facts and begin to designate scorn for these facts? It may be that accuracy of observations is not philosophy's primary concern; but does it follow that inaccurate observations are therefore philosophical? Voltaire treats philosophy no better than he treats the Bulgarians.

Voltaire never went to Bulgaria; he transmits no more than the commonplaces of his time. It is therefore important to read another illustrious writer who did travel through Bulgaria and who wrote about his travels: Lamartine, in his *Voyage en Orient* (*A Pilgrimage to the Holy Land*). Lamartine's project, such as he sets it out at the beginning of his book, is troublesome from the start when placed in the perspective of the mutual understanding of peoples and cultures. Lamartine wanted to go to the Orient no doubt because he was struck by certain images that themselves belonged to western Europe: the visual images in an illustrated Bible, the literary images of Chateaubriand. During this journey, Lamartine attempted to know only one person: himself. "If the reader desires to find in these volumes aught beyond the fugitive impressions of a passenger who proceeds to his object without pausing, he had better close them. . . . Sometimes the traveller, wrapt up in himself, in his own thoughts and feelings, forgets the scene before him, converses with himself, and listens to the enjoyments or sufferings of his own heart" (*A Pilgrimage to the Holy Land,* 1:vi).

Here, then, is a traveler who moves quickly, very quickly, who avoids acknowledging any object that could divert him from something that seems infinitely more interesting to him: himself. Here is a traveler who prefers listening to himself to listening to others. The entire Orient, from Syria to Serbia, serves but one end, namely, to allow Lamartine's poetic "I" to express itself:

> I always dreamed of travelling in the East; I never ceased arranging in my mind a vast and religious épopée, of which these beautiful spots should be the principal scene. . . . I should from hence derive the colours of my poem; for life in my mind was always a great poem. (1:8)

"My mind," "my poem": the Orient exists only insofar as it is necessary for the inner experience or the outer expression of the artist.

The images Lamartine uses to describe the encounter between the poet and the Orient evoke, in the background, the noble role of the male who must inscribe the admirable yet passive body of the part of the world he is discovering. In his mind, he is to the Orient what man is to woman, what the soul is to the body. Chateaubriand, "that accomplished writer and great poet passed but transiently over the land of miracles, yet has his genius imprinted for ever the traces of his steps upon the dust which so many centuries have swept" (1:iii).

On the one hand, the earth, dust that moves, pure expectation; on the other, the fecund genius who comes to imprint his trace there.

Let us observe how this hurried traveler, as he listens to himself rejoice or suffer, seeks the subject matter of his poem while crossing Bulgaria in July 1833. His journey leads him from Constantinople to Andrinople, and from there to Philippopoli (Plovdiv), to Tatar-Bazargik, to Sofia, leaving the Ottoman Empire at Nisch, his journey's end. Plovdiv is thus the first major Bulgarian city on his route. What does he tell us about it? "When we entered Philippopoli our party consisted of sixty or eighty horsemen. The people had assembled in the streets and at their windows to see us pass" (2:275). The only thing Lamartine sees is that people are trying to see him; the only thing he retains of the other is the other's attention to him. The horizon then expands somewhat, as he discovers some very beautiful landscapes from the windows and gardens of his host, a Mr. Maurides.

So much for Plovdiv. Lamartine then goes to Tatar-Bazargik, and from there arrives at the village of Yenikeui. This village does not suspect that it will become famous thanks to this French traveler. Lamartine spends twenty long days there—longer than anywhere else—not because of a sudden awakening of his curiosity about the Bulgarians, but because he contracts what was called at the time an "inflammation of the blood," treated by applying leeches to the chest and temples. Lamartine thinks about himself more than ever as he listens self-pityingly to his suffering. He imagines a theatrical setting for his burial: "I desired that I might be buried under a tree which I had observed on the road-side as we were coming to the village, and that a single word should be inscribed on the stone over my grave: this word was—God" (2:277).

As one might have guessed, the Bulgarians do not take up much room in all this. We first observe them upon entering Yenikeui: "On reaching the foot of the Balkans, we found all the principal inhabitants of the

Bulgarian village of Yenikeui waiting for us. They took the reins of our horse, ranged themselves on each side of our carriages, supported them on their shoulders, and occasionally lifted them up to prevent the wheels from slipping over the precipices" (2:276). Once again, the Bulgarians are reduced to a strictly auxiliary function. At another point, we learn that the (Turkish) prince of Tatar-Bazargik offers slaves to Lamartine. Are they Bulgarians? We are not to know. Toward the end of his journey, Lamartine passes through Sofia, but does not give us any description of it: "I spent one day in this town: the pacha sent me calves and sheep, and would not accept any present in return. The town of Sophia presents nothing remarkable" (2:279). At one point, it is true, Lamartine does examine the surrounding population more closely. This occurs at the end of his convalescence when he can allow himself to go out riding a bit. He tells us he had the occasion—apparently without getting off his horse—to observe "the domestic manners of the Bulgarians" (2:278). What he discovers from this study hardly differs from the image found in the works of other travelers: "They are a simple, mild and laborious people, full of respect for their priests and zeal for their religion.... their manners are pure." (ibid.). And he condescendingly adds an opinion for which the Bulgarians will be eternally grateful: "These people...are completely ready for independence" (ibid.). Thus he reserves for himself the right to decide whether a nation deserves its freedom or not.

In order to describe the outward appearance of the Bulgarians and their country, Lamartine does not look very far: they always remind him of something, even if it is not always the same thing. "These are the Savoyards of the European Turkey" (2:273). "The domestic manners of the Bulgarians...closely resemble those of our Swiss or Savoyard peasantry. Their costume resembles that of the peasants of Germany, and the women and children dress much like the mountaineers of Switzerland.... I saw some rustic dances of the Bulgarians, which are similar to those of our French villagers." (2:278). "These mountains are nearly similar to those of Auvergne" (2:279). One becomes somewhat skeptical of the way the mountain dwellers from all these countries are merged.

Lamartine cannot be accused of having betrayed his intention: he promised that he would tell us only about himself, and he keeps his promise. Like the eighteenth-century philosopher, the nineteenth-century poet has other interests than the faithful and attentive description of others. I leafed through these books in vain trying to find an image that revealed something of Bulgaria. What we learn from them is the intellectual, cultural, and political climate from which they arose; we learn something about France in the eighteenth and nineteenth centuries, but nothing about Bulgaria.

Yet we also learn something about the very process of knowledge. Does our disappointment mean that we must disavow exotopy, that its advantages are illusory? Rather, it shifts the problem. The naive and self-satisfied image that the native has of his own culture is a perfect match for the superficial and condescending portrait painted by the foreigner: the infinity of the former corresponds to the zero of the latter. It is precisely because these French travelers imagined that French culture was at the center of the universe that they were blind to the culture of others, in this case, the Bulgarians. It is not enough to be *other* in order to see, since, from his own point of view, the other is a self, and all the others are barbarians. Exotopy must be experienced from the inside; it is a matter of discovering, in one's very heart, the difference between *my* culture and culture in general, *my* values, and values in general. One can make this discovery for oneself, without ever leaving one's native soil, by alienating oneself progressively — but never completely — from one's group of origin. One can make this discovery by means of the other, but in this case one must also have experienced a questioning of the self, which is the only guarantee that one will be able to look patiently and attentively at the other. In short, it is the exile — internal or external — who stands the best chance here, and since I began with Herodotus's words about the innate pride of peoples, I will end by recalling that Thucydides, in seeking to explain why he was qualified to write the history of the war between the Athenians and the Peloponnesians, said that it was no doubt because, although he was Athenian, he had "lived for twenty years far from his country," and that he had learned, because of this exile, to know his own people, and others, better.

# 2 / Postscript: Knowledge of Others

But does one ever know others? In his *Essays,* Montaigne wrote, "I say others the better to say myself," and today his skepticism is shared by many. Does one ever know anything but oneself? We have just seen that the opposite idea—one that holds that the exteriority of the knowing subject is not only a disadvantage, but can also be an advantage—is equally widespread. Within the sixteenth century, one can contrast Montaigne's disenchanted lucidity with Machiavelli's epistemological project. In the dedication to *The Prince,* Machiavelli wrote: "For in the same way that landscape painters station themselves in the valleys in order to draw mountains or high ground, and ascend an eminence in order to get a good view of the plains, so it is necessary to be a prince to know thoroughly the nature of the people, and one of the populace to know the nature of princes" (32). Three hundred and fifty years later, Hippolyte Taine similarly justified the choice of the subject of one of his books: "I have selected England . . . since, because it is different, it presents, more so than France, characteristics striking to the eyes of the French" (*Histoire de la littérature anglaise,* 1:xliii). Rousseau, who had also reflected on the nature of this knowledge, stated it differently: one must know the differences between men, he said, not because the particular is in itself valuable, but in order to gain enlightenment about man in general.

Furthermore, the knowledge of the general can *only* be acquired by means of the particular: "When one wants to study men, one must consider those around one. But to study man, one must extend the range of one's vision. One must first observe the differences in order to discover the properties" (*On the Origin of Language,* 30–31). How can one choose among these general precepts?

Understanding a foreign culture is only one specific instance of a general hermeneutic problem: how does one understand the other? This other can differ from us temporally, in which case one's knowledge comes under history; or spatially, in which case a comparative analysis is called for (in the form of ethnology, "orientalism," etc.); or simply on an existential plane: the other is my fellow being, my neighbor, anyone who is not-I. The differences are specific in each case, but they all set in motion the opposition between self and other that is constitutive of the hermeneutic process. A variety of solutions — viewed at times as conflicting — to this general problem have been proposed, but I prefer to see them as successive phases of a single act, even if this process implies some backward movement, or as a gradual progression toward an immutable ideal.

The first phase of understanding consists of assimilating the other to oneself. I am a literary critic, and all the works about which I speak allow only one voice to be heard: my own. I am interested in distant cultures, but they are, according to me, all structured like my own. I am a historian, but I find only a prefiguration of the present in the past. The act of perceiving the others does exist, but it only reproduces several copies of the same thing. Knowledge grows quantitatively, not qualitatively. There is only one identity: my own.

The second phase of understanding consists of effacing the self for the other's benefit. This act may be experienced in many different ways. As a scholar devoted to accuracy and precision, I become more Persian than the Persians: I learn about their past and present, I accustom myself to perceiving the world through their eyes, I repress any manifestation of my original identity; by eliminating my subjectivity, I believe I am being objective. As a literary critic or literary historian, I pat myself on the back for making the writer I am reading speak, without adding or subtracting a thing, as if he were speaking himself. As an ardent lover, I give up my self in order to better fuse myself with the other; I become merely an emanation of him or her. Here again, there is only one identity; but it is the other's.

In the third phase of understanding, I resume my own identity, but after having done everything possible to know the other. My exotopy (temporal, spatial, or cultural exteriority) is no longer a curse; it is, on the contrary, what produces new knowledge, now in a qualitative rather than quantitative sense. As an ethnologist, I do not claim to make others speak, but rather, to establish a dialogue between myself and them; I perceive my own categories as being just as relative as theirs. I abandon the prejudice of imagining that one can abandon all prejudice: I prejudge, necessarily and always, but it is precisely in this that the interest of my interpretation lies, my prejudices being different from those of others. I affirm that all interpretation is historical (or "ethnic"), in the sense that it is determined by my spatiotemporal belonging: this does not contradict the effort to know things as they really are, but rather complements it. Duality (multiplicity) replaces unity; the "I" remains distinct from the other.

During the fourth phase of knowledge, I "leave" myself once again, but in an entirely different way. I no longer desire, nor am I able, to identify with the other; nor can I, however, identify with myself. The process can be described in these terms: knowledge of others depends on my own identity. But this knowledge of the other in turn determines my knowledge of myself. Since knowledge of oneself transforms the identity of this self, the entire process begins again: new knowledge of the other, new knowledge of the self, and so on to infinity. But is this infinity indescribable? Even if the movement can never reach an end, it has a specific direction, it leads toward an ideal. Let us imagine the following: for a long time I have lived within a foreign culture and this has made me conscious of my identity; at the same time, it sets this identity in motion. I can no longer subscribe to my "prejudices" as I did before, even if I do not attempt to rid myself of all "prejudice." My identity is maintained, but it is as if it is neutralized; I read myself in quotation marks. The very opposition between inside and outside is no longer relevant; nor does the simulacrum of the other that my description produces remain unchanged: it has become a space of possible understanding between the other and myself. By interacting with the other, my categories have become transformed in such a way that they speak for both of us and—why not?—for third parties also. Universality, which I thought I had lost, is rediscovered elsewhere: not in the object, but in the project.

Human experiences are infinitely varied. What is surprising about this is not that untranslatable feelings and uncommunicable specificities remain, but, on the contrary, that—provided one is willing to pay the price—we can manage to communicate and understand one another, from one being to another, one culture to another. That there is misunderstanding goes without saying; but understanding does exist, and it is this understanding that needs explaining. Things are not universal, but concepts can be: one must simply not confuse the two so that the road to a shared meaning may remain open.

# 3 / The Conquest as Seen by the Aztecs

The discovery of America is a unique event in the history of humanity: two great masses of people were living in ignorance of one another, only to discover, virtually overnight, their mutual existence. Nothing comparable had previously existed in the history of either half of the universe: discoveries had been progressive and gradual. Nor did the like exist in their later history: as of that day, the world became closed and finite (even if its dimensions have since doubled). This encounter unsettled not only the lives of the Americans but also — in a way just as profound though less visible — the part of the "old world" whose inhabitants had made the decisive journey. Our modern history also begins on that day.

This exceptional event gave rise in Europe, and in Spain in particular, to descriptions and analyses that are as inexhaustibly interesting as the event itself: from travel narratives to missionaries' efforts to understand *others*. The unique opportunity to describe a complex civilization that was entirely independent of our own did not go unnoticed, and some of the most interesting pages in the spiritual history of Europe can be found on this subject. These European texts are accessible and well known (even if they are not as well known as they should be). What is less well known, however, is that a similar phenomenon occurred on the other side: the invasion of America by the Europeans gave rise to a rich literature, written by the conquered

Indians. These texts are not only of exceptional value for the study of the Americas themselves, but also are valuable to us, today's Europeans, because of their intrinsic literary worth and their unique representation of our ancestors *viewed from outside.*

Can one speak of a shared vision in all of these Indian texts? It is true that only two of these narratives—the ones transmitted by Sahagún and Durán—cover the totality of the events from the arrival of the first Spaniards (or even before) up to the surrender and death of Quauhtemoc. (The texts with which this chapter deals concern only the conquest of Mexico City; they have been collected in *Récits aztèques de la conquête.*) Even if they take into account the entire history, the other narratives emphasize certain episodes in particular: Muñoz Camargo dwells on Cortés's passage through Tlaxcala, before and after his first stay in Mexico City; the *Ramírez Codex* stresses the interaction between the Spaniards and the inhabitants of Texcoco, which occurs after the passage through Tlaxcala; the *Aubin Codex* provides greater detail about the first battles in Mexico City, whereas the *Historical Annals* deals with the final battles. Furthermore, in addition to the differences introduced by the various narrative modes, these narratives do not tell exactly the same story. Yet it is still possible to isolate a few moments, or themes, that are common to all the Aztec narratives of the conquest and that reveal the vision that the Indians had of the event.

## The Announcements

The first striking characteristic of these narratives is that they begin not with the arrival of the Spaniards, as one might expect, but well before that, with the description of the announcements of this event. The *Florentine Codex* [hereafter in references as *FC*—Trans.], collected by the Franciscan Sahagún through meticulous investigation, reports eight marvels that the Aztecs considered as signs foretelling this event: a comet, a fire, lightning, other comets, the bubbling of the waters of the lake, a woman's strange voice, a bird with a diadem, and men with two heads. Muñoz Camargo, who must have been familiar with Sahagún's materials, took up in his turn these same marvels and added a few more from Tlaxcalan tradition: more comets, a swirl of dust. The *Aubin Codex* in addition mentions the descent of a column of stones. Durán—a Dominican monk and the author of another remarkable compilation—recounts in detail three amazing marvels: a comet; a heavy stone that cannot be lifted, which then speaks and later returns on its own to its original location; and the story of a peasant carried off by an eagle that forces him to burn the thigh of the sleeping Moctezuma, and then to go to the palace.

The very fact that these marvels are placed at the beginning of the narratives implies that they are considered as omens of the events recounted later. In addition, the narratives report other scenes, related or not to the first ones, where certain characters prophesy about what will arise. In the *Florentine Codex,* a drunkard—who is suspected of being the divinity Tezcatlipoca—announces: "Nevermore will there be a Mexico." According to Muñoz Camargo, the Tlaxcalan chiefs were familiar with an ancient prophecy that white, bearded men, wearing helmets as a sign of authority, would come from the east. The *Ramírez Codex* refers to a prediction made by the emperor of Texcoco, Nezahualpilli, about the arrival of the Spaniards (chapter 2) and to another prediction, according to which "Ixtlilxochitl would be the craftsman of the ruin of the Mexicans" (chapter 12).

The prophecies of events to come play a particularly important role in the version transmitted by Durán; so much so, in fact, that a good half of the entire narrative of the conquest is devoted to them (Durán, chapters 61–70). The starting point is Nezahualpilli's prophecy, recounted here in great detail (chapter 61); the comet in the sky then comes to confirm these statements. In the fantastic story of the heavy stone, it is the stone itself that undertakes to explain the meaning of the event: "Warn Moctezuma that his power and his rule are coming to an end" (chapter 66). The eagle that carries off the peasant also immediately interprets this marvel: "His power and his pride are coming to an end" (chapter 67). Other characters join in this chorus of prophecies: "Those who must avenge our affronts and sufferings have already begun their march" (chapter 68). In the end, Moctezuma himself begins to prophesy the result of the events: "And I want to warn you of one thing; that is, without any doubt, we will all be killed by these gods and the survivors will become their slaves and vassals" (chapter 71).

First, we can question the veracity of these narratives. Did such prophecies really occur, did these marvels take place? In regard to the first question, their precision is sometimes such that the answer appears beyond doubt: they were fabricated a posteriori, and with full knowledge; they are "retrospective prospections." The case is slightly different for the second question: the apparition of comets, tornadoes, or earthquakes certainly could have occurred; but it is the later event—the Spanish invasion—that allowed them to be construed as a series and transformed them into omens. What these narratives prove is that the Indians of Texcoco or Tlatelolco believed, in 1550, that the conquest had been foretold; they do not prove, however, as they state, that Moctezuma believed it in 1519, the year of the Spaniards' arrival. It is also interesting to note that the oldest narrative, the *Historical Annals,* has nothing to say on this subject.

Although one cannot maintain the literal veracity of these narratives on this point, this does not mean that they do not contain another, analogous, kind of truth. Their authors were Mexican dignitaries, sometimes direct descendants of the princes of various cities. Their way of understanding and narrating is as close as we can come to understanding the mentality of Moctezuma and his advisers. It is plausible—even if it is not true—for them to have sought portents of the events that were taking place.

How does one interpret this aspect of these narratives (which makes them similar on this point to *The Odyssey* or the legend of the quest for the Holy Grail)? There is a clear refusal here to accept an entirely new event, a totally unprecedented act: only events that have been foretold can occur. The Aztecs' entire conception of time favors the cyclical over the linear, repetition over difference, ritual over improvisation. When such an unprecedented event does occur, however (and what was more unprecedented than the appearance of the Spaniards?), an attempt will be made to transpose it to a familiar mental schema in order to make it intelligible and, thereby, at least partially acceptable. This kind of interpretation of history is an act of resistance against Spanish domination; it is a final act of war. And yet the move is ambiguous: isn't making an event acceptable already resigning oneself to accepting it?

An episode found in Durán's narrative clarifies this attitude. In this instance, it is no longer a matter of omens or prophecies, but of a truthful account made to Moctezuma by his emissaries, who had encountered the Spaniards from the first expedition. How does the Aztec ruler react? "Moctezuma wondered how he could know who these people were and where they came from. He decided to seek out, by all available means, old Indians who could tell him, in the greatest secrecy" (chapter 69). Why, in the face of this unprecedented event, which had been clearly described by its observers, was it necessary to consult *old* Indians, if not because only events that have already existed in the past can occur in the present, even if only in the form of a prediction?

The account of this search takes up chapter 70. First Moctezuma has a portrait of the Spaniards drawn according to the descriptions of those who saw them; next he shows this portrait to various old men, but they remain silent. He then tries another tactic: he keeps the picture at home and asks the oldest painters of the kingdom for their early drawings representing strange beings. Another disappointment: he is shown men with one eye or one foot, men with fish tails or grass snake tails, but nothing that resembles the Spaniards. He then discovers an old man from Xochimilco, a painter and scholar. He replies to Moctezuma's question by unfurling a "painting which my ancestors bequeathed me"; and—what a coincidence!—it depicts beings who are similar in every way to the Spaniards, except some of them are mounted on eagles instead of on horses. Moctezuma is distressed but, at the same time, almost relieved: yes, the event had indeed been predicted.

Concrete information is thus treated in the same way as omens: as a confirmation of the cyclical nature of time and the repetition of history.

## The Arrival of the Spaniards

The arrival of the Spaniards is indeed an absolutely unprecedented event. Muñoz Camargo speaks of "events so strange and unique, never seen or heard until then" (Muñoz Camargo, chapter 1). An earlier version of the narrative in the *Florentine Codex* is particularly revelatory. It begins:

> No knowledge here, really nothing,
> no word said about the Spaniards
> before they arrived here, before their reputation was known.
> First there appeared an omen of misfortune in the sky,
> it was frightening, as if it were a flame . . .

The two sentences contradict one another, but this is because one is a response to the other: it is precisely *because* nothing of the Spaniards was known beforehand that it was necessary to devise the omens.

Once the Spaniards were there, how were they perceived? The lack of any preliminary familiarity gives rise to what may be called a "distantiated" form of perception. Harquebuses become "trumpets of fire," boats become hills that move by themselves, houses that float with the help of large sheets. Horses are "roebucks"; at first the Indians do not know if they are really separate from the riders or if they eat the same food humans do. All these objects do not exist in the Indian world and are, in fact, described quite plausibly. Other traits of the Spaniards are depicted very precisely, revealing an attentiveness to everything that is different: the complexion of their skin, the color of their hair and beards, their clothing, food, and weapons.

For us today, some of these descriptions have exceptional power, a power due to a gaze that is at once direct and removed. Chapter 15 of the *Florentine Codex* is a fine example of this: it is as if a movie camera had been installed on the outskirts of Mexico City and trained on the troops of conquistadors as they slowly filed past. Other, earlier descriptions from the same text emphasize the metal on the Spaniards' bodies, transforming them progressively into supernatural, almost extraterrestrial beings. Other descriptions are of the newcomers' dogs — and we know the sinister role they were to play (they were "extremely efficient," wrote Muñoz Camargo coldly, in chapter 5):

> Their spears of metal, their bat-like spears, it was as if they threw off lightning. And their metal swords undulated like water. It was as if their metal shirts, their metal helmets, reverberated. And others are coming, all in metal, they come made entirely of metal, they come throwing lightning. . . . And their dogs are leading them, they come before them, they come leading the way, they come gasping; their slaver falls in little drops. (chapter 11)

This view "from the outside" also extends to interpretation. And here we find an additional characteristic of the encounter between Indians and Spaniards. At first the Spaniards are believed to be gods. The *Florentine Codex* repeatedly offers proof of this: "And Moctezuma had acted thus in this way because he thought them gods, he took them for gods, he worshiped them as gods. They were called, they were named the 'gods come from heaven.' And the black ones were said to be dirty gods." (*FC,* chapter 21). Muñoz Camargo described the Mexicans' doubts: "If they were gods, they would not overturn our oracles, nor would they mistreat our gods, since they would be their brothers." On the other hand, however, "they were gods because they came mounted on very strange animals, never seen nor heard in the world" (Muñoz Camargo, chapter 1). Durán also reports that the Spaniards were called "gods" and once explains this by the workmanship of their boats: "work more fitting of gods than of men" (Durán, chapter 69).

The belief that the Spaniards were gods is given additional precision in both the *Florentine Codex* and in Durán's account: they are not just any gods, but Quetzalcoatl, the legendary god and king who, driven from his throne, had vowed to return one day. Moctezuma was said to believe that Cortés was Quetzalcoatl or, if not Quetzalcoatl himself, one of his descendants (*FC,* chapter 16; Durán, chapter 74). There is no reason to doubt the good faith of the authors of these accounts: it is clear that they believed this version. Nonetheless, the same may not have actually been true for Moctezuma and his relations. The Spaniards appeared for the first time in

1517, whereas Quetzalcoatl was supposed to have returned in a One-Reed year of the Aztec calendar, for example, in 1519. Furthermore, he was not the most important god in the Tenochca (another name for the inhabitants of Mexico City) pantheon. We do know, however, that Cortés tried by every means possible to make the Mexicans suspect that he was in fact the returned Quetzalcoatl; this was his way of speaking the "language of the others," and of manipulating them through their own myths. The Indian accounts are in fact too similar to the version given by Cortés himself in his reports to Charles V, and to those communicated by his chaplain and biographer Gomara, for one to believe that they are truly independent of one another.

Yet if Cortés himself influenced this particular identification, he had nothing to do with the widespread belief in the divine nature of the Spaniards, of which there exists much evidence. How could such a thing occur? The words used to describe the fact also provide its explanation: it is because of their newness, their strangeness, their difference, and their technical superiority that the newcomers are classified as gods. Moctezuma sent sorcerers and enchanters to fight the Spaniards, to cast nightmarish visions at them, to spread disease, to make their hearts stop. The magicians' attempts failed, and here is the explanation offered: "These people were very different from them, in mood and matter. The flesh of these gods was hard, no magic arts could penetrate it and make the least impression upon it, for they could not reach their heart. The gods had very dark entrails and chests" (Durán, chapter 71). There is a direct movement here from "very different" to "gods." Until then, the Aztecs had lived in a relatively closed world, despite the vastness of their empire; they were unaware of radical human alterity and, upon encountering it, they used the only category available to them that allowed for this radical strangeness: gods.

The misunderstanding did not last long, but it occurred when the Spaniards were particularly vulnerable; and because it had a paralyzing effect on the Indians — who venerated the newcomers rather than fighting them — it played an important role in the outcome of the encounter. At the same time, or shortly afterward, another image of the Spaniards arose (but it was probably already too late). The "gods" were revealed to be less than human, moved only by material instincts. All the texts mention their "appetite for riches" (and they threw themselves with equal gluttony upon real food), which inspired the Mexicans' scorn: "As if they were monkeys, they seized upon the gold; they stuffed themselves with it; they starved for it; they lusted for it like pigs" (*FC*, 31).

Significantly, this description is immediately followed by another: "It was as if they babbled. What they said was gibberish" (*FC,* 31). In the eyes of the Mexicans, the Spaniards appeared as beings poor in symbols who barely knew how to speak and who were ignorant of the social and ritual dimensions of life. They were offered the most prestigious gift, the finery of the gods: they rejected it with scorn, seeing in it nothing more than a heap of feathers. They were given elegant jewelry: they destroyed it in order to extract nuggets of gold. "And as all the gold was detached, at once they ignited, set fire to, applied fire to all the various precious things which remained. They all burned. And the gold the Spaniards formed into separate bars" (*FC,* 48). During one of the earliest battles — the massacre in the temple of Mexico City — the conquistadors first attacked the professionals of symbolic activity: the personifiers of the gods, the drummers. "Thereupon they surrounded the dancers. Thereupon they went among the drums. Then they struck the drummer's arm; they severed both his hands; then they struck his neck. Far off did his neck and head go to fall" (*FC,* 55).

In contrast, the Mexicans represented themselves (and appear to us) as deeply attached to ritual and little inclined to imitate the pragmatic behavior of the Spaniards: whereas the latter gladly stuffed themselves with the gifts offered by their hosts, the former, on a similar occasion, carried the food offered in a ritual procession, sang appropriate hymns, and buried it in the temple (Durán, chapter 69). And when they seized a canon, they immersed it ceremonially in the water of the lake. In addition, they reproached the Spaniards for waging war "without warning."

## Moctezuma's Reactions

When the first news of the Spaniards reached Moctezuma, how did he react? It is not surprising that he entrusted the interpretation of omens to the gods; but it must be recalled that, faced with factual information, his behavior did not change — he rushed to the ancient manuscripts in order to find answers to the new questions. He was very careful to learn about the comings and goings of the Spaniards, but at the same time his behavior was not encouraging to his messengers or interpreters: each time the information or its interpretation displeased him, he threw its bearers into prison or had them killed, which discouraged any other candidates for the job. He was particularly frightened to learn that the Spaniards were apparently continually asking for news of him, as if their sole goal were to acquire information.

To say that Moctezuma was ill-at-ease with the news about the Spaniards is an understatement; he was plunged into a veritable stupor. "And when Moctezuma so heard, he was terrified. It was as if he fainted away. His heart saddened; his heart failed him." "Moctezuma, when he heard it, only bowed his head. He hung his head; he sat with head hanging down. No longer did he speak aloud; he only sat dejected for a long time, as if he had lost hope" (*FC,* 34). He felt deeply shaken: "Alas, until now, I. In great torment is my heart.... Where in truth may we go, O our lord" (*FC,* 34). Durán also shows Moctezuma plunged in deep silence, "as if dead or mute" upon hearing the news (chapter 69).

Why this paralysis? The very fact that the Spaniards could land on the Mexican coast seemed to have determined the direction his response would take: faced with this radically new fact, there was no reaction possible; for this fact, by its very existence, signified the collapse of the old system of thought in which it was inconceivable. The only thing left to do was to re-sign oneself:

> How could this have happened? From where did these calamities, this anguish, these torments come to us? Who are these people who are arriving? From where have they come? Who led them here? Why did not this happen in our ancestors' time? There is no other remedy, my lords, other than to resign your hearts and souls patiently suffering your fate, for it is already at your door. (Durán, chapter 73)

This is the speech that Moctezuma addressed to the other Mexican kings. If only the event had occurred in the time of their ancestors!

His stupor thus expressed resignation and fatalism. Moctezuma decided to let himself die; he wanted to hide deep in a grotto as a kind of transition to the world beyond. He would rather have seen the bad omens come true than live in uncertainty, and he asked his emissaries to let themselves be eaten by the newcomers, if the latter so desired. The very existence of the Spaniards, because it was so unexpected, was proof of their superiority. "What has been determined can be avoided by no one"; "one cannot es-cape the decrees of fate" (Durán, chapter 67).

Moctezuma was not alone in this attitude. The *Florentine Codex* describes the entire population as if struck with paralysis, immobilized by pain. Peo-ple cried upon meeting, they hid in their houses. "They were in great ter-ror; they could not control themselves for fear; they were astounded. Fear prevailed; fear was widespread. No one dared do anything. It was as if a

fierce beast were there; it was as the deep of night." Muñoz Camargo explains that "the Indians were not distressed by the fear of losing their lands,
their kingdoms or their goods, but by the certainty that the world had
reached its end, that all the generations were going to disappear and perish,
since the gods had come down from the sky and one could no longer
think of anything but the end, the ruin, and the destruction of all things."
This stupor seems to originate precisely in the newness and the unintelligi-
bility of the things that had occurred: "And they went about like this, lost
and sad, without knowing what to think of events so strange, so remarkable, never seen nor heard until then" (Muñoz Camargo, chapter 1). Durán
also recounts the appeals to submission and the widespread conviction that
the old gods were dead.

When Moctezuma favored a more active opposition to the Spaniards,
he again resorted to soothsayers and sorcerers. He asked them to blow on the
Spaniards, to bewitch them to make them ill or to discourage them from
coming; but the sorcerers proved powerless and confirmed the superiority
of the new gods: "They declared that they were gods against whom their
power broke." They did not know that the Spaniards, however, had acknowledged the power of the spells: "Sometimes they saw the heads of
men jumping in the courtyard; other times, they saw a foot or a thigh coming at them, or corpses rolling.... And it was a religious conquistador who
spoke to me of these visions, well before this story had explained it all to me,
still frightened of the things he had seen at that time" (Durán, chapter 75).

Moctezuma thus continued to react within the same sphere whose relevance had been challenged by the very coming of the Spaniards; and the
absence of palpable results from his efforts confirmed his resignation, or kept
him in a state of perplexity. He thus acted alternately in two contradictory
directions, either sending out his sorcerers or offering hospitality to these
gods. But it appears that the benevolent attitude prevailed; consequently, at
the end of his life, a new sector of Mexican public opinion accused him of
having become the wife of the Spaniards — the worst insult for the virile
Aztecs — while other versions even say he converted to Christianity.

## Internal Discord

At the beginning of the sixteenth century, Mexico was not a homogeneous
state, but a conglomeration of populations dominated by the Aztecs of
Mexico-Tenochtitlán; in some cases, this domination was recent and pre-
carious. In addition, the relations between neighboring populations were

often hostile. This is why the arrival of the Spaniards led to a series of contradictory reactions that together served Cortes's cause well. For example, the Tlazcaltecs, who were outside of the Aztec Empire, suffered constantly from its assaults; they therefore willingly entered into Cortés's service. The inhabitants of Teocalhueyacan also complained: "Moctezuma and the Mexicans have much afflicted us, much wearied us. To our very noses have they brought affliction" (*FC,* 75). Another chief declared: "May the Tenochcas be annihilated one by one!" (*Historical Annals*). All of these old animosities were revived with the coming of the Spaniards. An intense rivalry existed between the neighboring cities, Tlaxcala and Cholula: Cortés's arrival gave the inhabitants of the former the opportunity to take revenge on the inhabitants of the latter; according to Muñoz Camargo's chronicle — and he was from Tlaxcala — this was motivated by the Cholultecs' own hostile acts.

Within each population, each city itself, discord flourished. In Mexico City, both Moctezuma and Quauhtemoc received contradictory counsel. On the one hand, the Mexicans were executing the local chiefs who dared to oppose Cortés; on the other, they persecuted those whom they suspected — sometimes wrongly — of being his collaborators. In Tlaxcala and Texcoco, similar conflicts erupted. Ixtlilxochitl, a prince who had been removed from power by a half brother, was one of the first to convert to Christianity. When his mother learned of this, she "asked him if he hadn't lost his mind and reproached him for having let himself be conquered in such a short time by a handful of barbarians. Don Hernando Ixtlilxochitl retorted that, had she not been his mother, his response to her would have been to tear her head from her shoulders, and that he would become a Christian whether she wanted him to or not" (*Ramírez Codex,* chapter 3).

Thanks to his "intelligence network," Cortés learned of the existence of these internal frictions early on and decided to use them: he "had found what he wanted, that is, this discord" (Durán, chapter 73), and he cultivated it carefully, thus bringing one population after the other over to his cause: "Neither did the good Marquis renounce winning these nations over, and he sent embassies and missions in order to declare that he was coming to deliver them from the tyranny and the yoke of the Mexicans" (Durán, chapter 76). During the war's last phase, an impressive army of Indians entered Cortés's service to fight the Mexicans. The *Ramírez Codex* breaks off at a very significant scene in which Hernando Ixtlilxochitl knocks over the idols he had so recently venerated: "Cortés grabbed the mask, Don Hernando caught the idol, which he had once adored, by the hair, and decapitated it.

Holding the head with outstretched arms, he showed it to the Mexicans and said to them in a stirring voice: 'Behold your god and his feeble power; acknowledge your defeat and receive the law of God, unique and true'" (*Ramírez Codex,* chapter 14).

The Indian narratives describe this friction and often deplore it. Yet they unwittingly attest to the vigor of these fratricidal hatreds since, as we have seen, they always adopt the point of view of regional patriotism and, even some ten, twenty, or thirty years after the conquest, still attempt to lay blame on their neighbors. "And when this had occurred, the people of Tenochtitlán entered here into Tlatilulco. . . . But the Tlatilulcans again already went there to Tenochtitlán to fight" (*FC*, 91). "And during the whole time that we were being beaten, the man from Tenochtitlán was never seen, on any road here. . . . Simply, everywhere, it was up to us, the Tlatilulcans" (*Historical Annals*). These are tragic words uttered by people who did not know what role the feelings that generated them would play in the fatal outcome of the combat.

## The Confrontation

The first battles were not between the Spaniards and the inhabitants of Mexico City, but between the Spaniards and the inhabitants of other cities that were nearer the Atlantic coast. The *Florentine Codex* relates one of these encounters as a total victory for the invaders. "But the Otomis, the men of Tecoac, they completely annihilated, they completely destroyed them. They trampled upon them" (27). Durán describes a type of man-to-man combat that seems to have come straight out of romances of chivalry: two horsemen throw themselves at two Indian warriors who are on foot; at the last minute, each of the Indians springs to the side and kills the horse thrown against him, thereby incapacitating his adversary. Even in this instance, however, the Spaniards' metal swords, harquebuses, and cannons lead them to victory in the end. Muñoz Camargo tells of an unusual military tactic developed by the Cholultecs:

> According to legend, when the facing of the wall cracked off, water began to seep through the fissures; and, so as not to perish by drowning, they sacrificed two- and three-year-old children and, kneading their blood in lime, made a kind of coating to stop up the leaks. . . . The Cholultecs proclaimed that, should they suffer setbacks in the war against the Tlaxcaltecs or the white gods,

they would strip the coating off the walls, and the fountains that would spring from the cracks would drown their enemies. (Muñoz Camargo, chapter 5)

But the Cholultecs drowned in their own blood, for they were the victims of the first great Spanish massacre.

The open hostilities with the Mexicans began with another massacre, the massacre of the Tenochca nobility in the temple during the festival of Uitzilopochtli. Cortés had left to fight the troops of another Spaniard, Pánfilo de Naváez; Alvarado, who remained in charge of the Mexico City garrison, "authorized" the festival to go on, then locked up the defenseless participants and exterminated them. The Indian narratives have retained a vivid memory of these events: "Of some they slashed open their backs: then their entrails gushed out. Of some they cut their heads to pieces; they absolutely pulverized their heads. And some they struck on the shoulder; they split openings, they broke openings in their bodies. . . . And when in vain one would run, he would only drag his intestines like something raw as he tried to escape. Nowhere could he go" (*FC,* 55). Durán visualizes some divine intervention at this point, but not on the side one would have expected: the Christian God becomes involved precisely because he condemns the act of his zealots and he saves them from death so that they will have time to atone for their sins.

The next major event is the death of Moctezuma. In the Indian narratives of the resistance, this emperor, with his ambiguous behavior, is not a hero. Although they never admitted responsibility, the Spaniards stabbed Moctezuma in secret and then returned his body to the Mexicans.

According to the *Florentine Codex,* the Mexicans arranged a hasty cremation (in contrast to that of another Mexican chief), and the body of Moctezuma, the text points out, "smelled foul as it burned" (*FC,* 66). The *Aubin Codex* presents a more comical scene: the corpse is loaded onto the back of a Mexican who brings it to a first site. People come to see it, but they refuse to accept it. The same occurs at a second and then a third site. Weary from carrying this body without finding a burying place, the bearer arrives at a fourth site and cries: "Ah, the unhappy Moctezuma! Am I to spend the rest of my life carrying him on my back?" The body is then accepted and burned without ceremony.

The Spaniards fled from the city during the *Noche triste,* and then, almost a year later, returned with reinforcements of Indian allies, bringing with them swift brigantines that dominated the fighting on the waters of the lake that surrounds Mexico City. The final battle lasted another several months. The Indian narratives relate many significant episodes. At times they tell of the exploits of a particularly heroic warrior who resembles Diomedes in the Iliad: Tzilactazin in the *Florentine Codex,* or, in the *Ramírez Codex,* Ixtlilxochitl on the side of Cortés's allies. At other times, it is the miseries of the besieged, suffering from hunger and thirst, that are emphasized, rather than the Spaniards' assault. An elegy, preserved in the *Historical Annals* and perhaps written at the time the events occurred, powerfully expresses this experience:

> The shields were able to protect us,
> but in vain did we want to people the solitude
> with shields.
> We have eaten the colored wood of *tzompantli,*
> we have chewed the couch grass of natron,
> the clay bricks, lizards,
> mice, plaster dust
> and vermin.
> . . . Gold, jade, cotton mantises,
> the feathers of quetzal,
> everything that is precious
> counted for nothing.

The Spaniards' vise around the city became tighter and tighter and the Mexicans ceded ground, house by house. The Mexicans' last attempts to make an impression on the Spaniards are particularly moving: Quauhtemoc takes out a parade costume that his father—the former emperor of the Mexicans—had bequeathed him, and places it on an intrepid fighter before loosing him on the Spaniards. "And when our foes saw him, it was as if a mountain had crumbled. All the Spaniards indeed were terrified" (*FC,* 118). But the outcome of the war could no longer be changed. Durán reports another of Quauhtemoc's ruses: "Wanting to make the Spaniards believe that he was lacking neither men nor force to defend himself, he asked the women of the city to dress in men's clothing and, in the early morning, to take up arms and shields, and to go up on all the terraces of the houses and to make gestures of contempt at them" (Durán, chapter 77). At first, the strategy succeeded, but soon the truth was discovered and the Spaniards' advance continued, inexorable.

The last act of the drama is Quauhtemoc's surrender, about which the narratives offer abundant details. Quauhtemoc is dressed only in a torn coat. Cortés looks at him, and "he continually stroked Quauhtemoc" (*FC*, 121). Yet this did not prevent Cortés from torturing Quauhtemoc shortly afterward, burning his feet in an attempt to discover where Moctezuma's treasure might be hidden. In order to avoid the concupiscent stares of the Spaniards, the Indian women covered their faces with mud and dressed themselves in rags. The Spaniards were severe: the imprisoned chiefs were hung or given up to the dogs to be devoured. The stench of corpses was so strong that it nauseated the Spaniards, and "all of them pressed against their noses with fine white cloths" (*FC*, 122).

"*Finally the battle just stopped; thus silence reigned; nothing took place*" (*FC*, 118).

## The Meaning of the Story

Do this defeat and destruction have meaning, or are they simply absurd? Since the transmitters — and sometimes even the narrators — of these accounts are Christian, it is not surprising that their interpretation of the story is influenced by Christianity. This interpretation attempts to justify not the Spaniards' misdeeds, but rather the end result of the encounter: "The divine will was to save and deliver these miserable nations from the intolerable idolatry that was blinding them" (Durán, chapter 76). God, in a way, had condescended to accept the gift the Spaniards were offering him, even if he condemned the manner in which they went about it. In chapter 4 of his *History of Tlaxcala*, Muñoz Camargo recounted the veritable theological debates that took place between Spaniards and Mexicans (in reality they occurred after the conquest, and not between Cortés and the Tlaxcaltec chiefs). The imposition of the Christian faith gave meaning to the cruel story of the conquest.

Can one arrive at another, more authentically Indian answer to the above question, through these same texts? Certain passages in the *Florentine Codex* and in Durán's narrative allow a glimpse of this other answer: they establish Moctezuma's guilt — he was held responsible for the disaster — outside of any reference to the Christian canon. "He hath committed a fault; he hath abandoned the common folk; he hath destroyed the people," declares the prophet-drunkard in the *Florentine Codex* (33). And the eagle who carried off the peasant maintains the same thing: "He himself unleashed the misfortunes that will strike him" (Durán, chapter 67). But what exactly was Moctezuma's error? The texts seem above all to criticize him for his pride. During the cremation of his body, his disdain for those around him is recalled sternly. The eagle describes him as "drunk and filled with pride, he who scorns the entire world"; and the narrator himself notes "demoniacal pride, a haughtiness so unbounded that he no longer even feared the power of the gods" (Durán, chapter 66).

How does this pride manifest itself? It seems that the most spectacular proof of it is offered by Moctezuma's attitude toward the Spaniards themselves: he resists them too much, he is not resigned enough. The drunkard says this about it: "What do you yet require? What would Moctezuma still wish to do?" (*FC*, 31). And the stone that refuses to be moved says, "May he not oppose destiny" (Durán, chapter 66). The entire episode of the stone confirms that Moctezuma's pride consists in wanting to act on his own authority, in not sufficiently yielding to the signs of the gods.

An answer such as this is somewhat paradoxical. There is no happy outcome to this situation: were he to submit, Moctezuma would bring about a Spanish victory by his very weakness; were he to resist, he would still bring it about, but he would also provoke the wrath of the gods. Since the Spaniards could not have arrived on the Atlantic coast without the consent of the gods in the first place, their arrival carried within it the seed of all that was to follow; the Spaniards would remain because they had already arrived. The mere sequence of events does not suffice, as it did with Caesar, to explain the events. The Spaniards came *and* they conquered? No: they conquered *because* they came.

Today's reader might think that the causes of Moctezuma's defeat—his fatalism, his slowness to adapt, his inability to improvise and to take personal initiatives—were what distinguished him from the Spaniards. The Indian narratives offer the opposite point of view: it is precisely his similarity to the Spaniards—his lack of fatalism, his desire to act outside the established codes—that causes his downfall. Thus, in affirming the guilt of their emperor, the narratives in fact reject the new ideology brought by the Spaniards. The very existence of these narratives becomes an act of resistance—not military, but spiritual—to the conquest that Mexico undergoes. Moctezuma was punished for having violated the traditional Indian spirit that the narratives themselves loudly proclaim. To give such a meaning to the conquest-defeat is at the same time to overcome it.

Frightened by the omens of misfortune, Moctezuma decided to ensure that he would be remembered for eternity, and he called on the sculptors in his kingdom, asking them to carve his likeness in the rock of Chapultepec:

He went to see his statue when he was told it had been completed and began to shed tears, lamenting in this way: "If our bodies were as durable in this life as this portrait of stone that will last for eternity, who would fear death? But I see clearly that I am going to die and that this is the only memory that will remain of me." (Durán, chapter 66)

Here again Moctezuma was mistaken, not because he understood his mortality, but because he believed the image of stone to be eternal. Once they had become the masters of Mexico City, the Spaniards' first task would be to eliminate all traces of the Mexicans' past grandeur that could incite them to revolt: temples were destroyed and stone statues broken. Yet the name of Moctezuma and the saga of his compatriots were preserved and will never be forgotten, not because of stone, but because of the words that captured the event, the narratives that managed to transmit them. This lesson, it seems, had already been learned by another people of pyramids. An Egyptian papyrus of the nineteenth dynasty of Ramses reveals:

A book is more useful than a graven stele
or a solid wall.
It takes the place of temple and pyramid,
in proclaiming the name.
Man perishes, his body will become dust once again,
all his fellow beings return to the earth,
but the book will cause his memory to be passed from mouth to
    mouth.

# 4 / The Conquest as Seen by the French

Beginning in the sixteenth century, a great variety of attitudes and a searching reflection about the events that were taking place could be found in Spain, the principal country involved in the conquest. The debates surrounding the conquest can be said to have reached their apogee in the public debate that took place in 1550 at Valladolid. The opposing opinions were held by two major figures: on one side, Bartolomé de Las Casas, a Dominican and a tireless defender of the Indians, who denounced the conquistadors' crimes; on the other, Juan Ginés de Sepúlveda, a man of letters, a translator, and a commentator of Aristotle, a champion of the intrinsic superiority of Christian Europe who supported the conquest in the name of the values of his civilization.

Today, choosing between these two positions seems easy: who would not prefer to espouse Las Casas's generosity rather than what appears to us as Sepúlveda's racism? And yet, if we follow the controversy from beginning to end, it becomes obvious that things are not so simple. Las Casas acknowledged the a priori equality of all peoples, yet he did not abandon his belief in the superiority of his own religion, Christianity. Thus, he attributed the characteristics of ideal Christians to the Indians. In other words, his egalitarianism led him to an unconscious assimilationism; and the image of the Indians found in his works is relatively paltry (although he did accumulate an impressive mass of facts), since he tended to brush aside everything that contradicted his apologetic project, and to interpret his observations from a Christian point of view. Sepúlveda, on the other hand, was on the lookout for differences because he needed proofs for his thesis of European superiority, and he willingly emphasized things that Las Casas had glossed over, such as sacrificial and cannibalistic rites, and the absence of phonetic writing, draft animals, and money. But his European prejudices prevented him from exploring these differences further, and he contented himself with a quick, negative sketch. For entirely different reasons, the knowledge of Indians that one can acquire from Sepúlveda's writings is at least as unsatisfactory as what can be found in Las Casas's work.

Still, it is not a matter of declaring a draw more than four hundred years later between these adversaries of old: Las Casas's attitude is without a doubt more admirable, and the thousands of pages he devoted to the Indians obviously carry more weight than the few pages left by Sepúlveda. But the ambiguities that exist in both positions are cause for reflection. Despite the many differences that separate them, the generous assimilationism of Las Casas and the proud ethnocentrism of Sepúlveda lead to the same point: ignorance about the Indians themselves. If one projects one's ideal onto the other, one is just as liable to misunderstand him as one is if one were to project that ideal onto oneself. That is, the egalitarian attitude threatens to be transformed into an affirmation of sameness, whereas the perception of differences runs the risk of being swallowed up in the brutal affirmation of the superiority of one culture over another. At the same time, one realizes that knowledge is not a neutral attitude that can be opposed outright to value judgments made about others: through its determinations and its consequences, knowledge is closely linked to the ethical stance one takes and the values one praises. Science is not the opposite of ethics, since there is an ethics of science.

The antagonism between Las Casas and Sepúlveda has the disadvantage of being too extreme. Their positions are hyperbolic and do not aid in perceiving nuances. A little distance would be useful here, distance in time and in space. When we move from Spain to neighboring France, we find that French philosophers and moralists have often used the conquest of America as a subject of their reflections. In this chapter I analyze two of these reflections—those of Montaigne and those of Montesquieu—because they seem to me both complex and representative.

# I

Montaigne analyzed the conquest of Mexico (and of Peru) in his essay "On Coaches," and for four centuries it has been admired by anticolonialists. One of them, the historian Charles-André Julien, summarizes a widely held opinion: "In these generous, so profoundly human pages, among the most beautiful ever written, an unequaled power of the French tradition of the defense of the oppressed against the strong is affirmed" (*Les Voyages de decouverte,* 418). In point of fact, doesn't Montaigne clearly express his condemnation of the conquering Spaniards, and his regret that the conquest even took place? "So many cities razed, so many nations exterminated, so many millions of peoples put to the sword, and the richest and most beautiful part of the world turned upside down for the traffic in pearls and pepper! Base and mechanical victories" (*Essays,* 695). Still, reading Montaigne's essay, one discovers some difficulties in adhering to this interpretation.

One cannot help being struck by the fact that Montaigne seems to vacillate between two positions that at first appear to be contradictory. Let us take, for example, the questions related to material and technological civilization. On the one hand, Montaigne mentions the Indians' characteristic lack of know-how in relation to road construction: "They had no other means of carrying than by strength of arm, dragging their load along; and they had not even the art of scaffolding, knowing no other device than to raise an equal height of earth against their building as it rose, and remove it afterward" (698). On the other hand, seeing their botanical and zoological collections, he acknowledges the splendor of their cities and the delicacy of their workmanship, which "show that they were not behind us in industry either" (694). And the same roads inspire this opinion: "Neither Greece nor Rome nor Egypt can compare, whether in utility or difficulty or nobility, with the road which is seen in Peru" (698). "Nobility" seems to refer here not only to the height of moral inspiration but also to technical perfection.

The same is true of his descriptions that deal with the moral sphere. On the one hand Montaigne writes:

> Why did not such a noble conquest fall to Alexander or to those ancient Greeks and Romans? Why did not such a great change and alteration of so many empires and peoples fall into hands that would have strengthened and fostered the good seeds that nature has produced in them, not only adding to the cultivation of the

earth and the adornment of cities the art of our side of the ocean, in so far as they would have been necessary, but also adding the Greek and Roman virtues to those originally in that region! (695)

Implied here is that these peoples do not possess all the necessary virtues and remain, in part, savages; and that some kind of colonial intervention is desirable, provided it were conducted by those who possessed the necessary virtues. At the same time, however, Montaigne assures us that "they were not at all behind us in natural brightness of mind and pertinence" (683) and that they even surpassed us "in devoutness, observance of the laws, goodness, liberality, loyalty and frankness" (694); as for "boldness and courage," "firmness, constancy, resoluteness against pain and hunger and death," they were equal to the "most famous of ancient examples that we have in the memories of our world on this side of the ocean" (694). But aren't these "ancient examples" the same Greeks and Romans mentioned elsewhere? And what, if not virtues, is enumerated here?

In the end, it is difficult to decide if Montaigne thought that these peoples belonged to humanity's infancy or not. It was a world, he wrote, "so new and so infantile that it is still being taught its A B C" (693); "It was still quite naked at the breast, and lived only on what its nursing mother provided" (693); "It was an infant world"; they were "souls so fresh, so famished to learn, and having, for the most part, such fine natural beginnings" (695). But elsewhere, having quoted a wise response from the king of the Mexicans, Montaigne comments ironically: "There we have an example of the babbling of this infancy" (696). One no longer knows if he believes it himself. Such a series of contradictions cannot be purely gratuitous.

One has the impression that Montaigne uses the stories about the conquest of America to illustrate two independent theses, and that this is what caused the discrepancies in his arguments. The first thesis is that humanity lives according to the model of the individual (which later leads to all his analogies between savages and children): it has a childhood, or an age of apprenticeship, and an old age, the age of the world "on this side of the ocean." The second thesis is the idea of the golden age—a time closer to man's origins, since with time what was naturally marvelous dissipates into artifice. This second thesis is what allows for the criticism of our society that is so often found in Montaigne's work. It is also the dominant thesis of "On Coaches," since the passages related to the conquest take up only the second half; the first part is devoted to the condemnation of our own rulers, who are contrasted with the wise kings of the American Indians.

In truth, one could, with a few readjustments, reconcile these two theses: one need simply make the biological model (or the myth of the golden age) slightly more complex by adding a third, intermediary instance between the Indians who embody childhood and our own decadence: the youthful maturity of the Greeks, the true golden age to which the Indians are closer than we are, yet nonetheless do not belong to. This would explain how, although they are superior to us, they still have things to learn from the Greeks. This interpretation, however, in no way changes another aspect of Montaigne's demonstration, which is that, rather than attempting to understand the Indians, he uses them to illustrate his ideas about our own society. The same fact—lack of technical knowledge, for example—can support, according to the dictates of the moment, either thesis indifferently. This is because the Indians are little more than allegory here. In addition, it is clear that Montaigne's reasoning is rarely supported by empirical observations: neither the idea of the infancy of humanity nor that of the golden age can be proved by such observations.

Montaigne's descriptions of the Indians are striking for another reason, which one could call their atomism. He isolates the Indians' characteristics (which he takes from the history of the Spaniard Gomara) and evaluates them one by one. He points out their "observance of the laws," but he never wonders about the reasons for this observance or what it entails in Indian society. The same is true of courage: the Indians' courage is directly comparable to that of the Greeks; it is an absolute value uninfluenced by circumstances. He speaks of their "indomitable ardor," their "noble, stubborn readiness to suffer all extremities and hardships" (694). He points out that, unlike us, they do not use gold as a universal equivalent: "The use of money was entirely unknown and . . . consequently their gold was found all collected together," whereas "we cut it up small and change it into a thousand forms; we scatter and disperse it" (697). Yet, with the exception of the implicit moral condemnation, this fact does not lead him to any conclusion about the societies that possess these very different characteristics, whereas Sepúlveda saw in this an indication of the level of civilization.

Montaigne's epistemological atomism is particularly striking in his explanation of the outcome of the military encounter. The facts, as we know, are enigmatic: how does one explain that a few hundred Spanish adventurers managed to overthrow the powerful empires of Mexico and Peru, with their hundreds of thousands of warriors? Montaigne answers this question by imagining what it would have been necessary to take from the former and give to the latter in order to change the outcome of the battle, and he concludes: very little. If one eliminated the Spaniards' ruses, if the use of metal and firearms were taken from them; if the Indians' surprise upon seeing such strange men and horses could have been contained, if their weapons—which were merely stones, bows, and sticks—could have been replaced, the outcome of the battle would have been uncertain: "Eliminate this disparity, I say, and you take from the conquerors the whole basis of so many victories" (694). Thus, at bottom, Spanish superiority does not exist.

This line of thought deserves some attention. Montaigne points out differences in behavior and technology between the two societies. But he draws no conclusions from these differences about the societies they characterize. Yet the metalwork and firearms did not come out of nowhere, without any relation to the life of the peoples who used them. The Indians were surprised, he said, at seeing "the unexpected arrival of bearded men, different in language, religion, shape and countenance" (694). But why don't the Spaniards experience the same paralyzing effect upon meeting beardless men who, obviously, were just as different in language and religion? The Spaniards' more rapid psychological adaptation and their technological superiority are undeniable, and they correspond to other characteristics of Spanish society of the time. How could they be "removed" without affecting the identity of this society? Reciprocally, there may be a relation between the Indians' "devoutness" and "observance of laws" on the one hand, and their uneasiness upon seeing someone unknown, someone other. Montaigne acts as if it went without saying that certain traits of a civilization are essential, while others are accidental and that the latter can be "removed" at will without jeopardizing the group's very identity. But who decides what is essence and what is accident?

In addition to this epistemological atomism, Montaigne also practices what can be termed an axiological (or ethical) "globalism." His description of Indian or European society consisted of a systematic listing of traits. But Montaigne's value judgment is global: "our mores" in their totality are characterized by "all kinds of inhumanity and cruelty," contrary to the mores of the Indians. Not only does each individual trait (courage, devoutness, etc.) of a society always retain the same value, everywhere, but the way that trait has been valued is immediately extended to the rest of the society in which everything is good, or else decadent.

The knowledge of societies that can be found in Montaigne's essay remains piecemeal and is in fact entirely subordinate to his didactic project, the criticism of our society. The identity of the *other* is never acknowledged, even if it is idealized for the needs of the cause. Not coincidentally, this epistemological negligence is accompanied by a political position that now appears to us as the opposite of anticolonialism: Montaigne is in favor of "good" colonization, colonization carried out in the name of his own ideals (incarnated by the Greeks and Romans). What the future colonized peoples themselves would think about it is never considered.

## II

Montesquieu did not leave a text devoted entirely to the conquest. Nevertheless, he had the intention of so doing, as the following note from his *Pensées* indicates: "I would like to make a judgment on Solis's history of Hernan Cortés, with comments; I have already written some" (Nagel edition, 796; Barkhausen [Bkn.], 104). Just as Montaigne had read and commented upon Gomara, Montesquieu had read Solis's history (from the late seventeenth century), and perhaps had in mind a work similar to *Considérations sur les causes de la grandeur des Romains et de leur décadence*. He did not write it, but the "comments" in question can be found throughout *De l'esprit des lois* and *Mes pensées*.

At first glance, Montesquieu's position regarding the conquest is similar to Montaigne's: he also condemns what was "one of the greatest wounds that the human race has received" (*L'Esprit*, book IV, chapter 6); he thinks the Spaniards brought nothing but superstition, slavery, and extermination, that they did only harm (X, 4), that their actions in America were "crimes" (XV, 4). But if we examine all of his comments, we find a very different attitude.

Let us again take the causes of the Indians' defeat as an example. Montaigne attributed this defeat to characteristics of Indian civilization that he deemed to be accidental, fortuitous, and that one could imagine being replaced by opposite traits; the very outcome of the combat did not seem inevitable. Montesquieu, however, sought these causes in what were for him the constitutive traits of states such as Mexico and Peru. These states, he believed, which were close to the equator, were predisposed to despotism; and historians' writings confirmed the presence of despotic structures. Now, in a tyranny, the subjects are reduced to the condition of beasts and know only how to be submissive:

> It is very dangerous for a prince to have subjects who obey him blindly. If the Inca Atahuallpa had not been obeyed by his people like beasts, he would have prevented one hundred and sixty Spaniards from taking him. If he had been obeyed less from his prison cell, the Peruvian generals would have saved the empire. . . . If Moctezuma, prisoner, had been respected only as a man, the Mexicans would have destroyed the Spaniards. And, if Guatimozin [= Quauhtemoc], once taken, had not made the war stop with a single word, his capture would not have been the moment of the fall of the Empire, and the Spaniards would have feared antagonizing his subjects by torturing him. (1983, Bkn. 648)

The a contrario proof of this interdependence is that other peoples of America, whose state structures were not despotic, managed to resist the Spaniards much longer.

But this is still only half the answer. The other half may be found in a long fragment (1265, Bkn. 614), in which Montesquieu imagines another outcome to the combat, but this outcome results from modifications quite different from those offered by Montaigne. And these modifications are so radical that Montesquieu's hypothesis aims only at showing their impossibility. The change, he claims, would be linked to the introduction of rational philosophy:

> If a Descartes had come to Mexico one hundred years before Cortés; had he taught the Mexicans that men, such as they are, cannot be immortal; had he made them understand that all the effects of nature are a series of laws and communications of movements; had he made them recognize in the effects of nature the shock of bodies rather than the invisible powers of Spirits: Cortés, with a handful of men, would never have destroyed the vast Mexican empire, and Pizarro, that of Peru.

If Cortés conquered, it was because he belonged to the same civilization that would produce Descartes: the relation between abstract philosophy and military art, far from being arbitrary, is necessary. The Indian emperors were conquered because of the superstition that dominated their representation of the world. "Moctezuma, who could have exterminated the Spaniards upon their arrival had he had courage, by using force, or who could have, without risking anything, made them die of starvation, only attacks them by means of the sacrifice and prayer that he undertakes in all the temples." In a word, "superstition removed from these empires all the strength that they could have drawn from their greatness and their police."

Thus Montesquieu sees the main causes of the defeat in the cultural characteristics of the Aztecs and the Incas. The effect of surprise itself is not an absolute given, inevitable "under all climes": "When the Romans saw elephants for the first time, fighting against them, they were surprised; but they didn't lose their heads, as did the Mexicans upon seeing horses." Technical superiority is not decisive, and Montesquieu would not have subscribed to Montaigne's belief that the Spanish harquebuses would have been "capable of troubling even Caesar": "The Mexicans, in point of fact, had absolutely no firearms; but they had bows and arrows, which were the strongest weapons of the Greeks and Romans. They did not have iron, but they had gun flints, which cut and pierced like iron, which they put on the ends of their weapons." The Spaniards' superiority was above all psychological: they "turned to their advantage the veneration or rather the internal cult that the subjects of Mexico and Peru had for their Emperors."

Montesquieu's methods, contrary to Montaigne's, may be characterized as stemming from an epistemological "globalism." Everything is related: despotism, superstition, and military defeat on the one hand; rationalism, the ability to adapt, and victory on the other. A society is a coherent whole, without accidental traits that can be "removed" at will. As a result, the road to knowledge is opened: it is in fact a description of Indian societies that Montesquieu proposes, even if it is summary and incomplete; the same could not be said of the use to which Montaigne puts the same materials.

The counterpart to Montesquieu's globalism is his axiological atomism. Unlike Montaigne, for whom the bravery of the ancients and that of the Indians were comparable and worthy of admiration, Montesquieu demands on the one hand that each action be judged in its context. The Spaniards themselves, from all evidence, showed exceptional courage; but this does not cause him to admire them:

> The tale of the greatest marvels always leaves in the mind something black and sad. I like to see a few Greeks, at Thermopylal, Plataea and Marathon, destroy the countless armies of the Persians: they are heroes who immolate themselves for their country, and defend it against usurpers. In this case, it is bandits who, guided by the greed that consumes them, exterminate a prodigious number of peaceful nations to satisfy this greed. (1268, Bkn. 617)

Yet at the same time, Montesquieu refuses to make a global judgment about every feature of these Indian societies; and he is satisfied to deplore some of those features—such as their despotism or their superstition—and to praise others, such as what appears to him as religious toleration. "When Moctezuma insisted so much upon saying that the Spaniards' religion was good for their country, and that the religion of Mexico was good for his own, he was not saying something absurd, because in effect the legislators could not prevent themselves from respecting what nature had established before them," he wrote in *L'Esprit des lois* (XXIV, 24), thereby provoking the ire of his theologian censors. Thus he had no need to see in the Indians an incarnation of the golden age, which would have blinded him in his perception; nor, as Sepúlveda had done, having observed a trait that he judged to be negative (such as despotism), to extend his judgment to all their other characteristics, driven by a unifying impulse, to approve of the conquest. Montesquieu judges each characteristic individually (all the while taking their context into account), which allows him to be more perspicacious than Sepúlveda and more generous toward the other than Montaigne.

Montesquieu praises a certain (religious) relativism in Moctezuma; its absence, on the contrary, often underlies his criticism of the Spaniards. The latter decided that the Indians deserved to be reduced to slavery because they ate grasshoppers, "smoked tobacco and didn't wear their beards the same way as the Spaniards did"; but isn't making such judgments abandoning the very principles of humanity (XV, 3)? Their execution of Atahuallpa reveals this same refusal to adapt to the customs of the country: "The height of stupidity was that they did not condemn him by means of the political and civil laws of his country, but by the political and civil laws of their own" (XXVI, 22).

One could thus imagine that Montesquieu places himself in a purely relativist position, and that he is simply defending the right of each individual to be judged on the basis of his own laws and to choose his own religion. But this is not the case, and it is clear that condemnation of despotism could not be based on the relativist creed. *L'Esprit des lois* is an immense effort to *articulate* the universal and the relative, rather than a choice of one or the other: on the one hand, there is natural right and the forms of government that are related; on the other, there is the spirit of each nation, which results from the interaction of geographical conditions, economic and cultural structures, and history. For each specific judgment, both elements must be taken into account, and the portion of the universal and the relative must be measured. Religious toleration is welcome, as is toleration toward other forms of dress and diet; but despotism is an evil wherever it is found.

Montesquieu was particularly clear on this question in an analysis of the behavior of the Spaniards in which he refers to the writings of Las Casas. Leaving aside any relativist consideration, he admits that he finds himself unable to think "without indignation of the brutality of the Spaniards toward the Indians" (207, Bkn. 1573). If he arrives at this verdict, it is not because the Greeks would have done better, but because such acts are contrary to the natural and universal right that he has so carefully made clear. And one should not protest that extermination was the "only way to preserve [their conquests] and that, as a result, the Machiavellists could not call [it] *cruel*. . . . The crime loses nothing of its blackness by what one gets out of it. Granted, actions are always judged by their success; but this judgment of men is itself a deplorable Moral abuse." The act should be judged not according to its results but in relation to universal principles. The maxim according to which "history has proved them right" is indefensible: history is on the side of force, not on that of reason, and it is not because things *are* as they are that they *must* be so. This conception of morality, which judges actions according to their success or failure, is already in itself profoundly immoral. Here Montesquieu assumes a position diametrically opposed to Machiavelli's.

The biological model Montaigne uses to characterize humanity (childhood—flowering—decadence) is replaced here by a systematic vision of different societies of which history is only one dimension. And, curiously, it is knowledge of these societies, thereby made possible, that allows one to make judgments about them—not as a whole, but about each one of their features.

## III

These two positions regarding the conquests seem to me exemplary in more ways than one.

Montaigne (in essays other than "On Coaches") starts with the principle of generalized toleration: all manners and customs are equal, and barbarity does not exist; it is simply that we call those who are not like us barbarians. This position of extreme relativism is untenable, however, and Montaigne's descriptions are, in fact, permeated with value judgments. Simply, these values are not explicitly presented as universal (since he is openly positing relativism), and it is not surprising to discover that their place is held by Montaigne's own preferences: his universalism is, in fact, of the most common sort; that is, it is ethnocentric (and egocentric). This exclusive interest in the self results in the presence of others as mere argument or example; their possible valorization rests on a misunderstanding: what if, in reality, they were not as close to the Greeks as he claimed? The idealization of others never really served their cause (even if it proves the good intentions of the author), for in the absence of any control stemming from actual knowledge, one can also easily invert the sign of the example, and turn it from good to bad. Respect for others begins by recognizing them as such, and not with a praise that derives from inverting our own portrait. The primary violence lies in the fact that they are reduced to being nothing more than a means of speaking about ourselves, and it matters little whether one speaks well or badly of them afterward. Today we know that it is not enough for the ideal of the colonizer to be a lofty one for the result of colonization to be positive: the colonization of Africa in the nineteenth century was, after all, carried out in a spirit worthy of Montaigne, in the name of the fight against slavery.

The mixture of relativism and universalism that one finds in Montesquieu is of a completely different type, since he explicitly admits the relevance of both of them and since his entire conscious effort (in *L'Esprit des lois*) consists in seeking how they are related. Radical relativism is an illusion; but we cannot for all that return to a universalism that does not take into account the plurality of cultures and the egalitarian aspirations of individuals. This kind of universalism — which was confused with Christian teachings — perished in the shipwreck of religion; but we have seen what care Montesquieu took to distinguish between toleration in religious matters and universal natural right. His epistemological globalism opens the road to knowledge of others: a given characteristic of their civilization will find its meaning not by being compared with similar facts in our civilization, but by being placed in relation with other features of the same culture. At the same time, Montesquieu's axiological atomism allows him to refuse the sterile dichotomy that would claim "all is good" or "all is bad," and leads him to formulate nuanced value judgments, either in the name of the criterion of local custom or in relation to a universal morality.

The reader will have guessed that I prefer this second position. Yet it is Montaigne's that has imposed itself as an ideal during the course of the centuries that separate us from him, whereas Montesquieu's has remained marginal. Even today the most widespread attitude is derived from Montaigne's:

an affective adherence to the cause of the "oppressed," seconded by de facto absence of knowledge about them, and closely followed by a naive ethnocentrism. Why this "injustice"? I am inclined to seek the answer in the fact that Montaigne's attitude is perfectly compatible with the spirit of Western Europe during these most recent centuries: it is the ideal complement to colonialist practices. Montesquieu's voice, on the other hand, could not be heard because it came too early, with his refusal of simple explanation and his intransigent adherence to pluralism—and, at the same time, his universalism.

However, things may be about to change in our time. Montesquieu is starting to be seen as a pioneer of ethnology and sociology; and we know that knowledge is not only an end in itself, but also, in and of itself, a moral attitude. Perhaps it was necessary to wait for the end of colonization (summarily speaking) in order to begin perceiving other civilizations first of all as *other,* that is, neither as an ideal nor as a foil. At the same time, this very knowledge determines the ethical and political choices to be made: our own ideals may be shaken if we learn the truth about others. Far from enclosing us in an untenable relativism, knowledge of others *as* others allows us to make judgments about them, and about ourselves.

# 5 / The Wrong Causes for the Wrong Reasons

In some ways, collective behavior resembles individual psychology: there is no necessary relation between an action's alleged motives and its true motives. Both the group and the individual often take action based on inadmissible motives; this is why other justifications—perfectly acceptable to individual conscience or public opinion—are advanced, even if they account poorly for the action, or are mutually contradictory. The ideological debates that accompanied the colonization process in the nineteenth century and the decolonization process in the twentieth century illustrate these elementary statements well.

## I

It was never obvious that colonization was a good cause. Why would one begin the conquest, subjugation, and exploitation of countries other than the one to which one belongs? Out of self-interest: to increase one's wealth and personal power, or those of the group with which one identifies. In the sixteenth century, the conquistadors' primary motive was, in fact, a personal one: it was individual Spaniards, not Spain, who conquered America. Cortés, who did the opposite, shocked his companions. Groups of individuals undertook expeditions; the state intervened only after the fact, and reaped the benefits of actions that had cost it nothing. In the nineteenth century, during the second great phase of European colonization, individual initiative retreated into the background (without, however, disappearing altogether), and instead governments decided on colonial wars. But the motives did not change in any noticeable way. The egotism of the group simply replaced that of the individual; national interest supplanted individual interest. In this respect, nationalist ideology is in fact nothing more than the transposition of individual egotism to the community: it is no longer I whom I want to make rich and powerful, it is my "country," that is to say, an abstraction with which I identify (rather than individuals other than myself).

Still, the defense of personal interests, or even of those of one's own group, was not something that ranked high on the scale of values of European societies in either the sixteenth or the nineteenth century. Neither Christian morality (which embodied this scale of values during the first period) nor humanitarian morality (which embodied it during the second) taught that making oneself richer and stronger at the expense of others was a good deed. The cause, therefore, was not good in itself, and thus good rationalizations for it had to be found. It is striking to see how, for example, during the famous debate already mentioned—which pitted the defenders of the Indians against their enemies—the parties on both sides agreed on one thing alone: colonization had to be maintained and expanded. But no one appealed to it in the name of the interest of the individual, or of the state. Sepúlveda, the Indians' foe, was obliged to go out of the framework of Christian reference: he found his reasons for pursuing the conquests in the Aristotelian doctrine of natural slavery, and hence in the affirmation of the inequality of men. The Indians' defender, Las Casas, however, wanted to reconcile colonization with Christian values: it was *because* the Indians were already, instinctively, better Christians than the Spaniards that they had to be brought the word of Christ. The propagation of Christianity—the only true religion, of course—would therefore serve to legitimate the colonization process, without for all that being its true cause.

More or less the same thing occurred in the nineteenth century, except that the official values had become humanitarian rather than Christian. Whoever wanted to legitimate colonial conquests avoided speaking in terms of self-interest, and instead chose essentially between two positions: calling on these same humanitarian values, and claiming, therefore, that the goal of colonization was to propagate civilization, spread progress, and bring good throughout the world; or else rejecting humanitarian values as a whole, and affirming the inequality of human races and the right of the strong to dominate the weak. These two strategies of legitimation are contradictory; but precisely because it was a matter of justificatory discourse and not of true motives, they were often found side by side in the work of the same ideologue of colonialism.

In nineteenth-century France, no one deserved the name "ideologue of colonialism" more than Paul Leroy-Beaulieu. This brilliant economist, sociologist, and professor at the Collège de France made colonization his privileged subject of study. In 1870 he wrote a paper entitled *De la colonisation chez les peuples modernes,* which he developed into a book in 1874. It was published in six editions, each one longer than the former. The very popularity of this book is significant: it was the mandatory reference in every debate. Of course, Leroy-Beaulieu was far from impartial; he was a propagandist, and this work, like all his other actions, corresponded to practical interests and aims. In it one can find the entire battery of arguments used by the defenders of colonization.

Two aspects of the humanitarian doctrine — under whose banner Leroy-Beaulieu still wanted to hide — are manifest in *De la colonisation:* first, the ideal of equality and second, education as the means for attaining this equality. In the preface to the first edition, he described the relations between the mother country and the colony (here he was thinking primarily of two groups of the same society — those who remain in the mother country and those who colonize distant lands): "One arrived at notions that were more in conformity with a natural law that maintains that all societies are equal and that no society, no matter how small or how young, should be sacrificed to an older or larger society" (1:xxiii). The ideal of equality is present here even if its application is somewhat problematic, since Leroy-Beaulieu extended to societies what could have been considered a right of individuals. The nonexistence of a "universal society" in which individual societies would be the "citizens" makes such a "right" completely fictitious. Even were one able to contemplate its possibility in some concrete way, it is still not obvious that this claim has anything whatsoever to do with the natural rights of man: the independence of a state in no way guarantees the preservation of the rights of its subjects. It is nevertheless plausible that the notion was related, in Leroy-Beaulieu's mind at least, to the humanist ideal.

The relation to this ideal is even clearer in regard to education. Here, Leroy-Beaulieu's attitude was similar to Condorcet's. "Colonization," he wrote in the same preface, "exists in the social, order just as not only reproduction, but also education, exist in the familial order" (xxi). "Thus it is for colonization as it is for education" (xxii). Here again society is confused with the individual, and this allowed Leroy-Beaulieu to speak of "primitive, at times childish, populations" (2:648). The metaphor of childhood is used throughout and sexual connotations begin to appear. "Algeria has left behind her first youth. Today she is a big, beautiful adolescent who has escaped childhood diseases, growth pangs, and who shows promise of a luxuriant youth and a productive age of maturity" (3rd ed. [1885], 1:xi). The colony is a woman.

At the same time that these elements of the humanist doctrine appeared, other doctrines—inegalitarian and racist—appeared that were directly opposed to it. Influenced perhaps by the contemporary viewpoints of such authors as Gustave le Bon and Léopold de Saussure (for the subject was developed especially in the fifth edition), Leroy-Beaulieu declared himself to be against the equality of peoples, and remained pessimistic regarding the possibility of remedying this inequality by means of education:

> It is not absolutely certain ... that, even after many centuries, the different human races will be able, under all climes, to bend to the same laws. At the present time, and already for the past fifteen years or so, there has been a very lively reaction against doctrines—and even more so against methods—which, based on the unity of human nature, have tended to submit the entire globe to the same political, administrative, and civil regime. (2:645)

Questioning the policy of assimilation (the same laws everywhere) leads in fact to doubting humanist philosophy (the singleness of human nature).

As he affirmed natural inequalities, Leroy-Beaulieu moved quickly from administrative structures to the very nature of minds: "There are also races that seem incapable of spontaneous intellectual development.... There are countries and races where civilization cannot flourish spontaneously, where it must be imported from the outside" (708). With slight modification, he adopted a classification of societies common in earlier centuries that divided them into savages, barbarians, and civilized beings. But he went further: he no longer believed that education could ever change this state of affairs. Not only could civilization not arise spontaneously in certain parts of the world, but it could not be maintained without the constant help of civilizing countries. As Tocqueville had remarked about Gobineau, Leroy-Beaulieu's arguments consisted in justifying present practices by means of extrapolations about the future: if the whites were to abandon Africa today, they would find it, in a few thousand years, exactly as it had been before they came! And the same is true of America: were we to discover Indians today who had never been in contact with whites, they would be exactly the same as the first Indians Columbus saw. Armed with these "proofs," Leroy-Beaulieu could draw a conclusion in direct contradiction to his ideas about natural law in societies: these inferior nations would always have to be held in tutelage, like children who cannot grow up (or like the natural slaves or the feeble-minded in Aristotle's version): "Thus colonization, in the milder form of the protectorate, would be destined to last indefinitely" (709).

This insurmountable inequality between societies gives rise to new "rights" that are also not reciprocal: "This situation of the world and its in-habitants implies for civilized peoples the right to an intervention — whose nature and intensity may vary — in the populations or small tribes of the last two categories" (707), that is, savages, barbarians, or simply "stationary people," as in India. Affirming this right to intervene is equivalent to openly endorsing imperialist wars. In the preface to the fourth edition (1891), Leroy-Beaulieu stated that, for about ten years, "we have been realizing that approximately half of the world, in a savage or barbarian state, was solicit-ing the methodical and persevering action of civilized peoples" (4th ed. [1891]), 1:vii). In concrete terms, this meant that it was the peoples of the colonies themselves who were asking the European soldiers to come and occupy them. Leroy-Beaulieu had the choice only between this preposter-ous postulate and another, in equally flagrant contradiction of the facts, ac-cording to which one half of the world (he was thinking of America and Australia in this instance) was actually empty, and was thus "soliciting" col-onies to populate it (we know that it is on a fiction of this nature that the United States was built). According to him, "vacant countries" actually ex-isted (2:565)!

Moving now from societies to individuals, we can ask ourselves if, in this context, individuals could still aspire to rights equal to those of the colo-nizers. Leroy-Beaulieu recounted this revealing anecdote:

> A singular decision was made on this matter in 1901 by the court of Tunis: Arab men of the upper and middle classes had been found in a hotel in this city in the company of European women of dubious morals, and in immoral postures. Although there were no circumstances that constituted a violation of the laws, the press considered it an insult that these individuals had had immoral re-lations with consenting European women, and called for their

punishment. The court, by a twist of the law, sentenced them to a
few days in prison. . . . The colonists do not want the indigenous
people to frequent European women of loose morals, under the
pretext that, in so doing, they would lose the respect of the woman
of Europe. (2:652–53)

There is a something of a structural scandal here: the colony is a woman
and inferior; Arab men want to make love to European women (even if
they are prostitutes); the men are therefore abandoning the role that has
been assigned them and establishing an unacceptable reciprocity. Leroy-
Beaulieu condemned the court's decision, but did not change his inegalitarian reasoning one bit, even if he knew that in practice, "the colonist
considers the native to be an enemy everywhere. He would willingly kill
him, like one kills the kangaroo or the fox" (696).

If Leroy-Beaulieu could nonchalantly combine such contradictory arguments (colonization is necessary because all peoples are equal; colonization is necessary because certain peoples are superior to others), it is because in reality it was always a matter of legitimations that were invented a
posteriori ("good excuses") and not a matter of true causes. Nevertheless,
certain causes also appear in his discourse, as they did at times in the works
of other apologists of colonization. In 1847, at the beginning of his report
on Algeria, Tocqueville indicated the perspective in which he intended to
place himself by means of the following question: "Is our continued domination over the former Algerian regency useful to France?" (*Oeuvres complètes,* 3:311). Leroy-Beaulieu, who was a "scholar" rather than a politician,
merely broadened the scope of this question in order to define his own
perspective: "The first question that we must ask — a question that governs
the entire matter — is the following: Is it good for a nation to have colonies?"
(*De la colonisation,* 2:472). Any consideration of justice was obviated here in
favor of a problematics of utility, of appropriateness to national interest, this
time accepted openly. Leroy-Beaulieu's answer, like Tocqueville's before him,
was an emphatic yes. Colonization was good for industry and commerce,
just as it was essential for political and military grandeur. "Colonization is
for France a matter of life and death: either France will become a great
African power or it will be, in a century or two, a secondary European power," he wrote, not without some clear-sightedness, in the preface to the
second edition of his book in 1882 ([1882], 1:xx). Moreover, colonization
was also necessary for the moral regeneration of the country (it favored a
rise in energy and heroism) and even for its artistic flourishing: it seems that
the writer who knew he would be writing for a large part of the world

would produce masterpieces. For all these reasons, "the people who colonize the most are the foremost people, if not today, then tomorrow" (2:705).

Leroy-Beaulieu was in favor of colonization; he found his arguments wherever he could, and was barely concerned with the lack of coherence among them. Doctrinal purity was much less important to him than the practical conclusions he was able to draw and which in fact all led to the same end: Let's colonize! One passage from his book deserves to be quoted in its entirety, for it illustrates especially well this intermixture of arguments, wherein the humanist idea of civilization serves to support an inegalitarian classification of peoples; material interests and intellectual growth mutually endorse one another; and justification by right is replaced by a kind of social Darwinism that is extended to the entire planet:

> It is neither natural nor just that Western civilizations be crowded in indefinitely and suffocate in the restricted spaces that were their first abodes; that they accumulate the marvels of the sciences, the arts, and of civilization; that they see, due to a lack of gainful employments, the capital interest rates decline every day; and that they leave perhaps half of the world to small groups of ignorant, impotent men, true retarded children, scattered across vast areas of land, or else to decrepit populations, populations without energy, without direction, old men who are incapable of any effort, of any farsighted, joint action. (707)

## II

Leaving behind the apologists of colonization, let us now look at the arguments put forward by colonialism's enemies in the mid-twentieth century. It is perhaps surprising to find here, one after the other, the protagonists of what appear in our eyes as a "good" and a "bad" cause, respectively. We are not dealing, however, with the political facts—colonization and decolonization—themselves, and they must not be placed on the same level; we are dealing with the discourses used to legitimate them and with the ideologies that underlie these discourses. The legitimation of decolonization raises a problem in its turn. Its nature is completely different from that of colonization because in this case it is not a question of personal or collective self-interest, enrichment, or increase in power, but rather a question of freedom from intolerable constraints. Colonialism is evil because in the colonies certain people kill others as if they were kangaroos, not because the former are French and the latter Algerian. What is odious is humiliation, shameless

exploitation, and loss of liberty; and they would be just as odious if practiced between members of the same nation, and thus, outside of the colonial framework. The colony is only that: a framework in which certain
reprehensible crimes or moral behavior — which would have been un-
thinkable at home — become not only possible, but legitimate. This is
where the problem lies: the good reasons for fighting colonialism are not
specific to it. In positioning oneself in the territory of anticolonialism, one
chooses to accept the framework imposed by colonialism itself, and to transform what could have been a fight for human rights into a fight between
nations.

It is for this reason that the slippage that threatens anticolonialist discourse is precisely a slippage toward nationalist discourse, which is itself supported by a doctrine of inequality among human beings, according to which
the colonized peoples are superior — morally and culturally, and not mili-
tarily, of course — to the colonizing peoples. In addition, such a justification of decolonization is untenable in general not only because it is false,
but also because it is useless: one does not earn equality; equality is everyone's right. Blacks do not need to be "beautiful," as the old slogan had it,
in order to demand being treated like every other member of our species.

Let us now look at Aimé Césaire's famous *Discourse on Colonialism* (1955).
In this work, Césaire appeals to a universal ideal; he longs for true civilization and condemns the pseudohumanism of the colonizers: one cannot but
agree with him here, and share his indignation at the degrading treatment
inflicted on the colonized peoples by the Europeans. This, however, does
not seem to be enough for him; he also resorts to a nationalist line of reasoning that is incompatible with universalist principles, wherein the colonized people are not only oppressed, but also particularly good. Colonization, he writes, has "destroyed . . . the wonderful Indian civilizations" of
the Aztecs and the Incas (20). But were these civilizations, in fact, so admirable to begin with? And supposing that they were not, would they therefore have deserved their colonization, would they have made it more legitimate? These civilizations were, he adds, "natural economies, harmonious
and viable economies"(20), and he concludes: "They were democratic societies, always. They were cooperative societies, fraternal societies. I make
a systematic defense of those societies that were destroyed by imperialism"(23). "Once again, I am systematically defending our old Negro civilizations: they were courteous civilizations" (31). Such statements are not only
false, or else devoid of sense, they are also open to criticism in that they
establish a rigid hierarchy of civilizations and imply that decolonization

cannot be otherwise legitimated. Colonial imperialism systematically defended European societies, and it was wrong; nationalist anticolonialism simply reverses these old assertions without, for all that, making them any more justified. We could say that colonialism carries off an oblique victory here, since even its adversaries adopt its arguments.

One finds similar slippages in the 1986 Nobel Prize acceptance speech of another great author, Wole Soyinka. Soyinka wages war against racism and colonialism. And yet he, too, adopts certain premises of their doctrines, most notably the idea that races—that is, both physical and cultural human groupings—exist and are pertinent to both human history and individual behavior. He sees the world divided between "the white tribe," "the white continent," "the white race" on one side, and "the black race," "the black nations" (he does not mention Asians) on the other. The blacks behave as a group: "The black race has no other choice"; "the black race knows what it is"; it has its "racial dignity." And apparently whites do, too, since it is the white race and not a particular country or culture "who gave an entire list of martyrs" and had, as a race, "an authentic conscience" in the person of Olof Palme. The cultural and physical are increasingly conflated, and value judgment makes its appearance, when Soyinka declares that African societies "never at any time of their existence waged war in the name of their religion. Never did the black race try to subjugate or convert by force, animated by an evangelizing zeal based on the conviction of holding the supreme truth." In this sense it compares advantageously to the white race or "Judeo-European" (?) thought; this latter served as the basis of war in the past, and can be seen at work today in "a state that claims divine selection in order to justify the perpetual annihilation of the indigenous people." (Could this be an allusion to the state of Israel?) "We also have our myths," Soyinka concludes, "but we never relied on them to enslave others."

It matters little if Soyinka's description of the history of Africa is correct or not; let us suppose it is. Nonetheless, it is somewhat ridiculous to establish a hierarchy among the dead, between those particularly ignominious deaths caused by religious motives and those deaths, relatively more pardonable, brought about for "political reasons," which Soyinka admits are familiar to Africans too (the massacres of the Tutsi in Rwanda, or the Ibo in Biafra are still remembered). More important, one cannot claim to be proud of "the black race" because of this fortunate course of history (supposing it were so), unless one believes that the one is due to the other, unless one takes the main assumption of racist doctrine as one's own, that is, that moral thought and behavior vary according to skin color. Isn't this subscribing to a new "theory of racial superiority," whereas Soyinka justifiably condemned its white version?

Finally, these warrior religions—Christianity and Islam—should perhaps be judged less categorically. They only attempt to convert others to their truth because their aim is universality. They are therefore the cradle of the idea of humanity and universality that, freed from its religious origins and the zeal of its missionaries, blossomed into humanist thinking. And this thinking—provided it is not used as mere camouflage—remains the best bulwark against racism; it is certainly better than the praise of a "race" other than the white race that was unjustly persecuted in the past.

The similarity between colonialist and anticolonialist discourse reaches its extreme in Frantz Fanon's 1961 book *The Wretched of the Earth*. According to Fanon, only the actors change in the move from colonialism to anticolonialism: their attributes, like their actions, remain the same. In both instances, radical difference is affirmed and universality is rejected: "We are nothing like you" is the cry raised by both parties, what Fanon calls "the untidy affirmation of an original idea propounded as an absolute" (41). In both instances, there is a belief that all the good people are on one side, and all the bad on the other: "The primary Manicheism which governed colonial society is presented intact during the period of decolonization"(50). In both instances, the world of others is considered perfectly homogeneous: "To the saying 'All natives are the same' the colonized person responds: 'All settlers are the same'" (92). In both instances, one chooses to speak the pure language of power: "The violence of the colonial regime and the counterviolence of the native balance each other and respond to each other in an extraordinary reciprocal homogeneity" (88).

What is extraordinary in the analogies Fanon thus establishes is that, all the while affirming this symmetry, he condemns colonialism absolutely and unequivocally defends decolonization. At times one wonders if he is conscious of all the parallels he is in the process of revealing; yet he must be, since he does not fail to point them out himself. "In fact, as always, the settler has shown him the way he should take if he is to become free. The argument the native chooses has been furnished by the settler, and by an ironic turning of the tables it is the native who now affirms that the colonialist understands nothing but force" (84). But there is no irony here: it is repetition, pure and simple, and the change of actor was predictable since the start (it is a question of violence as method, and not of a global project of course, since the Algerians are not in the process of colonizing France). Fanon adds: "Paradoxically, the national government in its dealing with the country people as a whole is reminiscent of certain features of the former colonial power" (118). But here again, there is no paradox: exploitation and repression do very well without national difference, and one reaps what one has sown.

With a somewhat incomprehensible joy, Fanon thus assumes all the characteristics common to colonialists and anticolonialists. If the colonizers were motivated by nationalism, nationalism will be used in its turn to advance decolonization. If colonialism is "violence in its natural state" (61), and "the agents of the government speak the language of pure force" (38), anticolonialism must do the same. This order "can only be called into question by absolute violence" (37), and "the people are decided to trust violent methods only" (84). This is, according to Fanon, because both "colonization [and] decolonization [are] simply a question of relative strength" (61). But if the resemblance between the two were really so great, why, after all, would one be preferable to the other?

Had he been consistent, Fanon's fascination with violence should have reconciled him to colonialism. "At the level of individuals, violence is a cleansing force," he writes. "It frees the native from his inferiority complex and from his despair and inaction; it makes him fearless and restores his self-respect" (94). "The colonized man finds his freedom in and through violence"(86). Sartre goes even further in his preface to Fanon's book, with the joy of a masochist who has just met a sadist: "To shoot down a European is to kill two birds with one stone, to destroy an oppressor and the man he oppresses at the same time: there remains a dead man, and a free man; the survivor, for the first time, feels a *national soil* under his foot" (22). But must everything really be sacrificed to the feelings of one's feet? How and why does the colonizers' defect transform itself into a virtue in the decolonized, when the defect remains the same? Or must one suppose that the colonizers were, after all, right to kill the natives because they were thereby getting rid of their own complexes — useless contemplative attitudes — and thus gaining freedom? It is like entering the world of Dostoevsky's Raskolnikov or Pyotr Verhovensky. If one admires the totalitarian side of colonialism, is there a "paradox" in the fact that the regimes that resulted from decolonization imitated it? Personally, I prefer the wisdom of Pascal: "Must one kill in order to prevent bad people from existing? This is creating two bad people instead of one" (*Pensées*, 911).

Fanon's response to all these questions is that no absolute values exist. Something is good when it serves my ends, and bad when it opposes them. This is why violence is good when it is in the hands of the oppressed and serves their struggle, while the colonizers remain forever detestable. Here again (ironically?), Fanon imitates the theoreticians of racism and imperialism. Maurice Barrès used to say: the true does not exist any more than the good; only what is true for France and good for the French exists. "The totality of these just and true relations between given objects and a specific man, the Frenchman: this is French justice and truth; to find these relations is the French raison d'être" (*Scènes et doctrines du nationalisme,* 1:13). Fanon, a faithful disciple, declares: "The true is what hurries on the break-up of the colonialist regime; it is that which promotes the emergence of the nation; it is all that protects the natives, and ruins the foreigners. In this colonialist context there is no truthful behavior: and the good is quite simply that which is evil for 'them'" (*The Wretched of the Earth,* 50). (Even Barrès, who was the author of a brochure entitled "Against Foreigners," did not dare to put it so bluntly.) Just as Barrès refused to ask himself if Dreyfus was guilty or innocent, and wanted only to know if his condemnation would be useful to France, Fanon, with a wave of his hand, sweeps away "all the Mediterranean values—the triumph of human individual, of clarity and of beauty" since "they have nothing to do with the concrete conflict in which the people is engaged" (47).

Fanon embraced the creed of moral relativism: values count only in and for the context in which they were born; Western values are bad because they are Western (all pretense to universality is a bluff), and the Third World must find new values, which will be good because they will belong to it. "When the native hears a speech about Western culture, he pulls out his knife—or at least makes sure it is within reach" (43). But is a knife raised against culture—because it is the weapon of the colonized—any better than Goebbels's revolver? By taking up the means used by colonialism so systematically, doesn't one run the risk of sharing its ends?

In the conclusion of his book, Fanon states: "Let us decide not to imitate Europe; let us combine our muscles and our brains in a new direction.... Let us not pay tribute to Europe by creating States, institutions, and societies which draw their inspiration from her" (313, 315). The problem is that Europe, contrary to what Fanon claims, is not a simple thing: it has practiced both universalism and relativism, humanism and nationalism, dialogue and war, tolerance and violence. In choosing one of the terms of these alternatives over the other, one is not choosing the Third World over Europe, but one European tradition over another, the tradition of Nietzsche, Barrès, and Sorel over that of Montesquieu, Rousseau, and Kant. Once again, colonialism and its ideology win a dark victory over their adversaries, since the latter have decided to worship the same demons as the former. Or, to look at it from another angle: if today one deplores the absence of democracy in the decolonized countries, and the violence and repression that prevail there, one does not have the right to conclude that "the colony was better." In fact, the quasi-totalitarian forms of government one sees in both instances correspond to the quasi-totalitarian aspects of colonialism itself. And this is the tragic error of ideologues like Fanon, who paved the way for and assumed this connection: by not wanting to imitate Europe, they imitated the worst of Europe.

The racist, nationalist, or relativist arguments that appear throughout anticolonial discourse do not make decolonization any less necessary, any more than Christian and humanist arguments justified the colonial cause. The very possibility of thus dissociating *causes* from *reasons* will perhaps lead us to recognize that basic political virtue lies in what the ancients called prudence, that is, not in the pure defense of abstract principles, nor in exclusive attention to particular facts, but in the placing of the former in relation to the latter, in the just evaluation of events in the light of ideals that indeed remain unshakable.

# 6 / The Journey and Its Narratives

I

What is *not* a journey? As soon as one attributes an extended figurative meaning to the word — and one has never been able to refrain from doing so — the journey coincides with life, no more, no less: is life anything more than the passage from birth to death? Movement in space is the first sign, the easiest sign, of change; life and change are synonymous. Narrative is also nourished by change; in this sense journey and narrative imply one another. The journey in space symbolizes the passing of time, physical movement symbolizes interior change; everything is a journey, but as a result this "everything" has no specific identity. The journey transcends all categories, up to and including that of change in oneself and in the other, since as far back as the most remote antiquity, journeys of discovery (explorations of the unknown) and journeys home (the reappropriation of the familiar) have been found side by side: the Argonauts were great voyagers, but so was Ulysses.

Travel narratives are as old as journeys themselves, if not older. The first great wave of modern journeys occurred at the end of the fifteenth and in the sixteenth centuries; and although it seems paradoxical, at that time the narratives preceded the journeys. From the High Middle Ages on,

60

the public favored narratives that were more or less fanciful and that aroused their curiosity. One learns in these narratives, for example, how it took the Irish monk Saint Brendan seven years to reach the Terrestrial Paradise after having braved every danger and met a variety of supernatural beings. Then there is Marco Polo's *Book of Marvels,* written in the early fourteenth century after his return from China, which, although it does not lapse into the supernatural, still lives up to its title. Soon afterward John Mandeville wrote his *Travels,* an inextricable blend of real facts and fabulous inventions; he too described the Terrestrial Paradise. During this time a number of compilation books also appeared, cosmographies or images of the world (Cardinal Pierre d'Ailly's famous *Imago mundi,* for example), inventories of all that was known about countries and peoples. These works were well known, and they paved the way for the narratives of later travelers, who in fact believed them to be reliable sources of information. Columbus, for example, took on his journey letters for the Great Khan who had been described by Marco Polo. And Vasco da Gama carried letters for Prester John, a legendary character who, according to Mandeville's narrative, lived in the Indies.

The public was not really surprised, therefore, by the first narratives of the new discoveries, and it is easy to imagine that the travelers themselves — who had also at one time been part of the reading-and-listening audience — were not shocked by their discoveries. In addition to the popularity of the ancient narratives, there is another reason for this lack of surprise, which has to do with a characteristic specific to European history. The geography of the Mediterranean enabled contact among populations that were physically and culturally quite varied: Christian Europeans, Muslim Turks and Moors, animist Africans. During the Renaissance, the Europeans' consciousness of their own historical diversity was added to this multiformity as they began to think of themselves as heirs to two quite separate traditions: Greco-Roman on the one hand, Judeo-Christian on the other; and this latter was not monolithic, since it offered the unique example of one religion that was built on another (Christianity and Judaism). In other words, the Europeans were already aware, through their own past and present, of the plurality of cultures. They had, in a sense, an empty slot where they could place newly discovered peoples without upsetting their general worldview.

This becomes obvious, for example, during the Spanish conquest of America. When the conquistadors saw the Indian temples, they spontaneously called them "mosques": the general procedure becomes obvious here, since the term begins at this point to designate any non-Christian place of worship. When the Spaniards discovered a somewhat larger city, they immediately called it "Great Cairo." In order to make his impressions of the Mexicans clear to his reader, Francisco de Aguilar, one of the first chroniclers, began his narrative with the following: "As a child and adolescent, I began reading many histories and tales about the Persians, Greeks, and Romans. I also knew, from reading, the rites carried out in the Portuguese Indies." The illustrations of the time also attest to this projection of the familiar (even if it is somewhat strange) onto the unknown.

## II

If one cannot isolate the journey from what it is not, one can, somewhat more successfully, attempt to distinguish within this vast confused medley several kinds of journeys, several categories that allow us to clarify particular types of journeys. The most general opposition we can establish is between the spiritual and the material, between interior and exterior. Two well-known examples of these categories from medieval narratives are Mandeville's *Travels* and the quest for the Holy Grail. The first describes two journeys (composed of real and imaginary elements, but let us leave this distinction aside for the time being), one in the Holy Land and one in the Far East. Here, the author discovers, to his readers' great delight, all kinds of fantastic beings in addition to Terrestrial Paradise itself. The second narrative describes the adventures of the Knights of the Round Table who set out from King Arthur's Court in search of a sacred and mysterious object, the Grail. Little by little these knights realize that the quest in which they are engaged is of a spiritual nature, and that the Grail is impalpable; this is why only the purest among them, Galahad and Perceval, can reach it.

Already one can see from these examples that, although the spiritual and material categories are opposed, they are not incompatible, nor do the narratives belong exclusively to one genre or the other. On the contrary, both categories are almost always present simultaneously; only the proportions and the hierarchies vary. Mandeville's book is primarily read as a tale of adventure, but, at the same time, it is a didactic work. The story of the Holy Grail, on the other hand, is an example of spiritual reinterpretation, a Christian reclaiming of legends that had originally had a different meaning. But whatever the original intention of the authors, the new readers and their guides — the commentators — can always provide a spiritual meaning where there had been none, or a meaning different from the one originally intended. In fact, journeys lend themselves particularly well to this reinterpretation.

Thus, from Hellenistic times on, Ulysses' return to Ithaca was viewed only as an image of flight from tangible beauties toward ideal beauty: Homer became an illustration of Plato. Particular narratives can thus occupy every imaginable point along an axis that leads from the purely exterior to the purely interior. Amerigo Vespucci's letters fall somewhere in the middle of this axis: they contain the narrative of some actual journeys, but they also contain the myth of the golden age. Although he was influenced by these letters, Thomas More is infinitely closer to the spiritual pole; on the other hand, Pigafetta, the narrator of the first journey around the world, is closer to the material pole: rather than constructing a utopia, he was content to recount a lengthy expedition.

If the opposition between the spiritual and the material does not allow one to classify narratives, but simply to understand them better, the same cannot be said of a second opposition to which these categories contribute, this time within one and the same text. In the new opposing categories, the relation between interior journey and exterior journey moves from complicity to hostility. This means that in our civilization, which favors the spiritual over the material (although it is not the only civilization to do so), the actual journey is at times valorized because it is the incarnation or prefiguration of the spiritual journey, and at times belittled because the interior has become preferable to the exterior.

At first, Christian religion seemed to lean toward complicity, and therefore it favored the establishment of a metaphorical relation between the exterior and the interior journey. Didn't Christ say "I am the way," and didn't he send his disciples into the world? Things changed rapidly, however, and as soon as Christianity was established as official doctrine, the motionless quest was favored over movement in space. An ancient Christian author speaking to other monks said: "Remain in your cell and it will teach you everything. Just as fish die if they are on dry land, monks perish outside of their cell." To venture forth was to participate in the spirit of worldliness that Pascal would castigate much later. In the late seventeenth century, in his *Les Aventures de Télémaque* (Adventures of Telemachus), a Christian variation of the *Odyssey*, Fénelon seemed to have forgotten that he was writing a narrative of a journey (even if it was an imaginary one), and it was within the very framework of material journeys that he succeeded in stigmatizing them. The inhabitants of Bétique, a country that embodies the golden age, are clever navigators, yet they scorn the results of their art, that is, journeys, as well as those who undertake them. "If those people — they say — have in their own country enough of what is necessary for life, what are they seeking in another country?" (270). More recently, at the end of his *Mémoires d'outre-tombe* (Memoirs from beyond the grave), Chateaubriand concludes in a spirit faithful both to Christianity and to the old Stoicism: "Man does not need to travel in order to grow; he carries immensity with him" (2:966).

If the journey is only vanity, the same will be true of its narrative. In Fénelon's book, this is what Telemachus learns at his own expense once he has enjoyed talking to Calypso about her wanderings. " 'Love of vainglory has made you speak without prudence,' Mentor scolded him. 'When, oh Telemachus, will you be wise enough not to speak from vanity alone?' " (177). The very existence of a narrative necessarily implies the valorization of its subject (because it is worthy of mention), and therefore also implies a certain satisfaction on the part of its narrator. Fénelon is unambiguous as far as his own narrative is concerned. What interests him in these "adventures" is not the pleasure to be derived from the journey, but the "truths necessary for government" that are presented in amusing fashion to the future prince, to whom the work is addressed.

Such an attitude is not exclusive to the Christian tradition. If we take another journey, this time to China, we see that the *Tao* of Lao Tzu also designates the way; but again, mere movement in space is belittled here. And in Chuang Tzu's work the men of the golden age hardly differ from Fénelon's Betiquians: "They are satisfied to stay at home. It can happen that the neighboring village is so close that one can hear the dogs barking there and the cocks crowing, but people can grow old and die without ever having been there" (quoted in Waley, 71–72). Like Chateaubriand, Lieh Tzu, another Taoist author from the fourth century B.C., preferred interior journeys:

> Those who take great pains for exterior journeys do not know how to organize visits that one can make inside oneself. He who journeys outside is dependent on exterior things; he who makes interior visits can find himself everything he needs. This is the highest way to travel; while the journey of the one who depends on exterior things is a poor journey. (ibid., 43)

In our own time, cultures that were previously isolated from one another have come into contact (yet another result of journeys!), and it is difficult to distinguish with precision the various sources—Eastern or Western—of this mysticism that belittles journeys in the name of the superiority of the interior over the exterior. During one of his very first journeys, to Latin America, the poet Henri Michaux discovered the vanity of travel and concluded: "You can just as easily find your truth staring for forty-eight hours at some old tapestry" (86). He did not follow his own advice, however, and set out again, this time to Asia; yet he arrived at the same conclusion, even if this time the filiation is oriental:

> And now, said Buddha to his disciples,
> at the time of dying:
> In the future, be your own light, your own
>     refuge.
> Do not seek any other refuge.
> Do not go in quest of any refuge other than
>     near you.
>
> . . . . .
>
> Do not trouble yourselves with others' ways of thinking.
> Stay on your own island,
> *Stick to Contemplation*. (*Un Barbare en Asie*, 233)

Alongside these traditions, which can be considered dominant and which disparage the journey, there are others — equally abundant if less glorious — in which the journey is praised, not because the material is preferable to the spiritual, but because the relation between them can be one of harmony rather than of conflict. Here again, it is the education of the soul that is the goal of these movements of the body: "If the water of a pond remains still, it becomes stagnant, muddy, and fetid; it only remains clear if it moves and runs. The same is true of the man who travels": so ancient Arab wisdom teaches us. Dante's Ulysses, while condemned to suffer in the eighth circle of hell, seems to have established a perfectly balanced relation between interior and exterior journeys: he moves in space in order to know the world, in particular, human vices and virtues; and he exhorts his companions to follow him since they were not "made to live like brutes / But to follow both science and virtue" (Canto XXVI). Along the same lines, Montaigne writes that the journey offers us the best means "to rub and polish our brain by contact with those of others" ("Of the Education of Children," 112). Although the goal is self-knowledge, the journey is no less indispensable: it is by exploring the world that one begins to discover oneself. "This great world . . . is the mirror in which we must look in order to recognize ourselves from the proper angle" (116). And countless travelers have proved by their example that they share these same convictions.

Must one be content simply to acknowledge the dialogue between these two traditions, or can one legitimately prefer one to the other? It is easy to see in what sense the contemplation of the wall hanging can offer the same knowledge as movement in space, or even greater knowledge, since it encourages concentration and meditation. Nonetheless, the limits of this solipsism are quickly reached. The existence of others around us is not purely accidental. Others are not simply solitary subjects comparable to the *I* plunged in solitary meditation, they are also part of it: the *I* does not exist without a *you*. One cannot reach the bottom of oneself if one excludes others. The same holds true for knowledge of foreign countries and different cultures: the person who knows only his own home always runs the risk of confusing culture and nature, of making custom the norm, and of forming generalizations based on a single example: oneself. The Betiquians must visit countries other than their own (and therefore undertake journeys) in order to seek what is necessary to the life of the mind, not of the body. The villagers described by Chuang Tzu can discover in the neighboring town more than dogs and roosters (which, in fact, probably do greatly resemble the ones they already know). They can discover other men and women whose vision of the world is different, even if only slightly, from theirs. This, in turn, could change them and lead them to be a little more just.

The relationship between spiritual and material journeys was modified with the advent of modern times. If we start from the mass of existing narratives, rather than from preestablished categories, we can say that the most general opposition concerns the *use* to which they are put rather than their *nature,* and that this change is in accordance with the increased subjectivization of the world in which we live. Rather than speaking of a spiritual journey, we would speak today of an allegorical narrative (since allegory points to something other than what it signifies), in which the journey is only a pretext the author uses to express his opinions. Still, there is no consecrated term; the Romantics spoke of a genre that, in order to distinguish it from allegory, they called *tautegory,* something that speaks only of itself. As we can see, the opposition is the same one that has structured Western identity for several centuries: the two kinds of travel narratives are opposed as autonomy and heteronomy, finding one's raison d'être inside or outside oneself; or again as those forms of social organization, modern individualism, or traditional holism, a society of individuals that judges itself to be free and equal and a community of members of a group who depend for their fate on the habits and decisions of this group. The most appropriate term with which to designate the nonallegorical travel narratives would perhaps be *impressionist,* since it has been historically tested and clearly suggests that the traveler is content to offer us his impressions, without attempting to teach us "something else."

In Western Europe there has undoubtedly been a movement away from allegorical narratives toward impressionistic narratives. There are numerous examples of this movement, yet none seems more eloquent than the works of Chateaubriand. Chateaubriand undertook two great journeys or, as he himself said, pilgrimages, to the West and to the East. As a young man, he went to North America and brought back a journal of his journey and an epic poem entitled *Les Natchez* from which he took the two pieces that brought him fame: *Atala* and *René*. Fifteen years later, he set out in the opposite direction, traveling to Athens, Jerusalem, Egypt, and Tunisia. The narrative of this journey, now called *Itinéraire de Paris à Jérusalem,* provides the prototype for countless later narratives. Chateaubriand himself sought to formulate the relation between these two journeys. At times he says that it is nature versus culture, or the civilization of the future versus that of the past. But from our point of view the most meaningful opposition lies in the genre of the two narratives: the one on America is allegorical, and the one on the Orient, impressionistic. The former submits the traveler's observations to a preconceived design that they are used to illustrate; the latter neglects the world and concentrates on the self, recounting the successive impressions of that self.

## III

If one were to ask uninitiated readers today what they expect from a travel narrative, they would no doubt find it difficult to give a detailed answer; and yet an expectation exists, and it constitutes one aspect of what is called a literary genre (the other being the internalizing of this same norm by the writer). This expectation is not the same today as it was in the sixteenth century: the texts themselves have not changed, but we read them with different eyes. I would like to propose a hypothesis regarding the nature of our contemporary expectations.

The first important feature of the travel narrative as it is unconsciously imagined by today's reader seems to me to be a certain tension (or a certain balance) between the observing subject and the observed object. This is what, in its way, the term *travel narrative* designates: narrative, that is, personal narration and not objective description; but also travel, and therefore a framework of circumstances exterior to the subject. If only one of the ingredients is present, we are no longer within the genre in question, but are sliding toward another. For example, *De la démocratie en Amerique* leans too heavily toward the description of its object to be considered a travel narrative, even if Tocqueville sporadically refers to the circumstances under which he obtained a certain piece of information. Conversely, if an author speaks only about himself, we once again find ourselves outside the genre. On one side, the boundary is science; on the other, autobiography. The travel narrative comes into being from the fusion of the two.

There is also a second feature of the genre, which its name does not indicate, but which is just as important: the situating in time and in space of the experiences reported by the narratives. In space: the "true" travel narrative, from the point of view of the contemporary reader, recounts the discovery of *others,* either the savages of faraway lands or the representatives of non-European civilizations — Arab, Hindu, Chinese, and so on. A journey in France would not result in a "travel narrative." It is not that such narratives do not exist, but they clearly lack the feeling of alterity in relation to the people (and the lands) described. There are journeys in Italy (a French speciality, though not exclusively) by Montaigne, de Brosses, and Stendhal. Yet here one must cite proper names, whereas typical authors of travel narratives are not professional writers; rather, they are people who take up their pens almost in spite of themselves, because they believe themselves to be the bearers of an exceptional message. Once this message has been delivered, they rush to return to their normal existence as nonwriters. A good number of these narratives are in fact anonymous; on the other hand, a journey in Italy is unexceptional in and of itself, and the Italians are not radically different from the French. It is the author alone who can justify the existence of the narrative.

The situating in time is perhaps more difficult, but I believe it is just as real. Travel narratives are written in our day; the next serialized article in *Le Monde* could easily be a travel narrative. Still, one senses a difference between books published in travel series and those strictly contemporary texts. And that difference is a lack of a certain distance in the latter (even if the financial means that the undertaking demands are not lacking) between the author of the narrative and his or her reader. I think therefore that, in addition to the first relation of alterity — the one that exists between the narrator and the object of his narrative — there exists another, less obvious no doubt, between reader and narrator, who must not share the same ideological framework. The narrator's discovery of the other, his object, is repeated in miniature by the reader in relation to the narrator himself; the process of reading imitates to a certain extent the content of the narrative: it is a journey within the book. The distance between narrator and reader cannot be precisely determined, but I would say that, in order to mark the boundary, at least one generation separating reader and writer is necessary.

And at the most? Travel narratives have been around forever . . . or at least since Herodotus's time. Yet here again I sense a boundary. The first "true" travel narrative (still from the point of view of today's reader) seems to me to be Marco Polo's; and I do not think it was by chance that this book played a decisive role in the departure of Columbus, who in his turn influenced so many other travelers. Before Marco Polo, in antiquity and the Middle Ages, there were of course travelers who told of their experiences, but they are *too* foreign to us: as foreign as the lands they visited. Herodotus's Greece is no less foreign to us than is his Egypt, even if the narrative perspective favors the former over the latter. And this is where I would view the essential feature of our genre to be: the narrator must be different from us, but not too different, not, in any case, as different as the people who are the subject of his narrative. The typical narrator would therefore be a European, belonging to the long period that extends from the Renaissance to about 1950.

If my reader has followed me up to this point, it is now necessary to take one more step. And that is that this same period, in the history of Western Europe, has a name: colonialism. If this structural feature were to be taken into account in the naming of the genre, it would be called: narrative of colonial journeys.

This becomes obvious if one examines the question from another angle. Who are the authors of these narratives? They are conquering warriors, merchants, missionaries, that is, the representatives of three forms of colonialism: military, commercial, and spiritual. Or they are explorers who put themselves in the service of one or the other of these three categories. They are not the only ones to travel, however, or to relate their journeys. But when the members of other groups write, the results are not "travel narratives." Scientists produce descriptions of nature or of people that, even if they are still imbued with a colonialist ideology, push personal experience into the background. Poets write poetry, as it should be, and at bottom we care little whether it was written during a journey or not. Adventurers in their turn can write tales of adventure without being concerned with the populations they encounter. In order to ensure the tension necessary to the travel narrative, the specific position of the colonizer is required: curious about the other, and secure in his own superiority.

Is it justified, however, to bring up colonialism in order to explain readers' present reactions, since colonialism can be considered dead, at least in its classic form? Granted, old-style colonialism is no longer exactly our problem; nor, however, and as a result, is decolonization. We are all in favor of people's right to self-determination, and we all profess faith in the natural equality of races. Yet for all that we have not stopped believing in the superiority of our civilization over "theirs"; and why would we, since they all seem to want to imitate us and dream of coming to work in our countries?

This could explain the popularity that travel narratives from earlier times still enjoy today. These texts are imbued with the sense of our superiority from the first line to the last. I am not speaking only of openly racist authors, such as Stanley, but even of more well-meaning travelers, even those who, like Cabeza de Vaca, Staden, or Guinnard, were conquered, made prisoners or slaves; the essential is not in the content of a statement, but in the very fact of its utterance, which is always from our side. In Marx's terms, they cannot represent themselves; they must be represented. Thus, as today's readers, we retain the advantage of colonialist ideology; but at the same time we derive the benefit brought about by the period of decolonization since we can still say to ourselves: but we are *not* those authors. The alienation so dear to Brecht, occurring here in relation to the narrators of these tales, allows us to retain our pleasure without having to face the criticism that could be leveled at our elders.

As I prepare for my trip, or upon arriving in a foreign country, I purchase, in addition to a practical guide, a slightly older travel narrative. Why? Because it offers me the prism I need in order to really take advantage of my trip: a slightly caricatural image of others that allows me to note with satisfaction the entire path that has been traveled; an image that separates me from the narrator, but that is sufficiently accurate on several counts to reassure me of my own superiority; an image of the traveler with which I identify while at the same time distancing myself from it, and which thus absolves me of all guilt.

"But in the end," my exasperated reader will say, "does it really matter so much if the vision of the Indians in these narratives does not conform to reality? You can't spend your life crying over the fate of the natives of every country! Let's change subjects already. How about going to see a western tonight?"

# 7 / Some Remarks on Contacts among Cultures

A specific difficulty arises when one attempts to consider intercultural relations: everyone already seems to agree on what the ideal state of these relations should be. This is somewhat surprising: although racist behavior abounds, no one seems to admit to racist ideology. Everyone favors peace, coexistence in mutual understanding, balanced and fair exchanges, efficient dialogue: international conferences proclaim this, congresses of experts agree on it, and radio and television programs repeat it. And yet we continue to live in a state of incomprehension and war. It seems that the very consensus about what is "politically correct" in this area, and the widespread conviction that good is preferable to evil, deprive this ideal of any effectiveness: banality results in paralysis.

We must, therefore, rid our ideal of its banality. But how? Obviously, not by embracing an obscurantist and racist credo so as to be original. I, for my part, see the possibility of action taking two directions. On the one hand, the ideal is effective only if it bears a relation to the real. This does not mean that it is necessary to lower our ideal in order to make it attainable, but that it must not be separated from the workings of knowledge. We must not have neutral scientist-technicians on one side and moralists who are unaware of human realities on the other; we must have scientists who are conscious of the ethical dimension of their research and people of action who are conscious of the results of knowledge. I am not certain, however, that the consensus about what is "politically correct" is as perfect as it seems at first glance. I have the impression that, quite the contrary, one often makes contradictory demands, combined in a single sweep of generosity; that one wants, as the saying goes, to have one's cake and eat it, too. In order to eliminate banality, one must accept remaining consistent. If this leads to absurdity, well, we must begin everything from scratch once again.

The comments that follow revolve around two main themes: judgments of others and interaction with others.

# I

I grew up in Bulgaria, a small country located at one end of Europe. Bulgarians have an inferiority complex: they think everything that comes from abroad is better than what they find at home; nevertheless, the various regions of the outside world are not equal and people from Western European countries represent the foreigner at his best. The Bulgarians have a paradoxical name for this foreigner, which can be explained by their geographical situation: he is simply "European." Fabrics, shoes, washing machines, sewing machines, furniture, even canned sardines are better when they are "European." Because of this, every representative of a foreign culture — person or thing — benefits from a favorable bias that blurs the differences from one country to another, even though these differences are the ones that shape the clichés of the ethnic imagination in Western Europe. For us as Bulgarians, then, when I was growing up, every Belgian, Italian, German, and Frenchman seemed to possess a glorious surplus of intelligence, finesse, and distinction; and we looked on them with an admiration that could only be spoiled by the jealousy and envy that we Bulgarian boys felt when one of these Belgians, passing through Sofia, charmed the girl of our dreams. Even after the Belgian had left, the girl was likely to continue to look down on us.

Because of this inferiority complex, Bulgarians are quite receptive to foreign cultures: not only do they dream of going abroad (preferably to "Europe," although the other continents will also do), but they also willingly learn foreign languages and, filled with goodwill, pounce on foreign books and films. When I came to live in France, this favorable prejudice toward foreigners was complemented by another: when I had to stand in line for hours at the prefecture in order to renew my residence permit, I could not help but feel solidarity with the other foreigners next to me, whether Africans, Maghrebians, or Latin Americans, who were experiencing the same difficulties as I was. Moreover, the employees there and, elsewhere, the guards, concierges, and other police officers—for once egalitarians— did not distinguish among us: all foreigners were treated alike, at least at first. Thus, here again the foreigner appeared good to me: no longer as an object of envy, but as a companion in misfortune, even if, in my case, the misfortune was relative.

But as I came to reflect on these questions, I realized that such an attitude was open to criticism, not only in those caricatural instances where it is so obvious, but in its very principle. This is because the value judgment that I was making was based on a strictly relative criterion: one is a foreigner only in the eyes of natives; foreignness is not an intrinsic quality. To say that someone is a foreigner is obviously not saying much about him. I was not attempting to find out if a certain behavior was in itself just and admirable; it was enough for me to note that it was of foreign origin. A paralogism that xenophilia shares with xenophobia, or with racism, even if it is a more generous impulse, can be found here; it consists in positing an equivalence between the different attributes of the same person: even if a given individual is both French and intelligent, and another is both Algerian and uneducated, this does not mean that one can deduce moral features from physical ones, nor that this deduction can be extended to an entire population.

Xenophilia has two variants: the foreigner belongs to a culture that is perceived as either wholly superior or wholly inferior to one's own. The Bulgarians who admire "Europe" embody the former variant, which can be called *malinchismo*—the word used by Mexicans to designate the blind adulation of Western values, previously Spanish, now Anglo-American. The word is derived from Malinche, Cortés's native interpreter. Malinche's case is perhaps less clear-cut than the strictly pejorative term malinchismo implies, but the phenomenon can be seen clearly in every culture in which there exists an inferiority complex in relation to another culture. The second variant is familiar to French tradition (and to other Western traditions): that of the noble savage, that is to say, foreign cultures that are admired precisely because of their primitivism, backwardness, and technological inferiority. This attitude is alive and well today and is clearly identifiable in ecologist or third-worldist discourse.

What makes these xenophilic behaviors not so much unappealing as unconvincing is that they share with xenophobia the relativity of the values on which they are based. It is as if I were to declare that a side view is intrinsically superior to a frontal view. The same is true of the principle of toleration to which we appeal so easily today. One likes to imagine that toleration and fanaticism are opposites, and that the former is superior to the latter. Under these conditions, however, the game is won before it is played. Toleration is only a positive quality if the things one is tolerating are truly inoffensive: why, for example, should others be condemned—as they in fact have been countless times—because their food, clothing, or hygiene differs from ours? On the other hand, toleration is inappropriate if the "things" in question are gas chambers or, to take a more distant example, the human sacrifices of the Aztecs. The only acceptable attitude toward them is to condemn them (even if condemning such acts does not teach us whether or how we must intervene to stop them). Almost the same thing can in the end be said of Christian charity or of pity toward the weak and conquered: just as it is inappropriate to declare that someone is right simply because he is the strongest, it would be unfair to declare that the weak always deserve our sympathy because of their very weakness; a passing state, an accident of history, finds itself transformed into an intrinsic characteristic.

I, for my part, do not believe that pity and charity, toleration and xenophilia must be radically cast aside; but they do not belong among the principles on which judgments should be based. If I condemn gas chambers or human sacrifices, it is not because of certain feelings, but rather in the name of the absolute principles that proclaim, for example, the de jure equality of all human beings and the inviolable nature of their person. Other instances are less obvious: the principles remain abstract and their application poses certain problems. All this may take time; meanwhile, it is certainly preferable to practice toleration rather than summary justice. At other times, one can see on what side the good motives lie; but misery, destitution, and pain are also important and must be taken into account. To allow daily behavior to be guided only by abstract principles quickly leads to the excesses of puritanism, where one cherishes abstractions rather than beings. Pity and tolerance therefore have their place, but this place belongs with practical interventions, immediate reactions, and concrete gestures, not with principles of justice or criteria on which to base judgment. In short, I share Spinoza's point of view:

Pity in a man who lives under the guidance of reason is in itself bad and useless. . . . he who is easily touched by the emotion of pity, and is moved to tears at the misery of another, often does something of which afterwards he repents: both inasmuch as we can do nothing according to emotion which we can certainly know to be good, and inasmuch as we are easily decieved by false tears.

But he immediately adds this qualifying statement: "I am speaking here expressly of a man who lives under the guidance of reason. For he who is moved neither by reason nor pity to help others is rightly called inhuman" (*Ethics,* part IV, proposition L, 175).

But isn't judging foreign cultures in itself reprehensible? This, in any event, seems to be the consensus of our enlightened contemporaries (as for the others, they avoid speaking in public). For example, the 1983 issue of *Le Français dans le monde,* the journal of professors of French outside France, is devoted to our very theme and is entitled "D'une culture a l'autre" (From one culture to another). In one article, an author—whose good intentions cannot be doubted—attacks the comparison of cultures:

Using comparison as a means to analyze cultures involves a certain amount of risk, in particular the hierarchization of cultures. . . . Theoretically and methodologically, comparison is dangerous. In effect, to seek to establish a parallel, to attempt to find in each culture the same elements in different forms or different degrees of maturity implies a belief in the existence of a universal cultural schema in which every culture has its place. In fact, as we know, everyone brings the universal back to himself. (41)

Juxtaposition is dangerous since it leads to comparative judgment and to hierarchy: one thing is better than another, and such moves are necessarily egocentric.

This notion, however, means viewing human beings as if they were physical particles or, at best, laboratory rats. No doubt human beings are determined by their personal history, by their material conditions, by their ethnicity; but is this true to such a degree that they can never free themselves from these things? What about human consciousness and freedom? And what do we do with all of humanity's aspirations to universality, present as far back as can be remembered? Weren't they the more or less cleverly disguised manifestations of ethnocentrism? Such hyperdeterminist discourse is not without political consequences: if one makes people believe that they are slaves, in the end they become slaves. Such discourse reveals, behind the "theoretical and methodological" claims, relativist ideological biases that cannot be justified.

I believe that behind this fear of hierarchization and judgment lies the specter of racism. One thinks that if one condemns human sacrifice, one runs the risk of appearing to be a champion of the white race. Obviously, Buffon and Gobineau were wrong to imagine that civilizations formed a single pyramid, the summit of which was occupied by blond Teutons or by the French, and the base of which, or rather, the bottom, by "Redskins" and Blacks. Their error, however, was not that they claimed that civilizations were different, yet comparable, since one can arrive, without such a claim, at denying the unity of the human race, which involves much more serious "risks and dangers." Their error was to have posited an identity between the physical and the moral, between skin color and the various forms of cultural life. In other words, the error comes from a certain determinist frame of mind that finds coherence everywhere; a frame of mind related to the attitude of the scientist, who does not want to admit that two series of variables—which can be observed at the same times and in the same places—bear no relation to one another. Further: even supposing that this correlation between the physical and the moral could be established (which is not the case today) and that one could establish a hierarchy of physical qualities, this does not mean that one must espouse racist positions. We are afraid of the idea that natural inequalities between human groups may be discovered (such as, women are less gifted than men for space perception, and men do not master language as well as women). But one must not be afraid of what remains a purely empirical question since the answer—whatever it may be—would not be capable of establishing inegalitarian laws. Rights are not established by facts, and science cannot fabricate the goals of humanity. The racist establishes a de jure inequality on a supposed de facto inequality. This is a disgraceful transition, but there is nothing at all reprehensible about the *observation* of inequalities.

There is no reason to renounce the idea of the universality of the human races; I should be able to say not whether a certain culture, taken as a whole, is superior or inferior to another (again, this would be perceiving coherence everywhere), but rather that a given characteristic of a culture (ours or another), a certain type of cultural behavior, deserves to be condemned or praised. By taking historical or cultural context too much into consideration, one excuses everything; but torture, to take one example, or excision, to take another, cannot be justified simply because they occur within the framework of a particular culture.

## II

Two different levels may be distinguished within the realm of international relations: relations between states on the one hand, and between cultures on the other; the two may also coexist. The relations between states that, despite the efforts of certain transnational bodies, rely on the balance of power and of interests, do not concern me here; instead I shall attempt to describe certain forms and aims of intercultural relations.

For as long as human societies have existed, they have maintained mutual relations. Just as we cannot imagine people living at first separately and only later forming a society, we cannot conceive of a culture that would have no relation to other cultures: identity arises from (the awareness of) difference. In addition, a culture evolves only by means of its outside contacts: the intercultural is constitutive of the cultural. And just as the individual may be philanthropic or misanthropic, societies may value either their contacts with others or, on the contrary, their isolation (though they can never manage total isolation). Here again we come across the phenomena of xenophilia and xenophobia with, for the former, such manifestations as infatuation with exoticism, the desire to escape, and cosmopolitanism and, for the latter, the doctrines of "racial purity," the praise of rootedness (*enracinement*), and the cult of patriotism.

How can we judge contacts between cultures, or the absence of such contacts? One could at first say (and here again the consensus is deceiving) that both are necessary: the inhabitants of one country profit from a better knowledge of their own past, their values, their customs, as well as from their openness to other cultures. But this symmetry is illusory: references to a specific culture and to the totality of cultures and thus, in the end, to the universal, do not form opposing categories. One could, in a preliminary juxtaposition, compare culture to language: both allow the individual to structure experienced diversity and at the same time to make it intelligible; both are composed of specific elements that provide access to a meaning that is, or can become, shared. From this point of view, immersion in a specific culture does not move us away from the universal; on the contrary, it is the only road that leads to it with any certainty.

But the comparison between culture and language rapidly reaches its limits; in other regards, the two are very different. First of all, a language is strictly organized by its grammar, which is the same for everyone, despite the existence of dialects and sociolects. The same is not true of culture. The image of unity and homogeneity that culture aims at presenting stems from a particular frame of mind; it partakes of an a priori decision. Within its own boundaries, a culture is constituted by a constant effort of translation (or should we say "transcoding?"), on the one hand because its members are divided into subgroups (based on age, sex, place of origin, socioprofessional category), and on the other because the means they use to communicate are not similar. Language cannot be divided by the image without a remainder, and vice versa. All of us, whether we know it or not, partake of several cultures simultaneously. "French culture" is the sum of all these subgroups, not their fusion. The constant "translation" between them is in fact what guarantees the internal dynamism of a society.

Furthermore, culture is not an "organic form," as the Romantics used to say, no more than it is "structured like a language"; that is, everything in it is not related, nor does the introduction of a new element lead to a modification of all the other preexisting elements. Populations, and thus cultures, that had been previously isolated from one another come into contact through encounters, journeys, fashions, and natural disasters; they then integrate segments of foreign cultures, without needing to transform themselves from top to bottom. History is replete with such examples. Cultures are not systems, in the strict sense of the word, but rather, composites of fragments of diverse origins. European cultures are typical examples of such assemblages: although they all have a common heritage (but one that, at the beginning, was formed from two traditions: Judeo-Christian, and Greco-Roman), they have each kept enough specific characteristics for their mutual contacts to elicit surprise and, as a result, modifications; and, from very early on, they have sought to come in contact with other cultures, in Asia, Africa, and America.

On a more practical level, it must be admitted that, even if the facts offer evidence of both the attraction to and the rejection of the foreigner, rejection is much more common. We need only observe the world around us to discover that the exclusion of others is easier than remaining open to them, whether we explain this exclusion by the social prolonging of infantile egoism, animal atavism, or least psychological expenditure. This same attitude is amply attested to in the theoretical discourses devoted to the question: the fear of miscegenation (what Pierre-André Taguieff, in his book *La Force du préjugé,* calls "mixophobia") has found eloquent advocates throughout history. And cultural crossbreeding has been just as disdained as its physical variant. Bonald, in the early nineteenth century, wrote, "This communication between all peoples, so praised by philosophers, has only resulted in a communication of vices; and this had to be: health is not won by contact; only diseases are contagious" (*De la chrétienté et du christianisme,* 318). This is why he also scorned "the excessive taste for travel" (*Théorie du pouvoir politique et religieux,* 1:490). The rejection of contacts between peoples and cultures has received support from unexpected quarters in our day: the liberal left fights for the "right to difference," and thus attempts to save minority cultures from the influence of dominant cultures; the nationalist right affirms that only the immersion in national tradition guarantees the blossoming of a people, and consequently recommends that immigrants go home. Finally, ethnologists, perhaps frightened by the rapid transformation of their favorite object of study—small rural communities—have ended up declaring that "complete communication with the other" represents a fatal threat to the survival of our own culture.

Such fears seem to me excessive: while society is becoming more homogeneous, it is also becoming diversified according to new parameters. Differences among cultures, a driving force of civilization, are not about to disappear, even if they have diminished as a result of technological discoveries in the field of communications. For all that, any effort to control the movement of populations on a worldwide scale would only bring us closer to this universal and uniform state that the enemies of crossbreeding rightly fear: the cure would be worse than the disease. Morally speaking, reference to the universal is inevitable and has everything to gain from a better knowledge of others. Northrop Frye called looking back on oneself with a glance informed by contact with others *transvaluation,* and we may judge it to be a value in itself, whereas its opposite is not. Contrary to the tendentious metaphor of rootedness (*enracinement*) and rootlessness (*déracinement*), we will say that man is not a tree and that this is to his advantage. Here we agree with Julien Benda who, in his *Trahison des clercs* (The betrayal of the intellectuals), recalled the wisdom of the ancients: "Plutarch taught us that 'man is not a plant, made to remain immobile with his roots fixed in the ground where he was born . . .' Antisthenes answered his brothers, who were proud of being natives, that they shared this honor with snails and grasshoppers" (56–57). Just as the progress of the individual (of the child) consists in passing

from a state in which the world exists only in and for the subject, to another state where the subject exists in the world, "cultural" progress consists
in a practice of transvaluation.

Obviously, for the individual, contact with other cultures does not play
the same role as the contact he has with his own culture. The latter is constructive; the former, critical: it enables me not to automatically consider
my values as a universal norm. This does not lead to a relativism wherein
everything is equal. Instead, it leads, first, to the discovery that certain elements of culture belong to transcultural moral judgment, and others do not
(human sacrifice and excision are not classified with customs of food and
clothing); and, second, to the decision to base this judgment on reason,
rather than on custom.

Contacts between cultures can come to grief in two different ways: in
the case of maximum ignorance, the two cultures are maintained but do
not influence one another; in the case of total destruction (wars of extermination), there is indeed contact, but it ends in the disappearance of one of
the two cultures: this can be said, with a few exceptions, of Native American populations. Effective contact has countless varieties, which could be
classified in numerous ways. Reciprocity is the exception rather than the
rule here: it is not because American television series influence French
productions that the opposite will or should be true. In the absence of
concerted action by the state, inequality is the very cause of the influence;
it is linked in its turn to economic, political, and technological inequalities.
One need not be annoyed by this state of affairs (even if one can regret it at
times): in this case, there is no reason to expect an equilibrium in the balance of payments.

From another perspective, we can distinguish between more or less
successful interactions. I remember feeling frustrated after animated discussions with some of my Tunisian and Moroccan friends who were suffering
because they were influenced by the French; or with Mexican colleagues
who complained about North American influence. It seemed to me that
they were offering themselves a sterile choice: either cultural malinchismo,
that is, the blind adoption of the values, themes, and even the language of
the metropolis; or isolationism, the refusal of "European" contribution, the
valorizing of origins and traditions, which often was nothing other than a
refusal of the present and a rejection of, among other things, the democratic
ideal. Each of the terms of this alternative seemed to me as undesirable as
the other; but how could one avoid choosing between them?

I found an answer to this question in a specific domain — literature — in the works of one of the first theorists of cultural interaction: Goethe, who promoted the idea of *Weltliteratur.* One could think that this "universal literature" is no more than the least common denominator of the literatures of the world. Western European nations, for example, have in the end recognized a common cultural source — the Greeks and Romans — and each of them has admitted into its own literary tradition some works from neighboring traditions: the French are familiar with the names of Dante, Shakespeare, and Cervantes. In an age of supersonic airplanes and information satellites, one can imagine the addition of some Chinese, Japanese, Arabic, and Indian masterpieces to this short list. The process is one of elimination, conserving only that which may suit everyone.

This, however, is not Goethe's idea of universal literature. What interests him is precisely the transformations that each national literature undergoes at the time of universal exchanges. And he points to a dual road to follow. On the one hand, one must not give up one's specificity; on the contrary, one must dig into it, so to speak, until one discovers the universal in it. "In each particular trait, be it historical, mythological, or coming from a fable, or invented in a more or less arbitrary manner, more and more we shall see universality shine and appear through the national and individual character" (*Ecrits sur l'art,* 262). On the other hand, faced with the foreign culture, one must not give in, but one must see in it another expression of the universal, and therefore attempt to incorporate it into the self: "One must learn to recognize the particularities of each nation, in order to leave them to it; this is precisely what allows one to enter into contact with it: for the particularities of a nation are like its language and its currency". To take an example from our own time rather than from Goethe's, Gabriel García Márquez's *One Hundred Years of Solitude* belongs to universal literature precisely because this novel is so profoundly rooted in the culture of the Caribbean world; and, reciprocally, it manages to express the particularities of this world because it does not hesitate to incorporate the literary discoveries of Rabelais and Faulkner.

Goethe, the most influential author in all of German literature, was himself tirelessly curious about all other cultures, near and far. In a letter, he wrote: "I have never looked or made a step in a foreign country without the intention of recognizing in its most varied forms what is universally human, what is spread and distributed throughout the entire world, and then of finding it in my own country, recognizing it and promoting it"

(*Ecrits sur l'art,* 51). Knowledge of others serves to enrich the self: to give, in this instance, is to take. In Goethe's work, therefore, we find no trace of purism, linguistic or otherwise: "The power of a language does not manifest itself by the fact that it rejects what is foreign to it, but by the fact that it incorporates it" (279). He therefore practices what he terms, somewhat ironically, "positive purism," that is, the incorporation into the mother tongue of foreign terms that it lacks. Rather than seeking the least common denominator, Goethe, in his universal literature, sought the greatest common product.

Is it possible to imagine a political culture inspired by Goethe's principles? The modern democratic state — the French state, for example — does not fail to use its authority and its resources in its international cultural policy. If the results are so often disappointing, it is due to reasons that go beyond this particular domain: it is because — to use a truism — it is always easier to organize those things that allow themselves to be organized. It is easier to bring together ministers, or their advisers, from two countries than creative artists; and it is easier to bring together creative artists than the artistic elements themselves within the same work (and this is why the organization of research is in the process of supplanting research itself). There are countless colloquia, broadcasts, and associations that propose to improve cultural interaction; these may not be harmful, but their usefulness may be questionable. Twenty meetings between the French and Greek ministers of culture will never equal the impact of a single novel translated from one of these languages into the other.

However, even if we leave aside this modern bureaucratic evil, there is one kind of intervention that we may find more admirable than others. Taking Goethe's principles as our inspiration, we could say that the goal of an intercultural policy should be importing others rather than exporting oneself. The members of a society cannot spontaneously practice transvaluation if they are unaware of the existence of values other than their own. As an outgrowth of society, the state must help to make these other values more accessible to the members of this society: the choice is possible only when one has been informed of the existence of such a choice. The benefits for these same members of promoting their achievements abroad seem less significant. In the nineteenth century, French culture had a major role to play, not because its exportation was subsidized, but because it was a lively culture and because, among other reasons, it avidly embraced what was being done elsewhere. When I arrived in France in 1963 from my small, xenophilic country, I was struck by the discovery that in the area of literary theory, people were unaware not only of what had been written in Bulgarian and Russian—exotic languages to be sure—but also of what had been written in German and even in English; thus my first intellectual undertaking in France was a translation from Russian into French. This absence of curiosity about others is a sign of weakness, not of strength: French thinking is better known in America than North American ideas are in France. Translations *into* French must be facilitated, rather than translations *from* the French: the battle of "la francophonie" is being waged above all in France itself.

The constant interaction of cultures results in the formation of hybrid, crossbred, creolized cultures at every level: from bilingual writers, through cosmopolitan metropolises, to multicultural states. As for collective entities, several equally unsatisfactory models come easily to mind. We may skip simple assimilation, which obtains no benefit from the coexistence of two cultural traditions. The ghetto, which protects and even maintains the minority culture intact, is certainly not a defensible solution, since it does not favor mutual enrichment. Nor is the melting pot—pushed to the extreme in which each of the original cultures brings its own contribution to a new mixture—a very good solution, at least not from the point of view of the flowering of cultures. It is a little like arriving at universal literature by means of subtraction, where each person gives only what the others already had; the results in this case are reminiscent of those dishes of indeterminate taste that one finds in Italo-Cubano-Chinese restaurants in North America. Here again, the other idea of universal literature could be used as a model: to speak of a (complex) culture, rather than of the coexistence of two autonomous traditions (from this point of view, emigration is preferable to migration), there must be integration; but the integrating (and therefore dominant) culture should, all the while maintaining its identity, enrich itself by the contributions of the integrated culture, and discover multiplicity rather than merely dull commonplaces. For example, and even if it was accomplished through bloodshed, one thinks of the way the Arabs influenced Spanish culture and even European culture as a whole in the Middle Ages and in the early Renaissance. Things seem much simpler in the case of individuals, and in the twentieth century, exile has become the point of departure for notable artistic experiences.

Transvaluation is, in itself, a value; but does this mean that all contacts, all interactions with representatives of a different culture are positive? To answer yes would be once again to fall into the aporia of xenophilia: the other is not good simply because it is other; some contacts have positive effects, others do not. The best result of the contacts among cultures is often the critical gaze one turns back on oneself. It in no way implies the glorification of the other.

# Part Two

*Entre Nous*: At Home among Ourselves

# 8 / Fictions and Truths

## I

Paul Valéry once remarked that, if we admire the portrait of a great figure of old, we tend to say it is a *true* portrait, even if we have no available means to *verify* such a claim. He extended this remark to books: in the case of the slightly distant past, and if one relies on the reaction of the reader, "there are no grounds for distinguishing" between the authors of history and the authors of fiction, between "books of actual witnesses and those of imaginary witnesses." "One can, at will, call them all *inventors,* or all reporters" (*Regards sur le monde actuel,* 11–12). This does not mean that we automatically judge all these books to be equally true; but the reasons that lead us to declare some tales truer than others have nothing to do with their actual veracity, about which we know nothing. What we do appreciate, one could say (even if Valéry himself does not use these words), is verisimilitude, not truth: the effect of the real (*l'effet de réel*), not the real and the true themselves.

Valéry was merely formulating in his own way a feeling that is quite widespread among modern authors (let us say since the mid-nineteenth century); still, he is not extreme in his formulation, since he does not fail to specify that the impossibility of distinguishing between texts of truth and texts of fiction occurs only "in their immediate effects on the readers," thus retaining the possibility of a later verification, a distinction that could be established by scholars. Many of our contemporaries are not burdened with such precautions: believing that there are no facts, only interpretations (this is Nietzsche's phrasing, but countless other writers have taken it up in one form or another), they extend the effects of this first impossibility—no *textual* sign can guarantee us the truth of the text—to the very nature of knowledge, and to that of the world. The formulation in its entirety would be as follows: there are no facts, only discourses about facts; as a result, there is no truth about the world, there are only interpretations of the world.

This is not, for all that, a discovery made by the moderns; the only new thing, perhaps, is the feeling of euphoria that now accompanies the pronouncement. Plato stated with much bitterness that in court the judges dealt with discourses and never, or rarely, with facts (they had not been present at the scene of the crime they were investigating). As a result, the pleading counsels who were hoping to persuade the judges relied on verisimilitude, on what would bring about agreement, rather than on truth, the effects of which are uncertain. At the tribunals, eloquence, or the capacity to produce the effect of truth, was valued more highly than the truth itself; hence the success of the Sophists, those masters of eloquence. From this fact, Plato arrived at the opposite conclusion from the majority of modern authors: rather than singing the praises of poets, those "imaginary witnesses," he recommended their banishment from the city.

In addition to this first interpretation of the relation between fiction and truth, our modernity offers an even more radical one, which claims not that fiction and truth are indistinguishable, but that fiction is truer than history: the distinction is retained, but the hierarchy is inverted. In a recent book, a book that itself combines several genres—novel, sociological work, autobiography, essay—and which is called *La Traversée du Luxembourg,* Marc Augé calls our attention to an advertising slogan in which a work of French ethnology is praised for being "as rife with truth as a Balzac novel [aussi criant de verité qu'un roman de Balzac]" (18–19). Commenting on this surprising claim (the novelist who vouches for the truth of the historian), Augé arrives at the conclusion that it is legitimate: the historian and the ethnologist must, according to the stubborn rules of their professions, report only what has taken place, only what they can establish as facts; while the novelist, who is not subject to "this cult of the true word" (26), has access to a higher truth, beyond the truth of details. Historians and ethnologists would thus do well, according to Augé, to follow in the novelists' footsteps.

Again, the idea is not original. To quote just one additional example from the more or less recent past, here is what Stendhal notes in his diary on May 24, 1834: "Mme. de Tracy said to me: 'One can no longer reach the *true* save in the novel.' More and more I see every day that elsewhere, there is nothing but pretense" (*Oeuvres intimes,* 2:198). The context of this remark shows that Stendhal considered the novel to be superior to history books on the one hand (biographies, his own *Life of Rossini,* for example), because it allows one to go beyond the factual; and, on the other, to be superior to philosophy books and abstract treatises (for example, his own *On Love*) because it stays within the realm of the specific, and because it remains rooted in detail. For Stendhal, the novel was a glorious middle ground since it was more philosophical than history, and more concrete than philosophy. It is probably for this same reason that, sometime earlier, Rousseau described *Emile,* his most ambitious and least understood book, as "the novel of human nature" (*Ecrits,* 2:161). Nevertheless, the term Stendhal chooses to describe this property is not efficiency or eloquence, but, in fact, truth. This "middle" quality brings to mind Aristotle, the heterodoxical disciple of Plato who, more than twenty centuries earlier, had already declared poetry to be nobler and more philosophical than history, for reasons similar to those of Stendhal and Augé (because poetry is more general, because it escapes contingents). The poets, rescued from the banishment to which Plato had consigned them, regained, inside the city, a worthier function. It must be pointed out that Aristotle did not say that poets were truer than historians; only (only?) that they were nobler and more philosophical.

Here, then, are two opinions, equally old, equally convincing, which share a refusal to give history preference over fiction. Yet if we move from the great thinkers toward the humble reality of daily life, we have a bit of trouble accepting this conclusion. Imagine yourself in the dock, charged with a crime you did not commit: would you accept as a preliminary principle that fiction and truth are equal, or that fiction is truer than history? Imagine that someone were to deny the reality of the genocide perpetrated by the Nazis: would you respond that, regardless of what the supporters of either point of view have to say about it, the debate is pointless because in any event we are invariably dealing with interpretations? Imagine that you were to read the following statement spray-painted on the walls of a building, as I did just recently on my way to the Bibliothèque Nationale: "Immigrants are Nazi occupying forces without a uniform." Would you be content to analyze the structure of the metaphor or even to make a moral judgment about the values implicit in this slogan? Wouldn't you ask yourself if the statement were true or false? If, then, you choose to retain the distinction in practical life, why would you refuse it a place in theory?

All right, you say. But then what status should be accorded to the "truth" of fictions? Were all these past writers mistaken in believing that poetry could tell the truth? Are we wrong to be touched by a human truth when reading Baudelaire's poems or Balzac's novels? And must we banish poets under the pretext that they do not tell the truth?

Perhaps we can answer these further questions by first accepting a more complex analysis of the notion of "truth," an idea that seems to be troublesome here. We must distinguish between at least two senses of the word: truth-adequation (*la vérité d'adequation*) and truth-disclosure (*la vérité de dévoilement*); the former can be measured only against all or nothing, and the latter, against more or less. It is either true or false that X has committed a crime, whatever the attenuating circumstances; the same can be said regarding whether or not Jews were incinerated at Auschwitz. If, however, the question involves the causes of Nazism or the identity of the average French person in 1991, no answer of this nature can be conceived: the answers can only contain more or less truth, since they endeavor to reveal the nature of a phenomenon, not to establish facts. Novelists aim only for this latter type of truth; nor do they have anything to teach historians about the former.

This distinction, though necessary as a point of departure, is insufficient. First of all, if it is true that the novelist aims only for truth-disclosure, the historian (or the ethnologist or the sociologist) cannot be content simply to establish indisputable facts. Historians are, in short, faced with a dilemma: either they stick to the facts, which are unassailable but hardly meaningful by themselves; or they must seek to interpret these facts, and then they open themselves to criticism. Very few, in fact, have chosen to do the former (no one is content merely to know the color of Henry IV's horse). But how does one move from the first to the second idea of truth? And if it is indeed a matter of two truly distinct things, is it worthwhile to retain this single term *truth,* which is then likely to lead to confusion? If one says that Balzac is *truer* than historians and ethnologists, or that he is nobler and more philosophical, isn't that putting into play other—and necessarily superior—criteria than those of truth-adequation, criteria that, in the end, can only arise from a moral position (since it is not knowledge that teaches me that one conception of man is nobler than another)? But if truth is bound by morals, if there are no other truths save pragmatic ones, who will make the decision about what is truer or more philosophical than the truth?

The philosopher-king? The majority of citizens? These solutions to the problem present some well-known drawbacks, which we tend to forget at times. Yet if we avoid subordinating one type of truth to the other, even if we avoid any connection between the two, how then do we situate them within a single framework?

Having arrived at this point in my questioning, I am tempted to change methods. After these indispensable but general preliminaries, I find it necessary to go into detail regarding some specific instances, in order both to test and to qualify my conclusions. Thus, I shall tell two stories, one that will lead us toward the East, the other toward the West, but both of which bring to life the interactions between truth and fiction. In so doing, I follow a tenet of Stendhal's, who claimed to prefer "the truth with a little detail" to everything else.

## II

In April 1704 a work was published in London, translated into French as of August that same year, and then published in Amsterdam under the title *An Historical and Geographical Description of Formosa*. A number of engravings illustrated this rather large book, which had two main subjects. The first was the one its title indicated: Formosa (or Taiwan) was little known at the time, and the author took advantage of this fact in order to acquaint the reader with its geography, history, and inhabitants. The reader learns that this island, separated from Japan only by a strait, is politically under its control. According to the book, the Japanese claimed Formosa after a war whose decisive battle had been won owing to a portable wooden house carried by two elephants, which the Formosans had unsuspectingly welcomed on their soil and which in fact was filled with ferocious Japanese warriors. The reader also learns about the language and the writing (phonetic) of the Formosans, and sees illustrations of their palaces and houses, the costumes worn by the aristocracy and the commoners, as well as their money (Figures 1 to 3).

But the most sensational details of this description of the Formosans' customs concern their religious life: we are told that they practiced cruel human sacrifices. Two prophets, or pseudoprophets, had converted the country to this barbarous religion, a religion that required the yearly sacrifice of eighteen thousand children under nine years of age. These rites were not lacking in macabre elements: the sacrificing priests tore out the hearts of

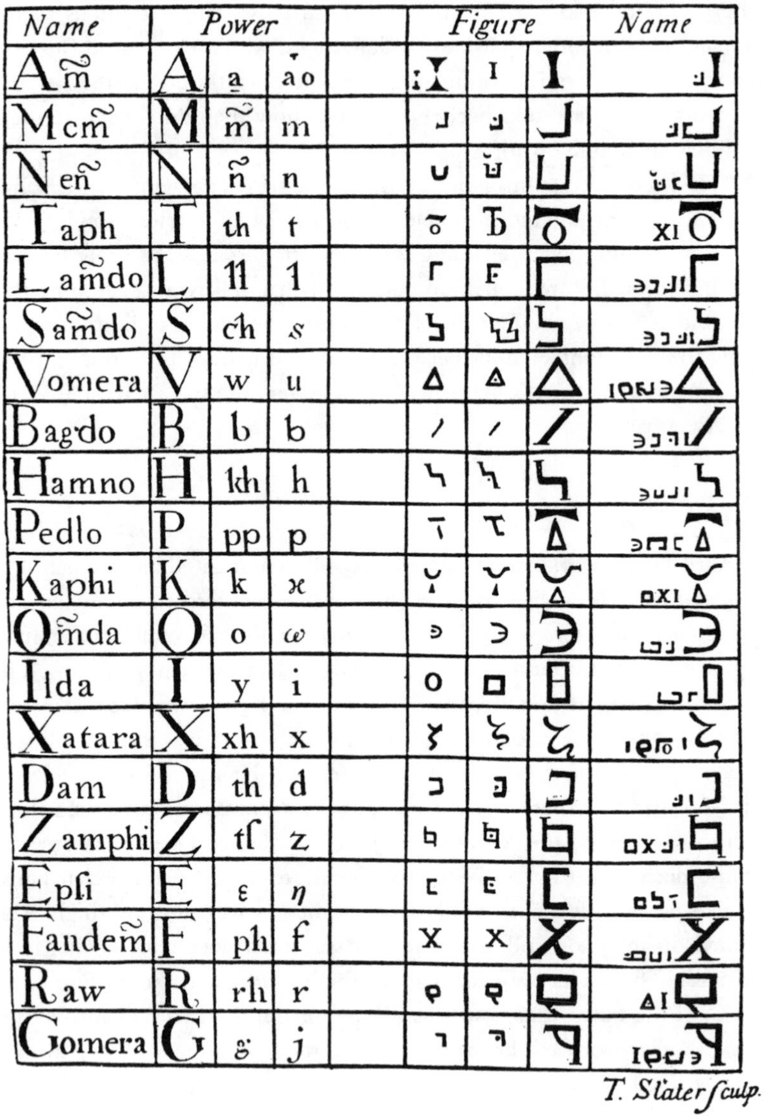

| Name | Power | | | Figure | | | Name |
|---|---|---|---|---|---|---|---|
| A m̃ | A | a | a o | | ːX | I | I | ꭥI |
| M cm̃ | M | m̃ | m | | ┘ | ┘ | ⎦ | ꭐⵊ⎦ |
| N en̄ | N | ñ | n | | ∪ | ʊ̈ | ⊔ | ʊⵊ⊔ |
| T aph | T | th | t | | ŏ | Ђ | ⌒ | xⵊ⌒ |
| L am̃do | L | ll | l | | Γ | F | Γ | ɜⵊⵣⴹΓ |
| S am̃do | S | ch | s | | ꓐ | ☒ | ꓘ | ɜⵊⵣⴹꓘ |
| V omera | V | w | u | | △ | △ | △ | ⅼꝹⴹⵙ△ |
| B agdo | B | b | b | | ⁄ | ⁄ | ⁄ | ɜⵊⵣ⅃⁄ |
| H amno | H | kh | h | | ꓶ | ꓶ | ꓶ | Ꝺⵃⵊⵊꓶ |
| P edlo | P | pp | p | | ⊤ | ⊤ | △ | ɜⵔⴻⴹ△ |
| K aphi | K | k | ӿ | | ⌣̣ | ⌣̣ | ⌣̣Δ | ⴹxⵊ ⌣̣Δ |
| O m̃da | O | o | ω | | Ɔ | Ɔ | Ɔ | ⴳⵑⴰⴶ Ɔ |
| I lda | I | y | i | | o | □ | ⊟ | ⴳⵀⴱ⊟ |
| X atara | X | xh | x | | ɣ | ɣ̧ | ⵒ | ⵊⴻꝊⵊⵒ |
| D am | D | th | d | | ⊐ | ꓕ | ⊐ | ⴹⵊ⊐ |
| Z amphi | Z | tʃ | z | | ꓸ | ꓸ | ꓷ | ⴹxⵁⴹꓷ |
| E pſi | E | ε | η | | ⵎ | ⵎ | ⎣ | ⴹⴱ⵿⎣ |
| F andem̃ | F | ph | f | | x | x | X | ⴷⴹⵊX |
| R aw | R | rh | r | | ꝗ | ꝗ | ⊡ | ⴰⵊ⊡ |
| G omera | G | g | j | | ꓶ̚ | ꓶ̚ | ꓒ | ⵊⴹⵙⴹꓒ |

T. Slater *sculp.*

Figure 1. English version of the Formosan alphabet (1704).

the children in order to offer them to the sun. A cannibalistic meal followed: "Then the Priests begin to pray for the Sanctification of the Victims, and after that they flay them and receive the Blood into a copper; they divide the Flesh into Pieces, and then Boil it with the Blood in a Chaldron which

Figure 2. Formosa (1704).

is upon the Altar.... And after the Flesh is boiled, the People draw near before the Altar, and every one of them receives a piece of it from the Hand of the Priest, bowing down his Head when he takes it" (182).

The second subject, whose relation to the first is only apparently tangential, deals with the story of the author of the book, one George Psalmanazar (some of the As in his name are doubled in different editions), a native of the island who lived there until he was nineteen and who had been taught by a European tutor. One day the tutor decided to return to Europe, taking his disciple with him. After a long journey, they disembarked in the south of France and from there traveled north to Avignon. They

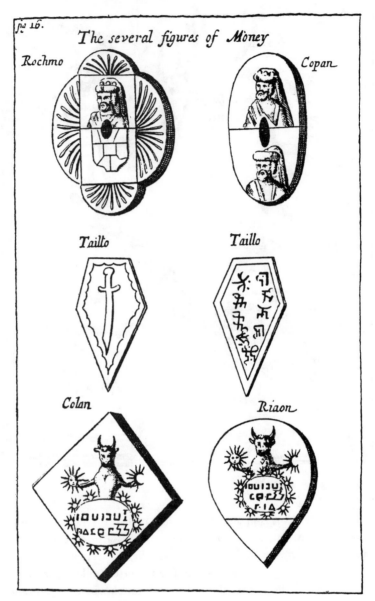

Figure 3. Formosan currency (1704).

then arrived at a monastery, where everyone greeted the tutor with respect; the young Psalmanazar discovered that he was among Jesuits and that
his tutor was one of them. The Jesuits demanded that Psalmanazar convert
to Catholicism. Although he did not scorn Christianity, he was hesitant to
submit to individuals whose virtue seemed suspect. Threatened with the
Inquisition, he managed to escape one night and head north. Upon arriving in the Netherlands, he met up with the British army, whereupon a
Scottish chaplain welcomed him, to his great satisfaction, into the Anglican
Church. Psalmanazar then left for London, where the bishop himself received him and granted him his protection. And there, he wrote his book.

Psalmanazar's work received lively attention. Translated, then, that same
year into French (a translation reprinted in 1708, 1712, and 1739), it was
published in Dutch in 1705 and in German in 1716. A second English edition also appeared in London in 1705, and in one season (but what more
can one expect from fashion?) he had become a household name. He became the guest of fashionable London, and everyone wanted to hear his incredible story from his own mouth; his youth and his eloquence made him
appealing to everyone.

Well, not quite everyone. Even before the book was published, Psalmanazar's story was known in London and piqued the curiosity of people in a
variety of circles. Even the Royal Society invited him, along with other
specialists, to its meeting of February 2, 1704. It was business as usual: Mr.
Collins related the case of someone who had managed to live for several
weeks without eating; another member exhibited the penis of an opossum
and some ovarian cysts; a third presented some new air pumps. Then it was
Psalmanazar's turn to speak. His story had already been heard during the
preceding meeting, but now people wanted to ask him more specific questions because doubt had arisen in some minds. Doctor Halley — famous for
his comet — asked him how long dusk lasted on Formosa. Because Psalmanazar's answer contradicted the already available astronomical data, Halley
accused him of being an impostor. Next, Jean de Fontenay, a French Jesuit
who had been to China at the request of Louis XIV, spoke. He claimed
that Formosa belonged to China, not to Japan. He did not understand the
Formosan language as presented by Psalmanazar; and he had never heard a
word about human sacrifices there.

Aware of these doubts, Psalmanazar decided to fight them in the preface to his work (thereby according them even greater notoriety), and he
used several types of counterarguments to do so. For example, the authority of other travelers had been used to contest his; but upon reading their

texts, one discovered that they recounted facts that were even more inconceivable. Candidius, for example, who was a great authority on the question, claimed that when a woman became pregnant before age thirty-seven, the priestesses laid her down and jumped on her stomach until she aborted: could one believe such nonsense, and have faith in the author who related it? In addition, continued Psalmanazar, unbelievable facts did indeed exist. The objection had been raised that, with eighteen thousand sacrifices each year, the population of the island must have had difficulty renewing itself. Psalmanazar explained that polygamy existed in order to make up for this lack. One could add that, in any case, considerations of verisimilitude do not affect truth: even had Psalmanazar omitted or modified the most implausible details from his story, one still could not affirm with any certainty that he was from Formosa or that the remainder of his narrative was truthful.

Another of his counterarguments was even more effective: it consisted in asking his opponents a question that had its moment of glory in France not so long ago: "From where are you speaking?" Faced with a particular statement, one does not question its truth, or its meaning, but asks instead: what are the *motives* of the person who utters it? To return to the modern parallel, we know that certain contemporary authors have denied the reality of the genocide of the Jews. When their theses were contested, they replied: but those who contradict us are all Jewish (or the servants of imperialism). This line of reasoning could have been convincing had we known as little about Auschwitz as the Englishmen of Psalmanazar's time knew about Formosa. In Psalmanazar's case, this parry protected him from two adversaries. On the one hand, it was well known that freethinkers such as Halley criticized the Christian institution. The fact that they were attacking Psalmanazar, then, became for the majority of believers proof that his narrative was *true:* if my enemies disparage something, it must be good. The affair involving the Jesuits is even clearer, since in Psalmanazar's narrative they appear in an unfavorable light: their "tolerance" toward foreign religions (here, the Formosan religion, with all its horrors) could be seen as bordering on indifference toward Christianity; and their brutality toward poor Psalmanazar became equally blameworthy. According to Psalmanazar, we cannot but question the word of such biased witnesses. How could they *not* want to destroy the author's credibility by showing that his description of Formosa was flawed? By affirming that the "Formosan" part of the narrative was false, the Jesuits were attempting to discredit the anti-Jesuit part of the work; Psalmanazar, for his part, called on the anti-Jesuit sentiments of his readers in order to authenticate his exotic descriptions: the two strategies come down to the same thing.

The newspapers of the time latched onto the affair. Opinions were divided. On the one hand, the implausible facts were pointed out, and Psalmanazar's adversaries, Halley and Fontenay, were quoted. On the other hand, the confidence placed in Psalmanazar by the Bishop of London (was he someone to take sides lightly?) and other respectable well-known men was recalled. Psalmanazar's work corresponded to a familiar genre — the tale of the journey to a distant land — with its juxtaposition of narrative and description; at the time this kind of literature afforded the reader great pleasure. The *Histoire des ouvrages des savans* [*sic*] relates, in its November of 1704 installment, that Psalmanazar was put to strange tests: "In London, someone attempted to test Psalmanazar, and to force him to establish the truth of what he was saying about the Formosans by eating the flesh of a hanged man himself. [Psalmanazar relates that this is common practice on Formosa, and that the flesh of young women who have suffered for a long time before their execution is particularly sought after.] He did it without revulsion, but far from convincing those who doubted, the horror that he provoked in them caused them to cover him with blows." Here again, as with Halley, the result was contrary to what one expected (the perverse effects of the proof). On the whole, the disbelievers were more numerous than the believers, but they did not go so far as to reject the entire testimony, by virtue of the underlying principle of calumny and rumor: there is no smoke without fire, as they say.

Several years passed and Psalmanazar and his adventures were slowly forgotten. But he had not died, and he obviously had not forgotten anything. The problem was that with age, Psalmanazar, who was leading a modest life and supporting himself by collecting texts, had become more and more religious, and the episode of his youth began to weigh on him. In 1747, when he was sixty-eight years old, he decided to reveal the deceitful side of the affair in an anonymous article on Formosa that he wrote for a geographical encyclopedia. In this article, he stated that Psalmanazar, whom he had known, had authorized him to reveal that his narrative had been, for the most part, fictive (*fabulous*). The news of the admission of the fictive nature of the narrative required a new fiction: that Psalmanazar and the author of the article were not one and the same. He saved the rest of the story for his *Memoirs,* which he finished writing in 1758 and which were published in 1764, a year after his death. At a later date, historians added some additional details.

In his *Memoirs,* Psalmanazar revealed many things, but—despite his increased devoutness—he continued to conceal others; thus, he revealed neither his real name nor where he was born. Some people believed him to be Gascon (because he was a liar?); others believed him to be Jewish (because he was a wanderer?). Apparently there was nothing Japanese about him. He spoke every language (not to mention "Formosan") with an accent; his *Description* was originally written in Latin. It seems that in his youth he lived with his mother in the south of France and went to a Jesuit school. Later, his mother sent him to his father somewhere in Germany; but his father did not want him, and he left for Holland. On the way—after all, one needs to eat, and the future Psalmanazar had no money—he begged in Latin from the clergymen he met and, one day, to attract even more attention, he decided to introduce himself as a Japanese man converted to Christianity. And, because the whole affair amused him, he invented a grammar, a calendar, and a religion; he also adopted the name Psalmanazar, which he found (without the *P*) in the Bible.

When he arrived in Holland, however, he became involved in another adventure: he introduced himself as a pagan who worshiped the sun and the moon, and who would convert to Christianity if offered protection. At this point, he met the Scottish chaplain who knew the whole thing was a hoax but who—far from denouncing Psalmanazar—decided to turn the affair to his advantage. He described the case to the Bishop of London and then "baptized" Psalmanazar. As a result, the chaplain was promoted and the bishop summoned Psalmanazar to London. All that remained for him to do was to write his book to corroborate his statements. It is at this point that he remembered the story of the Jesuit Alexander of Rhodes who, upon leaving Macao in 1645, had brought with him a young Chinese boy who later became a Jesuit himself. Psalmanazar gave the same name to his imaginary "tutor" and decided to participate, by means of his book, in the battle then being waged by the Anglican Church against Catholicism in general and against the Jesuits in particular. In fact, wasn't communion, as practiced by Catholics, a kind of cannibalism? The other details were acquired from books (the Trojan horse from the *Odyssey,* the human sacrifices from the Aztecs, the details borrowed from Candidius).

Today we know with certainty that *An Historical and Geographical Description of Formosa* was a hoax, that Psalmanazar had never been to China, and that, in addition, his name was not Psalmanazar. It is rare for a case to be so clear. Although I do not mean to imply anything, I wonder if all the descriptions of phonological systems brought back by linguists from their fieldwork, all the rites that have been observed and reported by ethnologists, can be situated with such certainty on one side or the other of the line that separates "actual witnesses" from "imaginary witnesses." Or, to take another example even closer to us: I doubt that many of my readers had ever heard of Psalmanazar before, or that the present work will inspire them to go to the Bibliothèque Nationale in order to verify if Psalmanazar really existed, or if he is an imaginary character (*fabulous*), similar to the authors to whom Borges refers at times.

What does Psalmanazar's story, as I have related it, tell us about the border that separates truth and fiction? The description of Formosa possesses neither truth-adequation nor truth-disclosure. And, because it *presents* itself not as fiction but as truth, it is *not* fiction but rather lies and imposture. What Edmund Halley and Jean de Fontenay did, by means of astronomy and history, respectively, was not to produce an "interpretation," a "discourse" to be placed alongside Psalmanazar's "interpretation" or "discourse": they told the truth, whereas he spoke falsely. It is absolutely essential, if one wants to know about Formosa and its inhabitants, to distinguish between the two. Psalmanazar's description of the Jesuits has absolutely no truth-adequation either, even if it has relatively more truth-disclosure: the characteristics by which the Jesuits are described in this story are not entirely invented. But this truth owes nothing to Psalmanazar: his text is a pure fake. Psalmanazar resembles Colonel Henry in the Dreyfus affair: in order to prove Dreyfus's guilt, in order to serve what he believed was a just cause, the colonel decided to fabricate false documents. Psalmanazar's calumnies were simply more innocent, since he did not attack any one person in particular (the real priest from Rhodes had been dead for a long time when Psalmanazar was writing); rather, he attacked an order and an ideology, an ideology that one will not leap to defend simply because it has been treated improperly.

As a historical text, Psalmanazar's *Description* does not deserve respect because it is false. As a fiction, it is not worthy of admiration because it does not present itself as such, and because its author was not particularly eloquent. But what if he *had* been?

# III

Today every child knows that "Columbus discovered America"; yet this statement is filled with "fictions." Let us first deal with the most obvious one, found in the word "discovered": the word is legitimate only if one has decided beforehand that the history of humanity is identical to the history of Europe, and that as a result the history of the other continents begins the moment the Europeans arrive. No one would think of celebrating the "discovery" of England by the French, nor that of France by the English, for the simple reason that neither of these peoples is considered more central than the other. If one abandons the Eurocentric point of view, one can no longer speak of a "discovery," but rather one must speak of the "invasion of America," the title of a book by Francis Jennings.

Next one realizes that Columbus was not the first explorer to have sailed across the Atlantic. To the north, and possibly even to the south, others had come before him; but their journeys obviously did not have the same consequences: it is in this that Columbus's role was unique. "Columbus" is thus no more justified than "discovery." And finally — and it is this paradox with which I will be most concerned here — it is curious that, having chosen Columbus as "discoverer," we gave the name *America* to the land that he "discovered," that is, the name of another explorer who came after Columbus, Amerigo Vespucci. Why America and not Columbia?

There is a simple historical answer to this question: the authors of an influential geographical treatise, *Cosmographiae introductio,* published in Saint-Dié in the Vosges in 1507, decided that Amerigo Vespucci's merits were such that it was fitting to give his name to the newly "discovered" lands. Little by little their proposal was adopted, first for what we now call South America, and then, some twenty years later, for "North America." Nevertheless, Spain and Portugal, who were at the time the main countries involved, did not accept this name until the eighteenth century, preferring instead to use "West Indies."

This answer, however, shifts the problem only slightly: why did the group of scholars from Saint-Dié who were responsible for the *Cosmographiae introductio* deem Amerigo's contribution more important than that of all the other explorers in general, and of Columbus in particular?

One could initially respond that Amerigo was the first to land on terra firma. We know in effect that during his first two voyages, in 1492–93 and in 1493–96, Columbus only reached the islands on the edge of the Gulf of Mexico. He reached the continent during his third voyage, at the end of 1497. Amerigo, on the other hand, reached these same continental lands during his first voyage, also in 1497, but several months earlier. This argument, however, does not hold for several reasons. First, it is not at all certain that Amerigo made the journey in question: it merely happens that his account of it — which is found only in a single letter — is the sole source of this information. Second, even if the account is true, Amerigo was not the commander, and the credit traditionally goes to the head of an expedition. Third, even supposing that it was Amerigo who made the journey in 1497, he would not have been the first at that time to have reached the continent: before Columbus, before Vespucci, it was Giovanni Caboto (John Cabot), a Venetian explorer in the service of England, who reached it first in 1497. In the fourth place, we must take into account what these explorers thought they had accomplished, and not only what we now know they actually did accomplish. Nothing proves that in 1497 either Cabot or Vespucci believed that they were on a continent; and as for Columbus, he believed he had arrived as early as 1494 because he did not want to admit that Cuba could be an island (in his mind he had reached Asia!). Fifth and last — and this is obviously the most important reason — it is not the question of who was first that motivated the Saint-Dié group. Neither are considerations supported by the analysis of the maps of the time pertinent. A map from 1500, drawn up by Juan de la Cosa, shows Cuba to be distinct from America; and it is probable that it was drawn based on information furnished by Amerigo and acquired during his 1497 voyage. But the Saint-Dié authors referred to Amerigo's writings, not to maps.

Thus a second answer is called for, and it is the one given by all the recent historians of the subject (the last to date being Edmund O'Gorman): Amerigo's merit was not that he was the first to have set foot on American ground, but that he was the first to have realized it; his was an intellectual discovery, not a physical one. Thus, Amerigo's discovery must be dated not from 1497 — a year that corresponds to a doubtful voyage — but from 1503, when his letter, very significantly entitled *Mundus novus,* appeared; and from 1506–7, when the Italian and Latin versions of his other famous letter, *Quatuor navigationes,* were published (the Latin version appeared in *Cosmographiae introductio*). In effect, the former affirms and the latter confirms the *consciousness* that Amerigo had of having reached an unknown continent, whereas Columbus believed, during the course of his first voyages, that he had reached Asia through the "Western route." From this perspective it matters little in the end if Amerigo made the journey or not; the main thing is that he *understood,* and he could have done that simply by staying in his study (assuming that he had one).

This second answer is certainly much closer to the truth than the first. And yet, it is problematic; Amerigo also has some significant rivals in the domain of intellectual discovery. The first of these rivals is, in fact, a man who never traveled, but rather was content simply to write: Peter Martyr of Anghiera of the Court of Spain, who wrote "open" letters to foreign dignitaries, in which he summarized news from the voyages as it arrived in Madrid. From the time of his earliest letter, dated November 10, 1493, and addressed to Cardinal Sforza, he offered a description of Columbus's journey that differed considerably from Columbus's own: he wrote that Columbus "discovered this unknown land" and that he had "found all the indications of a continent unknown until now" (*De orbe novo,* 16). One year later, in a letter to Borromeo dated October 20, 1494, Peter Martyr used the same expression, *orbe novo* (new world), which would serve as the title of the publication of his collected letters in 1530 and which is found in Amerigo's writings. Peter Martyr's letters were not private letters; they were, in fact, the main source from which cultured Europeans of the time obtained their information about the extraordinary voyages undertaken by the Spanish and the Portuguese.

Amerigo's second intellectual rival is none other than Columbus himself. The 1497 voyage during which Columbus reached the American coast provided the occasion for a *Relation* that he addressed to the kings of Spain and that was published shortly afterward. In it, Columbus clearly stated his conviction that he had touched terra firma and that this land was not Asia (he knew that Asia was in the Northern Hemisphere and that he had been traveling southward): it was, he wrote, "an infinite land that extends southward, and of which we had no prior knowledge." Amerigo would say the same thing.

But if Peter Martyr and Columbus wrote these sentences, of which the scholars of Saint-Dié could not have been unaware, why did these scholars nonetheless choose to honor Amerigo rather than either of his rivals? Lacking the ability to penetrate the minds of these men of old, and basing our opinion on the sole existing texts, only one answer can be found: it is because the accounts in which Amerigo is the main character are *better written* than Columbus's letters (and, in another way, than Peter Martyr's). It is not the intellectual discovery that the naming of the new continent celebrates; it is—whether its namers knew it or not—literary excellence. Amerigo owes his glory to the forty or so pages that make up the two letters published during his lifetime.

In order to substantiate this literary excellence, it is useful to compare two letters of similar length: the one Columbus wrote to Santangel in 1493, and the one—known by the title *Mundus novus*—Amerigo sent to Lorenzo de Medici (who is not Lorenzo the Magnificent) in 1503. These were, in fact, the two most popular texts of the time, and the ones that were reprinted most frequently (Amerigo's letter even more than Columbus's). It is the comparison between the two—implicit or explicit—that lay behind the decision of the Saint-Dié scholars.

First let us look at overall composition. Columbus's letter does not reveal any particular design. He describes his journey and the scenery on the islands (Haiti and Cuba), and then sketches a portrait of their inhabitants. Next he returns to geography, adding comments about the "Indians." He then continues with a chapter on monsters and concludes, first by assuring the kings that these lands are surely very rich, and then by thanking God for having allowed him to make these discoveries.

In contrast, Amerigo's letter reveals someone who has had a certain education in rhetoric. It begins and ends with several paragraphs that summarize his main points: it is in these paragraphs—and we will come back to them—that the astonishing assertion of the newness of this world is contained. Within this framework the text is clearly divided in two: the first part describes the journey (with a digression regarding Amerigo's excellence as a pilot); the second describes the new lands, with three subsections that are outlined at the end of the first part, concerning men, earth, and sky. Amerigo's letter has an almost geometric *form,* which Columbus's letter lacks and which is very appealing to the reader.

The reader, in fact, holds a place of honor in Amerigo's letter, whereas Columbus's letter hardly takes him into account. It must be pointed out that the positions of these two explorer-navigators are radically different. Whether writing to Santangel, a higher official and a ship owner, or to other persons of rank, Columbus is, in fact, always addressing, first and foremost, the rulers of Spain, Ferdinand and Isabella, whom he wants to convince of the wealth of the newly discovered lands and of the necessity of undertaking future expeditions (first to America, and then to Jerusalem); his letters are therefore instrument-letters, utilitarian letters. This is not at all Amerigo's case; he journeys for love of glory, not money, and he writes in order to "perpetuate the glory of my name," for "the honor of my old age." His letters aim, above all, to dazzle his Florentine friends, to amuse and enchant them. He has *Mundus novus* translated into Latin, so that all of cultured Europe "can know how many marvellous things are discovered every day." In *Quatuor navigationes,* written in the form of a letter to Soderini— another leading citizen of Florence—Amerigo again insists that he is certain that his addressee will take pleasure in reading him. And he concludes his preamble with a formal ending that, no matter how conventional, is no less significant: "Just as fennel is customarily served after pleasing dishes in order for them to be more easily digested, in this same way you may, in order to find rest from your great occupations, have my letter read to you." Columbus was writing documents, whereas Amerigo was writing literature.

Amerigo sought more to amuse than to undertake new expeditions, and he wanted to increase his audience; hence his concern with clarity of exposition, and the summaries at beginning and end. Thus, when he tackles the question of cosmography, a subject in which his reader was probably not well versed, he explains himself twice: "So that you may understand more clearly." He even adds a small diagram (Figure 4). In *Quatuor navigationes,* as an experienced narrator, he whets the reader's appetite with promises of what is to come: "On this journey, I saw things that are truly marvellous, as Your Magnificence will see"; "People who were worse than animals, as Your Magnificence will learn." But he had already done the same thing in *Mundus novus:* "As I shall relate later." We find nothing of the sort in Columbus's letters.

Amerigo flatters his readers by introducing a certain distance between the narrator he *is* and the character he *was;* he invites the readers to slip into the space that is contrived thereby, and even retains the possibility of their feeling somewhat superior to the travelers. Rather than describing the suffering endured during the passage, he calls it to mind by means of preterition. And, when he must justify his own decisions, he calls on the experience that the reader may share with him. Columbus, on the other hand, produces only one image in his letter: his own.

Amerigo also demonstrates a great concern for his reader in his choice of subjects. The facts as observed (or imagined) by Columbus and Amerigo are not very different. Columbus describes the Indians as naked, fearful, generous, without religion, and sometimes cannibalistic. Amerigo, using the same elements, will deploy them in three different directions. (1) He associates nudity, absence of religion, nonaggressiveness, and indifference to property with past representations of the golden age, producing the modern image of the noble savage: Amerigo is the main source for Thomas More, Montaigne, and countless other primitivist writers. (2) As for cannibalism, Columbus recounted it based on hearsay (he did not understand the Indians' language at all). Amerigo, on the other hand, launched forth into long commentaries: the Indians take prisoners of war in order to eat them later; the male eats his wife and children with pleasure. A man confided in him that he had devoured more than three hundred of his fellow beings; and during a walk through Indian territory he [Amerigo] saw salted human flesh hanging from the beams, like the pork we would see in our country.

ZENIT NOSTO

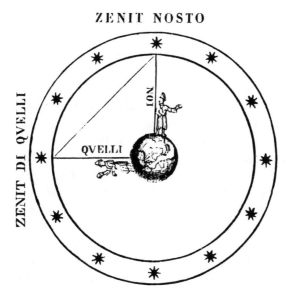

Figure 4. Amerigo Vespucci's explanatory diagram (1503).

Amerigo relates these "spicy" details to us before offering his opinion of the Indians, who do not understand the Europeans' repugnance for such a succulent dish. The choice of this topic is unquestionably judicious: one need only note the great extent to which it occurs in illustrations of the time or in later accounts (up to and beyond Psalmanazar). And lastly, (3) Amerigo enters the sphere of sexuality. Whereas Columbus had limited himself to saying, "In all of these islands it seems as if a man contents himself with a single woman," Amerigo's imagination was unleashed. Indian women are extremely lustful, he says again and again, and he offers these details to his readers (European males): the women cause venomous animals to bite their partners' penises, which then grow to incredible proportions and finally explode, making eunuchs of the men (the reader's reaction can be easily imagined). In the last French translation of *Mundus novus,* which dates from 1855, this passage is omitted and is replaced by the following note: "Here there were ten or twelve lines on the behavior of the women. This passage, which it is impossible for us not to omit, is perhaps not one of those which contributed the least to the popularity of the name of Americ Vespuce [*sic*]" (Charton, 201). Another bonus for the reader: he learns of the success that the European travelers had with the Indian women—the Europeans, we can suppose, did not undergo the same risky treatment as the native men. "When they have the possibility of copulating with Christians, motivated by an excessive lustfulness, they debauch and prostitute themselves." Amerigo even claims that "reasons of decency" do not allow him to tell all. This is a well-known technique for rousing the imagination of one's reader.

These sections of *Mundus novus* appeal to all of Amerigo's readers (once again all men, all Europeans). Other sections kindle the pride of the best among them — cultured men — and, at the same time, make them all feel that they belong to the cultural elite. In *Quatuor navigationes,* Amerigo quotes the moderns and the ancients, Pliny, Dante, Petrarch; in *Mundus novus,* after having described the noble savages, he offhandedly concludes: "We could describe them as epicureans rather than as stoics." Elsewhere, he does not fail to refer to the writings of philosophers. Another passage is significant: Amerigo complains that the pilot of the boat was ignorant and that, without Amerigo no one would have known what distance they had gone; he is the only one on board who is capable of reading the stars and of using the quadrant and the astrolabe; the sailors themselves "know only the waters in which they have already navigated." How could this haughty declaration of the superiority of intellectual-historians over sailor-practitioners not go straight to the hearts of the cartographer Martin Waldseemüller and the poet Mathias Ringmann, who had never traveled very far from Saint-Dié? And could they help but be grateful to Amerigo, and attempt to find a way to thank him? In recompense they offered him a continent. It is not by chance that the image of Amerigo that the engravings of the time transmit to us is also one of a scholar (Figures 5 and 6).

Finally, and independently of all the care Amerigo lavishes on his readers, they could find, in his writings, a universe that was similar to their own. As we have seen, his references draw upon Italian poets, philosophers of antiquity, and rarely upon Christian sources. Columbus, on the other hand, had only Christian texts, and the marvellous accounts of Marco Polo or of Cardinal Pierre d'Ailly in mind. Columbus is a man of the Middle Ages, whereas Amerigo is a man of the Renaissance. We find another clue in certain rudiments of cultural relativism that exist in Amerigo's writings: he transcribes whatever he knows about the Indians' perception of the Europeans (and not only his own perception of others). The avid readers of his news also belonged to modern times. Amerigo's world, as we have said, was prosaically divided into men, earth, and sky (the stars). In contrast, Columbus's world, in addition to the categories "men" and "nature," had another: monsters. It is obvious that Columbus had a list of monsters in mind and that he mentally checked off their presence or absence: Amazons, yes; men with two heads, no; men with tails, yes; men with dogs'

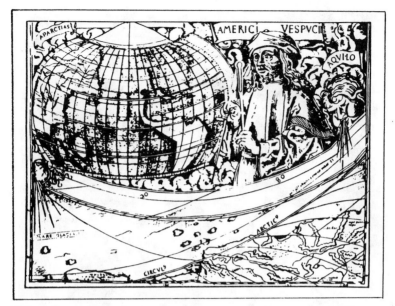

Figure 5. Portrait of Amerigo Vespucci as it appeared on the map of Martin Waldseemüller (1507).

heads, no. In comparison, Amerigo's world is purely human. He is also attracted to the monstrous, but only as an oddity. The word appears, for example, when he describes the Indians' adornments: their pierced cheeks or lips adorned with precious stones. The only implausible things we find in Amerigo are due to exaggeration; they demonstrate the bad faith of the tall-tale teller rather than the naiveté of the believer: the Indians live to be 150, he claims in *Novus mundus,* and in *Quatuor navigationes* he describes a population whose women are as tall as European men, and whose men are taller still. One need only see the references that Columbus and Amerigo make to the Terrestrial Paradise in order to gauge the difference between them: Columbus believes in it literally and thinks he caught a glimpse of it (in South America); Amerigo uses it as mere hyperbole (revived, perhaps, by Columbus's ecstatic evocations of it) and makes use of it to crown a perfectly conventional description of nature: "Needless to say if there is indeed a Terrestrial Paradise in this world, I do not doubt that it is to be found not far from this land."

*Quatuor navigationes* confirms Amerigo's literary talents. Here again, the general design is dictated by a concern for the reader. Amerigo devotes increasingly fewer pages to each of the four voyages, not because each voyage

Figure 6. Amerigo Vespucci meets America (1589).

is shorter than the preceding one (this is not the case), but because the
reader has less and less to learn. The description of the Indians, quite similar to the one found in *Mundus novus* (which dealt with the third voyage),
appears now in the first voyage: its place is dictated not by the chronology
of the voyage, but by that of the reader. Adventure tales alternate regularly

with peaceful descriptions. In addition, Amerigo develops in this work an art that was absent from *Mundus novus,* that of the narrative vignette: a small episode containing bizarre revelations or unexpected reversals. Thus, on the one hand we find the suggestive descriptions of the iguana (dragon without wings!), of hammocks (nets suspended in the air), the cultivation of pearls, ruminating Indians who can go without water; and, on the other, commentaries constructed on an identical schema: the Europeans believe themselves to be stronger, especially when it comes to women. Nevertheless, to their great humiliation, they experience defeat. For example, the episode of the giants that occurs during the second voyage: Amerigo and his companions are preparing to kidnap three young, very tall girls when thirty-six frightening bullies enter the cabin; the Europeans prudently beat their retreat. Or, again during the third voyage: when the Europeans see only women along the coast, they send a handsome boy to seduce and subdue them. But, while several of them are making eyes at him, another one comes up from behind and knocks him out with a large mace. The women then take his body and attach it to a large spit in order to cook him. The Christians, horrified, watch the scene from afar.

We now understand somewhat better the reasons for Amerigo's extraordinary success, a success demonstrated not only by the numerous reprints of his work and the choice of the scholars of Saint-Dié, but also by the fact that his texts were the most abundantly illustrated of the time. Columbus's letters are accompanied by strictly conventional engravings, showing castles and men similar to those found in Europe. The first images that attempt to grasp what is specific to America are the ones that illustrate Amerigo's narratives: this is because these narratives lend themselves to it (for example, the roasted Christian [on the Kunstmann II map, Figure 7]; or the same man, right before he was knocked senseless; or the Indians urinating in each others' presence [another detail revealed — or invented? — by Amerigo], Figure 8). The image and accompanying caption of one of the oldest and most interesting engravings, dating from 1505, summarize the entire *Mundus novus*: the Indians are naked except for feathers; they are sexually liberated and practice incest; they eat one another; they do not have private property; they live to be 150 years old and have no laws (Figure 9). It is obvious what it was that struck people's imaginations most.

These are the elements that explain Amerigo's success and the sympathy he elicits from the Saint-Dié scholars. We do not know exactly who proposed to name the new lands "America": Waldseemüller was the cartographer, but the text could have been written by Ringmann. Ringmann,

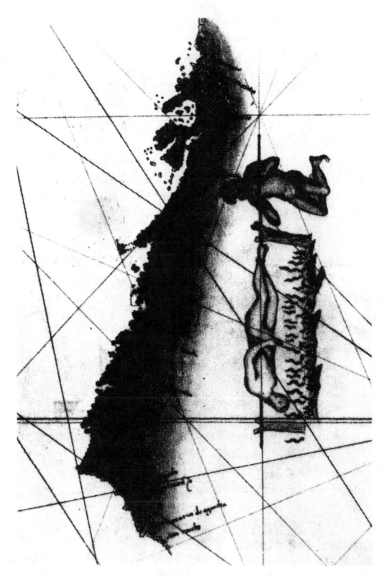

Figure 7. Amerigo Vespucci's companion being roasted on a spit. From the Kunstmann II map (1502).

who was twenty-five at the time, was a "humanist" and a poet; how could he not have considered Amerigo the kindred spirit he would have loved to be able to glorify, especially since Amerigo did not suffer from excess modesty: "as my last journey showed, . . . I discovered a continent" — these

Figure 8. Illustrations from *Quatuor nagivationes* (1509).

Figure 9. Illustration from *Mundus novus* (1505).

are his words. Above all, Amerigo knew how to turn something to his advantage, which neither Peter Martyr nor Columbus had known how to do: the entire first page of his letter proclaims the newness of his discovery (not, it is true, in relation to Columbus, but in relation to the older authors). He has discovered a continent, comparable to Europe, Asia, and

Africa; the title of the letter, *Mundus novus,* is in and of itself a stroke of genius. What a contrast to Columbus, whose words about the new continent
quoted above only revealed themselves to a very attentive eye, lost as they
were in a dogmatic account of the Terrestrial Paradise, an idea that was much
dearer to him than that of "America"! The latter, in fact, was only posited
in the event that the former proved to be a failure. "If this river does not
come from the Terrestrial Paradise...," wrote Columbus, hurrying to add,
"Nonetheless, I firmly believe deep in my heart that this place about
which I am speaking is the Terrestrial Paradise."

If we accept that Waldseemüller and Ringmann's decision is motivated,
however unconsciously, by the literary qualities of Amerigo's writings, another question arises: is this aesthetic justice, in fact, upheld by a historical
justice? In other words, does Amerigo's role, such as it appears in his own
writings, correspond to the role that he actually played? Does the name of
the continent glorify a fiction or a truth? All the arguments that I have just
enumerated in favor of Amerigo could in effect also be applied to an entirely false text, to Psalmanazar's, for example — had the latter lived during
another time and had he had Amerigo's literary talent.

This brings us to the controversial problem of the authenticity of the
letters. The term can be used to cover two autonomous though interdepen-
dent meanings here: Who is the true author of the letters? Do these letters
tell the truth? The letters may be the work of Amerigo and nonetheless be
pure fictions; or, conversely, they may be unduly attributed to Amerigo
and nevertheless tell the truth; or perhaps neither the one nor the other,
or perhaps both at once. Vespucci scholars have been mostly concerned
with the first question. *Mundus novus* and *Quatuor navigationes* are the only
letters that were published during the author's lifetime, but others have been
found since. Two are of particular interest because they are related to the
American voyages: the first, dated July 18, 1500, addressed to the same
Lorenzo de Medici, concerns the second voyage; the other, dated 1502,
also to Lorenzo, deals with the third voyage (they were published in 1745
and 1789, respectively). Up until quite recently, they were considered apoc-
ryphal, and the previously published letters were believed to be the only
authentic ones. One of the reasons given to justify this decision is the difference in style between the published letters and the manuscript letters.
Another reason has to do with the internal contradictions, and the implausible statements found in the latter.

Then, in 1926, an Italian scholar, Alberto Magnaghi, brought about a
spectacular reversal of the situation. Basing his argument on the incompati-

bility between the manuscript letters and the published letters, he drew the opposite conclusion: the only authentic ones are the handwritten letters, whereas *Mundus novus* and *Quatuor navigationes* are "forgeries" and, in addition, contain just as many internal contradictions and implausible facts as the handwritten letters. Furthermore, he claimed that the inauthenticity of the published letters could be easily explained: they were the work of Florentine men of letters, who used Amerigo's actual letters—preserved or lost—to produce amusing and instructive literature (it is much more likely that someone would have falsified a published letter rather than a handwritten one that was destined to be forgotten in the archives and rediscovered only some two hundred and fifty years later!). According to this hypothesis, the real authors of the letters were professional writers who had possibly never left their city. These letters, then, would have been written not only *for* readers, but *by* readers!

Magnaghi's conclusions were vigorously contested by a new Vespucci partisan, Roberto Levillier, who declared that all of the letters attributed to the explorer were authentic. We do not really need to enter into the details of these controversies, since they all primarily concern the question of the actual author, whereas the question that concerns us has to do with the veracity of the letters; nonetheless, certain arguments remain pertinent in both perspectives. But let us return to our subject, and ask ourselves, what does a reading of the letters tell us about their veracity?

We have already seen that there are some implausibilities (longevity, giantism) in *Mundus novus* and in *Quatuor navigationes;* no conclusions about their inauthenticity can be drawn if we recall that Columbus's letters, incontestably authentic, contain just as many, if not more. The travelers observe the unknown world, of course, but they also project their own prejudices and fantasies onto it. It is also true that *Mundus novus* contains internal contradictions; but they may be attributed to the translator from the Latin, or even to copyists (since the original text in Italian was lost and no manuscript exists).

But a comparison of the two letters leads to more troubling conclusions. *Quatuor navigationes* contains the narrative of the four journeys, *Mundus novus,* of the third. We can therefore compare two versions of the same voyage. And the differences are significant. According to the *Quatuor navigationes,* it is during the third voyage that Amerigo's companion is beaten and eaten before the horrified eyes of the other Christians. Yet *Mundus novus*—written earlier and therefore sooner after the return—

speaks extensively of cannibalism but does not relate any episode of this kind, which is hard to explain. More generally, this third voyage is, according to *Quatuor navigationes*, particularly poor in contacts with the local people (other than for supply purposes), whereas in *Mundus novus* the relations with the natives are described as "fraternal" and Amerigo affirms that he remained twenty-seven days among the "cannibals." If we follow *Quatuor navigationes*, it is hard to see at what moment this stay could have occurred. The rich portrait of the Indians found in *Mundus novus* seems impossible to establish on the basis of the third voyage as it is related in the *Quatuor navigationes*, which nevertheless situates a long "ethnographic" sojourn during the first voyage, the narration of which contains a description of the Indians that parallels the one found in *Mundus novus*.

Often one gets the impression that certain details easily "travel" from one voyage to the other. For example, according to *Quatuor navigationes*, it is during the first voyage that the Indians express their surprise to Amerigo: "They were surprised to hear us say that we did not eat our enemies"; but, according to *Mundus novus*, it is during the third voyage that the Indians speak of this: "They are surprised that we do not eat our enemies." According to *Mundus novus*, the consciousness that the discovered land is a continent dates from the third voyage; according to *Quatuor navigationes*, it dates from the first, and this first voyage is the only one that ends with the taking of slaves: 250 to be exact, of whom 222 had survived by the time of the arrival in Spain. The letter from 1500, however, which describes the second voyage, reports that *this* voyage ended with the taking of slaves, 232 upon departure, 200 upon arrival. The numbers are surprisingly close.

The comparison of *Mundus novus* (1503) and the manuscript letter (1502), both of which recount the third voyage, is equally troubling. First of all, both are addressed to Lorenzo de Medici; because their contents, as well as the dates of their composition, are similar, it is difficult to determine the necessity of the second letter (especially since Lorenzo had died in the meantime—but Amerigo could have been unaware of this fact). In many ways, *Mundus novus* resembles not an additional letter to the same person, but a new version of the same *work,* which corrects and organizes its predecessor. In 1502, Amerigo relates that an Indian whom he knew had eaten "more than two hundred" human beings; in 1503, they had become "more than three hundred." In 1502, an Indian man who is 132 years old is described as *old;* in 1503, 150 has become the average age of the Indians. In 1502, the human meat hanging from the beams was smoked; in 1503, it was salted.

Nor does a literary analysis of *Mundus novus* argue in favor of its veracity. The description of nature is purely conventional: "There exist over
there many wild animals, especially lions and bears, and countless serpents,
and other horrible and ugly beasts. The land is very fertile and pleasant,
with many hills and mountains, infinite valleys and powerful rivers; it is
watered by refreshing springs and is full of almost impenetrable vast and
dense forests, teeming with all kinds of ferocious animals." This kind of description may be calmly written while sitting in one's study in Florence
(this was not true of Columbus's descriptions of nature). The cosmographic
part is paltry and its function seems to be that of a marker: look how
knowledgeable I am (and at the same time, I presume that you, the reader,
are also knowledgeable). The description of men adds nothing essential to
the elements contained in Columbus's letter ten years earlier, even if it is
better written. The narration of the voyage itself contains not one single
memorable episode (except, perhaps, the confusion of the pilots, simple
practitioners). There is not one proper name. Nothing in *Mundus novus* indicates that we are dealing with the truth; everything, including the harmonious form of the whole, argues in favor of a fiction (of which Amerigo
is or is not the author).

The same cannot be said of *Quatuor navigationes,* where the abundance
of specific anecdotes can be interpreted as an indication of real experience;
but it is a narrative that obviously has been reworked. How many actual
voyages were there, two or four? Some have thought that Vespucci (or his
"editors") doubled each of the voyages in order to claim he had made four,
that is, as many as Columbus. At what point did Vespucci become aware of
the newness of his discovery? Aren't the episodes also arranged in this order
so that they might have the best effect on the reader, rather than because
the events actually took place in this order? Only one thing is certain: this
narrative cannot be considered to be pure truth, it cannot be treated as a
document wholly deserving of trust. It is a work made of the true and the
false combined.

What conclusions are we to draw from this statement? Is Amerigo's
glory undeserved? Must we conclude that the true cannot be distinguished
from the false, but that one moves imperceptibly from the one to the other?
Must we rejoice at this triumph of fiction, or deplore it? We know that
posterity varied greatly in its judgment. The superlative opinion of the
Saint-Dié scholars was widely shared in the sixteenth century. But, as early
as the middle of that century, Las Casas, in his *Historia de las Indias* (which
was not published until 1875), began the anti-Vespucci campaign, while at

the same time singing Columbus's praises; he was followed, in the early seventeenth century, by the influential Herrera; then, in the nineteenth century, by scholars such as Navarrete and Markham, or Washington Irving. The harshest phrases no doubt belong to Emerson: "Strange, that the New World..., that broad America must wear the name of a thief. Amerigo Vespucci, the pickle-dealer at Seville... whose highest naval rank was botswain's mate in an expedition that never sailed, managed in this lying world to supplant Columbus, and baptize half the earth with his own dishonest name" (*English Traits*, 148). In the mid-nineteenth century, however, the opposite opinion began to be expressed: it moved from Alexander von Humboldt and Varnhagen to Levillier and O'Gorman, through Harris and Vignaud, all of whom recognized the important role Vespucci had played in the discovery and identification of America.

My judgment on the matter runs the risk of disappointing both sides (if I am allowed to imagine them living at the same time, and listening to my arguments). Amerigo's voyages seem questionable to me, and their descriptions hardly trustworthy. They surely contain some true elements, but we will never know which ones. Amerigo is, for me, on the side of fiction, not on that of truth; and the historian must prefer actual witnesses to imaginary ones. Yet in other respects, I find Amerigo's writings incontestably superior to those of his contemporaries; the insufficient truth-adequation is counterbalanced by a greater truth-disclosure: not, I must add, of American reality, but of European imagination. His merit is great, but it does not lie where one thought. Far from regretting, as Emerson did, that Amerigo was nothing more than a confabulator, I rejoice in the fact that—and it may never happen again—half of the earth bears the name of a writer, rather than that of a conqueror, adventurer, or slave merchant. Certainly, the truth of poets is not the same as that of historians. This, however, does not mean that poets are liars and that they must be banished from the city; on the contrary.

We are not certain that Amerigo was the author of his letters, nor that he wrote them as we read them today; but there is no doubt that he is the character-narrator, and that it is as such that he must be celebrated. He does not make me think so much of Columbus or Cabot as of Sinbad or Ulysses, who, like him, were the protagonists of marvelous adventures (better than his, perhaps); and it is undoubtedly not a coincidence that his first name (Amerigo) rather than his last (Vespucci) was retained to name a continent, like Sinbad and not like Columbus: a first name is sufficient for a character. In this, he differs from Peter Martyr, a mere author. Also like

Sinbad, he promises himself during each journey not to begin his sufferings anew; but hardly has he returned than he again sets out toward new discoveries: "I rested from the great fatigue that I had felt on my two voyages, nevertheless deciding to return to the land of pearls." Like Ulysses, who invariably preceded the tales of his adventures with a phrase such as "I am going to answer you without pretense," Amerigo declares at the beginning of his narrative to Soderini that what drives him to take up the pen is "the confidence that I have in the truth of what I write." Far from wanting to rename America, I would propose to call Southern Asia, Sinbadia, and the Mediterranean, Odyssea. If I have one regret, it is that Amerigo was not content to be a half-imaginary character, but that he also wanted to be an entirely real author. When it leaves the book, a fabulation becomes a lie.

# 9 / Postscript: The Truth of Interpretations

The distinction between truth-adequation and truth-disclosure can help, I believe, to characterize the interpretative process itself. In order to do so a preliminary description, however schematic and incomplete, must be given.

I am calling "interpretative" any text that aspires to designate the meaning of another text. Every work of language brings a meaning to life; but apparently some of them do so in a way that does not entirely satisfy their reader, who in turn undertakes to reformulate this same meaning. This dissatisfaction is not a disapproval; on the contrary, one would not waste one's time on a writer whom one disliked. Rather, one believes that, for certain reasons, the text does not clearly state everything the interpreter sees in it.

But what are these reasons? In order to answer this question, we must first divide texts into two major classes: assertive and nonassertive. This distinction is not identical to that between history and fiction, a distinction that concerns the relationship between the text and the world (and which led me to speak of truth-disclosure and truth-adequation), for it has to do with another relationship: that between the text and its enunciator. Assertive texts are those we attribute directly to their author; in other words, they are texts in which there is no difference between the author as a historical person and the author as the subject narrating (*énonçant*) the text in question. These are, in general, scientific, political, didactic, or philosophical texts.

119

Nonassertive texts, on the other hand, are those that insert an imaginary subject, a character, between the empirical author and his discourse; this discourse is pronounced (*énoncé*) by the character, and we do not automatically know to what extent the true author shares the attitudes of this intermediary subject of the enunciation. This is the case of literature, where the author does not express himself directly, but constructs a lyrical "I" or a "narrator"; and perhaps we have here a minimal definition of literature itself: a discourse that the author does not present as his own enunciation. Of course, an assertive text may use literary techniques: for example, if a philosophical work is presented as a dialogue, it also shares some characteristics with literature.

The distinction between these two major classes—which poses several problems but which, for all that, is no less useful—will serve as our point of departure, since the members of one class or the other are not interpreted for the same reasons. Literary texts must be interpreted specifically in order to know what their authors "mean"—since they never tell us directly. The search can also be abandoned by deciding that the author had no thought, and that he simply wanted to please his readers by presenting them with a beautiful object. But too much evidence—direct and indirect—argues against such a decision; and so for a long time people have been asking themselves questions about the thinking of writers (and not simply about their art), according to methods that are not of interest to me at this point.

Let us stay with assertive texts for the moment. The reasons for interpreting these texts are different, since from the outset one grants that the author takes responsibility for what the text says. But one decides, in this instance, that the ideas contained therein must be articulated in terms that are closer to the contemporary reader, either more succinctly or more elaborately. Or—and this is the most interesting variant—one posits that a text can never reveal the totality of its meaning, and that it is the task of interpretation to unveil the part that is kept hidden. A text is the end result of an action; there is a path that leads to it and is as significant, if not more so, as the text itself. The reason I utter a certain sentence is no less revealing than the sentence itself; but I will never be able to explain this reason exhaustively within the text itself. Thus an interpretation is necessary to remedy the situation; and through this interpretative enterprise, the interpreter reveals a meaning that is, in fact, contained in the text but that the author did not state overtly.

How does one determine the value of an interpretation? The distinction between truth-adequation and truth-disclosure again becomes useful

here: we demand, in effect, that each interpretation offer us both. This duality is essential, and it allows us to understand certain contradictory descriptions of the interpretative process that are in reality simply partial descriptions (my itinerary here is parallel to the one I followed in describing
knowledge of others).

Interpretation aspires, first of all, to truth-adequation; in other words,
it is possible to establish empirically, by means of a juxtaposition with the
interpreted texts, whether the interpretation is true or false. This aspect of
interpretation concerns historical as well as structural facts: historical knowledge will give me access to the strict sense of words and phrases; structural
observations will teach me how the textual elements are arranged in relation to one another, and what their purpose is. This is what is rejected by
an entire trend of modern exegesis. This trend could be called nihilist and
its mottoes include such phrases as "everything is interpretation," or even,
"there are no facts, simply interpretations," meaning thereby that one can
never speak, in this area, of truth-adequation and that interpretations depend solely on the identity of the commentators, or even on the social milieu to which they belong. Such a position is, however, untenable: if one
reads previous interpretations of a certain work, one in fact perceives that
some of them are simply false and do not deserve to survive, whereas others have established undeniable facts that can be ignored only at one's own
expense.

But, contrary to what other interpreters—this time positivist rather
than nihilist—believe, truth-adequation is not the only requirement that
must be set forth in relation to an interpretation. I cannot help but quote
here a passage from Lanson, a literary historian representative of the positivist trend who expresses this ambition well:

> One would need to have paid scant attention to the movement of
> literary studies in recent years not to have noticed that the field
> for dispute is getting narrower and that the realm of factual sci-
> ence, of uncontested knowledge is continually expanding, thus
> leaving less room for the games of dilettantes and the prejudices of
> fanatics, unless they are ignorant; it is therefore not unrealistic to
> foresee the day when, in agreement as to the definitions, content,
> and meaning of works, people will only argue about whether they
> are nice or nasty, that is, sentimental qualities. (*Méthodes de l'histoire
> littéraire*, 36)

Yet it is not true that the meaning of works—literary or assertive in this
instance—can be definitively established, and that only debate about their

moral value continues; in other words, it is not true that the entire interpretative effort aims at truth-adequation.

How can this impossibility of coming to a definitive consensus about
the meaning of works be explained? The author of the original text has
himself established a preliminary itinerary between the specific meanings
elicited by each of his sentences. The interpreter believes that another itinerary, order, or hierarchy will be more revealing and will help us grasp the
author's meaning more clearly. But these interpretative itineraries through
any work — even disregarding those that imply a factual error — are numerous, even if not as numerous as those of literary works, the interpretations of which are practically limitless (the interpretation of Shakespeare
will always be more subject to discussion than that of Hobbes). Or, to put
it somewhat differently, each new interpreter asks a different question of
the same text (since he himself does not belong to the same century or the
same milieu, and does not have the same preoccupations or the same psychological profile); and he necessarily arrives at a different answer — an answer that nonetheless is to be found in the text under scrutiny, and is not
projected onto it by the interpreter. If one only uses the point of view of
truth-adequation, it must be said that the interpretation possesses an inferior threshold constituted by the category of falseness (error, ignorance,
deception), but that there does exist, at the other end of the spectrum, a
superior, symmetrical threshold where the interpretations would accede to
the status of truth. In order to point out the difference between these two
aspects of interpretation, Mikhail Bakhtin introduced a terminological distinction: he suggested that from this new point of view "the criterion is
not the exactitude of knowledge, but the depth of penetration." This is
what I myself call truth-adequation and truth-disclosure.

The criteria for the evaluation of interpretations, from this latter viewpoint, cannot be the same ones as were used previously; nevertheless, one
is constantly making judgments — all interpretations are not, in fact, equal,
as certain theorists, disappointedly or triumphantly, would have it. A comparison with a painted portrait can shed some light here. Imagine that we
are already familiar with the model. If in the portrait his eyes are blue,
whereas in reality they are brown, we would say that truth-adequation is
lacking; if, on the other hand, the two portraits are equally "adequate," we
would deem one more "revealing" than the other (or deeper, or containing more truth-disclosure, etc.). The final criterion here is intersubjective
and no longer referential: the truest interpretation, in the second sense of
the word "true," is the one that garners the strongest adherence among its

readers; the same holds true here for interpretations as for works of fiction that also possess truth-disclosure.

But can precise empirical content be attributed to words such as "deeper" or "truer"? It seems that it is possible to translate this demand into slightly less metaphorical terms by saying that what we ask of an interpretation, once it has been recognized as adequate, is that it be both rich and coherent. By "rich" I mean the taking into account of as much of the material of the interpreted text as possible; an interpretation that retains only isolated sentences from the text will inevitably be qualified as "poor." By "coherent" I do not mean that the interpretation should demonstrate that all the parts and levels of the text aim at affirming the same idea; rather, it should show that any discordance, inconsistencies, even contradictions, can be explained and justified.

The requirement of "richness," that is, the optimal taking into account of the text being studied, causes no controversy. The same is not true of "coherence," on which there is no agreement. On the contrary, sometimes the right to incoherence is called for and is justified either as the victory of "life" or as the defeat of reason (or of consciousness) by the "unthought" (*l'impensé*). The first attitude may be illustrated by another passage from Lanson, in which he responded to a well-known conundrum in the history of French philosophy: the question of unity in Rousseau's thought. Rousseau seems to demand at one and the same time the extreme autonomy of the individual and his or her submission to society; where is coherence? Lanson writes: "Aren't these attitudes of a vast and passionate soul who, possessed alternately by the two sides of things, affirms them successively with the same vehemence and does not consent to sacrifice one reality to another, preferable to the systematic narrowness of the dialectician who sees only one principle?" ("L'unité de la pensée," 29). The requirement of coherence here has a negative connotation ("systematic narrowness"), whereas incoherence is praised ("vast and passionate soul").

The second justification figures among the postulates of what is called "deconstructive" criticism, according to which no great text is entirely coherent, contrary to what haughty reason may claim; the task of interpretation is therefore imagined as the deconstruction of these pretensions, the bringing to light of inconsistencies. In fact, the two justifications are not mutually exclusive.

The discovery of an inconsistency is, in fact, the starting point for a number of interpretations of assertive texts; unless the author himself has declared his intention of expressing himself in veiled fashion (either allegorically or by means of allusion, etc.), what better justification for his own work can the interpreter find than the discovery of an inconsistency, a difficulty in relation to the demands of coherence? Two reactions, however, may result from this, calling for an additional distinction between categories of texts (still assertive): those of great writers and those of mediocre writers (with all the difficulties one can imagine in establishing the exact boundary between the two). For the latter, the discovery of inconsistencies or contradictions suffices to condemn them to oblivion: it confirms their mediocrity. It is pointless to waste one's time with an author who contradicts himself on every page! But if one deems that the author in question is a true thinker, it is no longer appropriate to relegate him to oblivion; and, unless one makes incoherence an article of faith, one must attempt to overcome it (which does not mean one must deny it). The discovery of incoherence is a good point of departure for an interpretation, but a bad point of arrival.

This interpretative principle has been expressed many times; the first of which I am aware occurs in Lessing's *Hamburg Dramaturgy:*

> Aristotle is not often guilty of a palpable contradiction. Where I would seem to find one in such a man, I prefer rather to mistrust my own reason. I redouble my attention, I re-read the passage ten times, and do not think that he contradicts himself before I perceive from the entire connexion of his system how and why he has been betrayed into this contradiction. If I find nothing that could so betray him, that must, so to speak, make this contradiction inevitable, then I am convinced that it is only an apparent contradiction. Else it would certainly have occurred first to the author who had to think over his matter so often, and not to me, the unpractised reader who has taken him up for instruction. (no. 38, 109)

Again to use Rousseau, and a remark by one of his commentators, it is not likely that our interpretations will be read two hundred years after their publication, as we read Rousseau today; what an ego one must have to claim to have discovered, in so little time, inconsistencies in Rousseau's thought, while he himself assures us, at the end of a life spent in reflection, that there are none!

But, one could ask, why did this great author leave behind what could, even if only superficially, be perceived as incoherence? There are several answers to this question; I shall recall two of them here, offered by two remarkable modern interpreters. The first, Leo Strauss, observed that as a rule up until the end of the eighteenth century, and then more sporadically until the present day, the climate in which authors thought, wrote, and published has been anything but liberal. If they wanted to express themselves freely but their ideas contradicted the dominant religious doctrine, the ideology of a party, or simply the general consensus, they had to practice a particular art of writing: one that forces the reader to read between the lines and that therefore presents an inoffensive, exoteric meaning to the general reader and to the censors, and an underground, esoteric meaning to attentive and well-disposed readers. In this case, the surface incoherence — of which the author is entirely conscious — can serve as a clue that elicits this necessary interpretation.

Strauss's suggestion deserves attention: the situations he describes are not exceptional. But there are other justifications for these seeming contradictions. Victor Goldschmidt, for example, treated Rousseau's "incoherence" in an entirely different manner from the way Lanson did: "It can be explained, in reality, by the very condition of modern man, which is contradictory, much more than by the analyses of Rousseau, whose main object — and worth — is to reveal this contradiction, before attempting to remedy it" (*Ecrits,* 2:161). Rousseau was not content to point out the contradiction from which, according to him, modern man suffered. He makes us experience it by placing us in contact with two (or even three) voices that reveal, each in a way coherent with itself, a partial truth. Rousseau's project, different in this from his voices, is precisely to bring these conflicting positions together, and to endeavor to overcome their apparent incompatibility.

For the moment, I will limit myself to these brief points about the truth-disclosure of an interpretation. What is important is to see that the two kinds of "truth" are not identical even if they are equally indispensable.

# 10 / Manipulation and Eloquence

"To manipulate someone" (this is the only use of the verb that I shall retain here) is a complex activity, and it is worthwhile to identify three of its related roles and three of its related actions. First there is *the manipulated person,* who engages in some action but—this is essential—thinks he or she is acting on his or her own authority. Then there is *the manipulator:* he or she acts on the manipulated person and is in fact responsible for that person's actions but, conversely, does not make it obvious; neither party, in other words, would accept the term *manipulation.* Finally, there is *the judge,* or *spectator,* who stands at a distance from the two, making a negative judgment about all the different operations and allowing them to be identified. An expression that is halfway between this meaning of "to manipulate" and its physical meaning (to manipulate substances in a laboratory) would be "to manipulate puppets": it is a material act, but the puppets do not have a will of their own; our verb "to manipulate" is, in fact, very close to the expression "to pull strings." "He let himself be manipulated like a child," that is, without offering any resistance and without being aware of it. One can also manipulate a community, a people, or levels of collectivities: to manipulate public opinion is to move it in the direction one wants it to go by using reprehensible means, and without its knowledge.

126

What is problematic in this delimitation of the concept is the judge's condemnation: to what may it be attributed? For action carried out on someone else in order to influence that person's behavior is not condemned in and of itself; if this were so, the majority of all communication would also be condemned. How does manipulation differ from instruction? From persuasion? From incitement? Although the alienation of the will of the other, its bending in the direction we want it to go, is still the stated goal of these actions, the words that designate them are not pejorative. One could think that, for those who are manipulated, it is ignorance of their state, and for those who manipulate, the desire to hide or to disguise their actions, that make all the difference; lucidity and sincerity would therefore be valorized, and their opposites, condemned. But we know just how unreliable our judgment in these matters is. Is total lucidity about my own actions, whether I am manipulated or manipulator, in fact possible? One could say that the wife of a man condemned to death who positions her weeping children in front of the television cameras is manipulating public opinion. But has she, for all that, ceased to be sincere? Nor is the public necessarily taken in, but it goes along with her, viewing the situation in a new light.

If, however, we abandon the criterion of an equivalence between acts and the consciousness we have of them, what reason do we have to condemn "manipulation"? Or should we say: I call "manipulation" acting on another person in view of ends I deem contemptible; and I speak of incitement, persuasion, and the like, in those instances where I agree with the goals? Would the cause of evil be, therefore, in the ends rather than in the means? Yet what is considered manipulation by one person could be considered, by another, a noble action that enlightens the mind.

# I

The debate surrounding the morality of acting on another is not new, and a detour through its history may be beneficial. One tradition seems particularly relevant: that of rhetoric. In the Western world, rhetoric is a discipline that developed around the fifth century B.C. in Sicily and in Greece, the goal of which was the learning of eloquence, that is, the art of speaking in such a way that one succeeds in persuading one's interlocutor. It becomes immediately clear that the field of rhetoric does not coincide exactly with that of manipulation: first of all, only action on another by means of language is taken into consideration; second, any moral condemnation and thus any restriction as to the end being sought is lacking from the outset. In this sense "manipulation" is merely one possible variant of rhetoric. Nonetheless, their relatedness is quite obvious and is reinforced by the idea of "technique" that can be found in both instances: the manipulator possesses a certain "art" that could, if necessary, be codified, just as the orator was supposed to learn his art in the treatises (or schools) of rhetoric. And, early on, rhetoric also provoked a moral debate: was it permissible to learn a technique that could be used to serve both just and unjust causes?

In order to advance our reflection on manipulation, I am going to recall some of the principal attitudes toward rhetoric, isolating certain exemplary positions. The authors whose names will be used to represent these positions are in reality more complex, more eclectic, more contradictory, and more nuanced.

## The Immoral Attitude: The Sophists

Tradition has it that rhetoric was born in Sicily, with Corax and Tisias, and was then rapidly transplanted to Greece, where the most famous masters were Protagoras and Gorgias. This is the Sophist school, which we know only through the writings of its adversaries, Plato in particular. In the Platonic dialogue that bears his name, Gorgias defines rhetoric in these terms: "The orator has the power to speak to everyone indiscriminately and on any subject, in such a way as to be, in the presence of the crowds, more persuasive than anyone" (*Gorgias,* 457a). Rhetoric was born of the need to win over the hearer, in particular in two kinds of public circumstances: in political meetings at the forum and in the courts, before the judges. The inventors of rhetoric supposedly realized that in these situations one did not have the time to patiently seek the truth; and, in addition, that those who had to decide were not necessarily capable of carrying out such a pursuit. It was therefore deemed possible to persuade them, without bothering with the truth, as long as one possessed the appropriate technique of persuasion. Thanks to this art, the Sophist orator could make the same thing appear just or unjust, good or bad, single or multiple, mobile or immobile, to his interlocutors. And he could prove himself superior to any specialist in any particular area.

The Sophist was therefore entirely uninterested in the relation between

discourses and their subject, and was concerned only with the relation between these discourses and their addressees. According to the Sophist,

> The intending orator is under no necessity of understanding what
> is truly just, but only what is likely to be thought just by the body
> of men who are to give judgment; nor need he know what is truly
> good or noble, but what will be thought so; since it is on the lat-
> ter, not the former, that persuasion depends. (*Phaedrus,* 260a, 119)

*Verisimilitude*—that is, the received opinions and commonplaces of a society—was in effect the basic category of this rhetoric; in return, the search
for truth played no role in it, any more than did the reference to absolute
justice.

The individual who possessed rhetorical technique found in it immediate gain: he won his trials, whatever injustices he may have committed;
having become a lawyer, he also won the trials of others and thus became
rich. He succeeded at everything in life, for what was necessary in order to
do so was "not to really be a man of good, but to have the reputation of
one" (*The Republic,* book II, 362a). And if he was engaged in political life,
he had access to power, which in turn would open every door. This attitude, too, was explicitly adopted by the Sophists (one thus moves imperceptibly in Plato's dialogues from rhetoric to ethics and politics), who
claimed that there was nothing blameworthy about it. According to them,
the common idea of justice, based on moral universals, was an invention of
the weak who, being more numerous, had managed to impose themselves;
it was a last resort that everyone had accepted for fear of being subjected to
the outrage of those stronger than themselves. But if one could have had
the benefit of impunity, everyone would have been tempted by the possibility of doing everything, at the whim of one's desires and pleasures, since
"self-seeking [is] the way which every creature naturally follows as a good"
(ibid., 359c, 157). Thus, it is enough to be strong in order to base one's behavior on another principle, one that consists in taking advantage of one's
superiority: this is another conception of justice, according to which might
makes right: "The same thing is just in all states, the advantage of the established government. This I suppose has the power, so if you reason correctly, it follows that everywhere the same thing is just, the advantage of the
stronger" (ibid., book I, 339a, 137). The praise of rhetoric here is bound
up with the defense of immorality, or rather of strength as the sole source
of ethics.

## *The Moral Attitude: Socrates*

Socrates rejected this conception of ethics in its entirety, as well as the role reserved for rhetoric. His attack against the latter was based on a concept of language according to which words were pure reflections of things and as such did not possess laws that one needed to know. Thus, he claimed not to understand the difference between rhetoric and any other "art," architecture, medicine, or arithmetic: according to him, words could not be considered in the same way as objects or actions, but only as labels for other objects and actions that, each in their turn, belong to their respective "arts." Sophistic rhetoric was wrong to neglect this relation between words and things, that is, the essential. "The rhetorician need not know the truth about things; he has only to discover some way of persuading the ignorant that he has more knowledge than those who know" (*Gorgias,* 459b–c, 517). Because it values verisimilitude (the opinion of the vulgar) over the true and the just, rhetoric deserves only blame.

Rhetoric therefore privileged the intersubjective communication dimension of language, and neglected its referential and cognitive dimension. Socrates admitted that the Sophist orator had, by nature, "the habit of a bold and ready wit, which knows how to manage mankind" (*Gorgias,* 463a, 521), but it was the totality of these activities that had little value in his eyes: for him, there was no other persuasion than that which comes from truth (arithmetic has no need of rhetoric), and, in any case, he preferred to see truth triumph, even at his own expense, rather than to benefit from a factitious persuasion. The interlocutor had no particular status in his universe: he was either on the side of the knowing subject, or on that of the object to be known. Because it was ignorant of the relation of knowledge that links words and things, rhetoric was not a science, nor an "art," but mere know-how: it accommodated appearances without worrying about realities and was similar in this respect to other practices of illusion that, instead of making things more beautiful, simply make them appear so. Sophistic eloquence is to the discourse of justice what the "art" of adornment is to gymnastics; and Socrates has little esteem for makeup, which is "knavish, false, ignoble, illiberal, working deceitfully by the help of lines, and colours, and enamels, and garments and making men affect a spurious beauty" (*Gorgias,* 465b, 523).

What makes these "flatteries" morally reprehensible is that they are based on the feeling of the agreeable, which is individual and subjective, rather than on the good and the true, which belong to the universal and

the absolute; to be guided by the former rather than by the latter is to take
the first steps toward the "ethics" of strength (*la force*). Socrates places these
absolute values above that which is most precious to the individual, life itself: "For no man who is not an utter fool and coward is afraid of death itself, but he is afraid of doing wrong" (*Gorgias,* 522e, 583). Socrates' position is perfectly coherent, but that of the Sophists is no less so; and his most
important interlocutor in the *Gorgias,* Callicles, never accepts his reasoning.
If Socrates seems to prevail over him, it is because, on the one hand, Callicles admits his exhaustion from the long interview (it is therefore strength
that prevails), and, on the other, because Socrates has recourse to a myth of
the last judgment in which, after their death, the just are rewarded and the
unjust, punished: it is a deus ex machina.

Socrates also envisions — although without great enthusiasm — the possibility of a moral rhetoric. It is obviously one that is based on ideas of just
and unjust, true and false, and which contributes to the acquisition of these
distinctions by others. Addressing his fellow citizens, the orator will aim
"to implant justice in the souls of his citizens, and take away injustice, to
implant temperance and take away intemperance, to implant every virtue
and take away every vice" (*Gorgias,* 504e, 566). But of what can this rhetoric
consist, since language becomes exhausted in its role as reflection of the
world? When Socrates has to formulate concrete precepts in view of the
acquisition of this particular eloquence (in the *Phaedrus*), he is satisfied with
recommending the practice of the sciences (to know the nature of things),
a psychology of receivers of discourse (since it is on the soul of the interlocutor that one acts, one must know what a soul is, how many kinds of
souls there are, and what a soul's various parts are), and finally logic, synthe-
sis and analysis, generalization and subdivision. In all that, language itself
remains perfectly transparent and transitive.

But even this concession quickly appears to Socrates as being one too
many: "There is, as the Spartans put it, no 'soothfast' art of speech, nor as-
suredly will there ever be one, without a grasp of truth" (*Phaedrus,* 260e,
120). In order to truly speak well, one must become wise; but if one becomes wise, one no longer worries about pleasing one's interlocutors: "And
this skill he will not attain without a great deal of trouble, which a good
man ought to undergo, not for the sake of speaking and acting before men,
but in order that he may be able to say what is acceptable to God and always to act acceptably to Him as far as in him lies" (*Phaedrus,* 273e, 277).
Consequently Socrates claims for himself the title of "friend of wisdom,"
of philosopher, and will take no further interest in "writer" or "maker of

discourse," firmly stating: "For of course I don't lay claim to any oratorical skill myself" (*Phaedrus,* 262d, 126). Future generations will not, however, invariably be convinced of this.

## The Amoral Attitude: Aristotle

After all of Plato's arguments to prove that rhetoric cannot be an "art," one of his disciples—who calmly set about writing an art of rhetoric in three volumes!—offers him no small challenge. Although Aristotle never polemicizes against Socrates' theses in his text, the very existence of his work and the act that led to it are themselves extremely polemical. The meaning that each of them gives to *techne* is not exactly the same, but they remain quite close: for Aristotle, this "technique" does not come under theory, inasmuch as it does not find its goal in itself, but in an objective outside itself—the persuasion of interlocutors. Nor, however, is it pure practice, for it cannot be reduced to particular instances, has its own rules, and can be learned; it is a kind of "applied science." "Since no art examines the particular—for example the art of medicine does not specify what is healthful for Socrates or Callias but for persons of a certain sort (this is artistic, while particulars are limitless and not knowable)—neither does rhetoric theorize about each opinion—what may seem so to Socrates or Hippias—but about what seems true to people of a certain sort" (*On Rhetoric,* book I, 1356b, 41). The goal, which is to persuade, must never be forgotten; but the perspective having been so defined, the task of the rhetorician becomes that of drawing up an inventory of the forms of language, of reasoning, and of expression; this is what fills almost the whole of Aristotle's work. Language has come out of its transparency.

But what has happened to ethics? Aristotle does not embrace Callicles' creed at all; he is, as much as Socrates, convinced of justice's independence in relation to strength. Rhetoric must be used to serve the true and the just, and one must not persuade of anything that is immoral (*On Rhetoric,* book I, 1355a). But "be used to serve" does not mean "be": Aristotle claims that technique, *as* technique, is morally neutral. In truth, Gorgias had already held this position in Plato's dialogue of the same name, a position of compromise between the extreme but more coherent theses of Socrates and Callicles; but Aristotle gives it new life, and his move is fraught with incalculable consequences. He states: "And if it is argued [and this argument no doubt comes from Socrates] that great harm can be done by unjustly using such power of words, this objection applies to all good things except virtue, and most of all to the most useful things, like strength, health, wealth, and military strategy; for by using these justly one would do the greatest good and unjustly the greatest harm" (*On Rhetoric,* book I, 1355b, 35). A material tool, a hammer, is in itself neither moral nor immoral; it is amoral. This is even truer for that instrument of the mind that is the word, inasmuch as it is mankind's specific characteristic: to refuse to use it well would be even more incomprehensible. In addition, the fairness of a thesis as well as the honesty of the orator are excellent arguments for winning over interlocutors. Aristotle's position is, in fact, moral; but that of Aristotelian rhetoric is not.

Socrates compared rhetoric to the art of adornment in order to denigrate it. Aristotle also uses analogy, but he does so in order to compare rhetoric to dialectic: both of them are related to the art of reasoning and persuasion. The difference is in the interlocutors, who are not the same in both instances. The ideal addressee of dialectic is the philosopher, a professional thinker, in a sense. Yet Aristotle knows that the majority of people are not philosophers, especially those who have decision-making power in the assemblies and law courts (this is still a Sophistic argument). They are "listeners [who] are not able to see many things all together or to reason from a distant starting point." Those who must make decisions are, hypothetically, simple men (*On Rhetoric,* book I, 1357a).

Faced with this situation, and being realistic, one would arrive at the conclusion that it is neither useful nor possible to practice dialectic, and that it is preferable to rely on rhetoric, whose ideas will be modeled on logical categories. Thus we see that, instead of the true (and Socrates would have been shocked), verisimilitude appears — that is, what happens most often, but not necessarily. *Enthymeme* — rhetorical syllogism based on the probable — replaces rigorous deduction; exhaustive induction is replaced by the *example:* the conclusion will not necessarily be true, but it will always be able to win over the hearer.

One could say that by positing the amorality of technique, Aristotle made rhetoric possible; everything that came before him is merely prehistory. And in the breach that he thus opened more than twenty centuries of works of rhetoric have passed — perhaps in part because of the dominant influence of Cicero, who immediately situates himself in a post-Aristotelian context. Like Aristotle, Cicero is against immorality; but also like Aristotle, he places rhetoric outside moral questions. The relations between rhetoric and philosophy are, in Cicero's work, symmetrical and inverse to what they were for Socrates: rather than rhetoric being in the service of philosophical teaching, it is philosophy—moral or not—that becomes a part of "general culture," declared, by Cicero, necessary for a good orator. This having been posited, his works of rhetoric (and in particular the voluminous central treatise *On Oratory and Orators*) consist of an inventory of linguistic and discursive forms; Cicero's answer to the question, who will be the best orator? is not, the one who is the most moral; it is, the one whose discourse is the most appropriate (to the subject, to the audience, and to the circumstances).

## *The Aesthetic Attitude: Quintilian*

Quintilian was not only, at the end of the first century A.D., the last of the great rhetoricians of the Greco-Latin era; he was also an assiduous reader of his predecessors. Thus we find a certain eclecticism in the solutions he proposes to the various problems of rhetoric: he makes use of Socrates' attacks, as well as of the defenses that the Sophists or Aristotle might have devised (and, of course, of Cicero). Nonetheless, in the key passages of his work, he takes yet another position, one that may not be of his own invention, but for which he is our main source.

He begins with a critique of the traditional definition of eloquence, that is, "the art of persuasion." Quintilian first counters it with the two classical arguments.

First, eloquence is not the only thing that persuades: money, power, beauty (the famous example of Phryne) may be even more convincing. And the objection must not be raised that in this instance it is only a question of persuasion by means of speech. "Others besides orators persuade by speaking or lead others to the conclusion desired, as for example harlots, flatterers and seducers" (Quintilian, book II, 15, 11).

Second, eloquence does not only persuade, and furthermore it is not limited to the law court or to the forum: "For my own part, and I have authority to support me, I hold that the material of rhetoric is composed of everything that may be placed before it as a subject for speech" (book II, 21, 4). In addition, all aspects of eloquence do not visibly contribute to persuasion—style, for example. A third argument, one that is more revealing of Quintilian's personal position, is then added to these two: Quintilian criticizes the defining of an "art" by means of the results that it must lead to rather than by its very being; in the event of failure, would we have called the action differently? The doctor is the one who attempts to cure the patient; in the event of death, he does not cease to be a doctor. "The speaker aims at victory, it is true, but if he speaks well, he has lived up to the ideals of his art, even if he is defeated. . . . So too the orator's purpose is fulfilled if he has spoken well. For the art of rhetoric, as I shall show later, is realised in action, not in the result obtained" (book II, 17, 23–25).

In effect, the new definition, of which Quintilian is quite proud, is "independent of the result"; it is the "science of speaking well" (book II, 15, 34). All reference to the interlocutor disappears; discourse is deemed eloquent in terms of its intrinsic qualities. Whereas all other discourses find their finality outside themselves, for rhetoric, the perfect discourse is one whose finality is in itself: it is autotelic. As Quintilian says, in a somewhat obscure manner, "We are not in a position to see clearly what is the end, the highest aim, the ultimate goal of rhetoric, that 'telos' in fact which every art must possess. For if rhetoric is the science of speaking well, its end and highest aim is to speak well" (book II, 15, 38). Elaborating on this line of reasoning, Quintilian is even led to say that the best speech is the one that is useless: "Perhaps the highest of all pleasures is that which we derive from private study, and the only circumstances under which the delights of literature are unalloyed are when it withdraws from action, that is to say from toil, and can enjoy the pleasure of self-contemplation" (book II, 18, 4). Thus a discourse will be appreciated not because it is useful but because it is "beautiful in itself" (book II, 16, 19). And this is the point of departure for aesthetic reflection.

It is on this definition that Quintilian bases his claim that there is an inherent morality to eloquence. He breaks here with Aristotelian (and Ciceronian) amoralism, and joins Platonic moralism, but he comes to a diametrically opposed conclusion: now rhetoric is necessarily moral. Why is this? Very often, Quintilian contents himself with a *petitio principii* ("no man can speak well who is not good himself") (book II, 15, 34). Other times, he attempts to accommodate the arguments of Gorgias, Socrates, or Aristotle. But there is also his own response: it is a definition of virtue, based on criteria that are strictly within an individual; rather than a hierarchy of faculties, virtue is their harmony, the mutual adequation of the parts of the being. "If self-consistency as to what should and should not be done is an element of virtue . . . the same quality will be revealed as regards what should be said and what should not be said" (book II, 20, 5). There is no possible virtue if what is inside and what is outside, intentions and words, are not in harmony. Inverting the Socratic precept—no rhetoric without virtue!—Quintilian seems to affirm that there is no virtue without rhetoric. Reciprocally, one would be unable to speak well without the help of reason; but maliciousness is a proof of the absence of reason; thus speaking well is a sign of virtue (book XII, 1, 4). We can see here that Quintilian values "speaking well" very highly; this is because, for him, it is a matter not of counting metaphors, but of appreciating the general act of language. Of all the means the orator has at his disposal and must bring into play, "the highest is that loftiness of soul which fear cannot dismay nor uproar terrify nor the authority of the audience fetter further than the respect which is their due.... Without constancy, confidence and courage, art, study and proficiency will be of no avail" (book XII, 5, 1–2). The quality of speech is measured in terms of the risks it takes. Quintilian, although he is a moralist, is poles apart from Socrates: whereas Socrates wanted to moralize aesthetics, Quintilian, on the other hand, aestheticizes morality.

It goes without saying that Quintilian refuses the Aristotelian restriction according to which rhetoric was good only for the common people: why would it displease the educated? However, he introduces another restriction, which limits rhetoric's wider application, not in terms of the interlocutors, but in terms of the aims one has:

> If all that was required of [the eloquent speaker] was merely to indicate the facts, he might rest content with literalness of language, without further elaboration. But since it is his duty to delight and move his audience and to play upon the various feelings, it becomes necessary for him to employ those additional aids which are granted to us by that same nature which gave us speech. (book XII, 10, 43)

The role of eloquence would thus be minimal when language is used descriptively, where the essential of linguistic action would be played out between words and things; it would be vital, however, in any situation where the interaction between subjects is more important than the description of facts.

## II

These diverse notions, developed during the debate on rhetoric, have all left a rich heritage. For example, the Sophistic attitude finds new life in the work of Machiavelli, who affirms the precedence of what *seems* over what *is*; one version of Socrates' moral rhetoric is put to use as early as antiquity by Saint Augustine, the creator of the first Christian rhetoric; and the criticism of rhetoric in the name of truth returns, intact, in Locke's *Essay concerning Human Understanding.* The idea according to which technique is amoral still prevails today, for the sciences as well as for the "techniques" (and not only for rhetoric). The aesthetic attitude becomes Kant's—who, in his *Critique of Pure Reason,* valorizes the art of speaking well over the art of persuading—as well as that of all German Romanticism, which uses it to establish the modern definition of literature.

But let us return to manipulation. The attacks to which it is subject all belong to a Platonic context: one condemns a technique that can be used indifferently to serve both good and evil. The history of rhetoric offers three possible defenses: making effectiveness a principle of ethics, affirming the ethical neutrality of technique, or positing that beauty is virtuous. We could use each of these defenses, or any combination of the three, to justify our refusal to accept the condemnation that the very word "manipulation" implies. For my part, and although I acknowledge the validity of some of their arguments, I realize that none of these positions coincides exactly with my own. This does not mean that examining them has been of no use to me: I had to formulate them in order to realize it, and it is based on these positions that I shall attempt to express my way of judging—a way, as I immediately see, that has the rhetorical inconvenience of not applying to everything uniformly; instead, it offers different approaches to different subjects. In fact, the ancient concepts of rhetoric—no matter how opposed to one another in their theses—share an essential common trait: for all of them, eloquence is either all good or all bad, entirely amoral or entirely beautiful. The impulse to totalize thought, to explain monistically, may be inherent to the human mind; but one can also attempt to resist it.

My starting point will be a distinction made by the ancients, which specifically maintains the heterogeneity of the subject. Quintilian said that eloquence plays a minimal role when it is a matter of reporting facts, but that it is essential when one wants to act on another. Yet these two situations are not really in opposition to one another, for a relation between language and the world can only be opposed to another relation between these same entities. Here, we do not learn what the relationship between words and things is once one has decided to act on another. Is this still description? Does the decision to act on another bear no relation to what one is speaking about? Were we to make Quintilian's remarks more explicit, we would arrive at something like the following: either describing the facts exhausts the essential of what one wants to say (and then it follows that the persuasion of the interlocutor is secondary and subordinate); or else the relation between my discourse and the world is not one of description, but is of another order (and thus it is interaction with the person to whom I am addressing myself that becomes essential). But what is this "other order"?

Let us take an example. As a historian, it is important for me that others know that the largest genocide in the history of humanity was the one that followed the discovery and conquest of America, since in two generations the population of that continent was reduced by seventy million. This is a fact. Obviously there are those who are set on denying it and claim this fact is nothing but propaganda. But I shall not attempt to persuade them by means of my eloquence. My entire effort will be concentrated on establishing irrefutable facts; my affirmation will be either true or false.

But now I offer another example — that of the history of rhetoric, which my readers, if they have been patient enough, must have assimilated a short while ago. The portrait I painted was not false; I can prove it by the use of additional proper names, dates, and citations. Here, too, the facts are present. But can I say that this history is not only not false, but, in addition, true? Among hundreds of competing ideas, I have retained only four. Why? Of all the possible conceptual divisions, I chose one: does it mean anything to say it is *true*? Yes, but only if, once again, we use the distinction between truth-adequation and truth-disclosure, a distinction that lies beyond the accuracy of reported facts. I can only aspire to truth disclosure in a historical interpretation.

Here I must add a word about the very form the explanation of my interpretation will take. It is more or less irrelevant if my calculation of the number of victims of the genocide is presented in one way or another; I can also ask that a collection of statistics be organized in a pleasing manner, but this will have nothing to do with its merit. Truth-adequation is indifferent to its form. The same, however, is not true of truth-disclosure, which aims for intersubjective consensus, in other words, for persuasion. From this new point of view, interpretation is indissociable from its own literary form. Here, I recall the analogy with the portrait: to say that it is true (in this sense of the word) is to affirm at the same time that it is beautiful. To be convinced of this, one need only remember of what interpretation consists. To interpret an event (a work, an idea) is to (re)construct it. In other words, one selects some of its elements that one deems of particular importance, and arranges them in a temporal and logical hierarchy, providing the missing links. The choice and order are the work of the interpreter, even if he seeks in them the confirmation of what is easily observable. As H.-I. Marrou rightly claimed, the polysemy of the words *histoire* (history/story) or

*Geschichte* (also history/story) is no accident: a series of facts and its expression in words are one and the same thing.

In fact, it is not only a matter of (hi)story, and this is why a general term such as "construction" is preferable to "narrative" or "plot," words that imply the presence of a temporal dimension in the facts observed. Not only the historian, but also the ethnographer or the literary critic, or the author of descriptions of psychological cases, are led to interpret, thus to construct. The shaping of their discourse is based not on an arbitrarily chosen "expression," but on the very conception of their work.

From this standpoint, the interpreter's activity is not unlike that of the writer, which also results in constructions. A novelist or an interpreter observes different material, but they are both subject to the demands of truth-disclosure: just as the painter produces a portrait that is unfalsifiable and yet true, the novelist reveals the truth to us, even if only of an infinitesimal piece of the world. If he didn't, he wouldn't deserve to be read. This is why, as has often been said, Shakespeare and Dostoevsky teach us more about human beings and the world than a thousand authors of scientific works (and, we must add, than a thousand other writers of plays and novels). Authors of fiction and authors of interpretations are related through the very identity of this construction work, whereas their verbal procedures may differ completely.

This is hardly an original statement, but usually all its implications are not taken into consideration. We know that, at least since Kant, it is up to the scholar to construct the totalities that constitute his object; and at the time of German Romanticism one could clearly see the relation between the activities of the poet and those of the historian. Apparently it was Schiller who said, "Why shouldn't the historian behave like a poet? After having collected within himself the material content, he must reproduce it outside of himself, in recreating it once again" (*Goethes Briefwechsel,* 254). And Novalis, pushing the description of their similarity even further, wrote in *Heinrich von Ofterdingen* that the historian must also and necessarily be a poet, since only poets can get along in an art that consists of relating facts cleverly. Von Humboldt would base his definition of the "task of the historian" on this, and the image would remain in Germanic epistemological tradition until the time of Raymond Aron, who had this laconic remark to make: "History narration is a true novel" (*Introduction à la philosophie de l'histoire,* 509). Yet if this is so, the presentation and expression selected by the historian, the critic, or the ethnographer will not be external to his work of interpretation; in fact, they are not even distinct from it: the form they give to the reconstructed totality is also its meaning. "Eloquence" in this kind of work is not a superfluous ornament, but the mark of a greater "truth-disclosure."

In the end, then, I do not find the word "manipulation" to be of great usefulness, but the reasons for this affirmation vary according to the domains in which the word is applied. The appellation is not strong enough in the area of the establishment of facts: it almost ennobles a fraudulent action, in which the only appropriate reaction would be to denounce the trickery, to correct the error, and to supply the missing information. In the areas of interpretation and human interaction, however, the a priori negative judgment seems too strong, and the boundary between manipulated interactions and others impossible to establish.

Yet someone who thinks this distinction is crucial might object that Socrates refused to manipulate his judges by bringing before them his weeping children during his trial. Is this as true as all that? Socrates' goal was not to save his life but to defend the idea of justice. If he had brought his children, he would have harmed his cause. By not bringing them, and, in addition, by drawing everyone's attention to this refusal, he acted in the most effective way to reach his objective; the proof is that some twenty-five hundred years later, we still use him as an example of a man who preferred his ideals to his life. It remains true, however, that, even previously, he was not lacking in eloquence; otherwise we would no longer speak of him today. Thus I am abandoning here manipulation, and retaining the virtue of eloquence.

# 11 / Toleration and the Intolerable

In order to better apprehend the problems of toleration, I have chosen to question some pages from the history of ideas in Western Europe between the sixteenth and the nineteenth centuries in which the stakes of current controversies are already clearly perceptible.

## I

The idea and the practice of toleration enter into relation with the two great principles of modern democratic states, principles that are designated by the two recurring key words: equality and freedom. Let's begin with equality: obviously, I can only be tolerant toward other human beings if I posit from the outset our common participation in the same human essence, implying that others are just as worthy of respect as I am. This is, for example, the basis of the toleration I could practice toward foreigners and their customs. Unlike a traditionalist view of humanity—which holds that *we* are the only human beings or, in any case, the best embodiment of humanity, and that the farther others live from our borders, the less human they are—those who believe in the universality of the human race are willing to tolerate the differences they observe in people from other countries.

141

This faith in the universality of humanity and in the essential equality of individuals is the basis of classic *humanism*.

The humanist idea was not born in the sixteenth century; it can already be found in early Christian thought and even in antiquity. But it was in the sixteenth century that it received fresh impetus. One of the factors of this impetus was the discovery of new worlds and, consequently, the taking into account of a much greater human diversity than that which had been previously known. Obviously, there is nothing mechanical or linear in the move from empirical facts (the geographical discoveries) to the new doctrine (humanism), since the most prevalent attitude toward the newly discovered countries was one of distrust and misunderstanding, followed by massacre. It is, however, precisely in response to such immediate reactions that the constitutive ideas of humanism would be forged. The most exemplary case is that of the Spanish Dominican Bartolomé de Las Casas, defender of the Indians. Moved by their fate, he relinquished his evangelizing activities to devote himself to the safekeeping of what he considered to be the natural rights of all human beings: In a letter to Prince Philip, he insisted that natural laws and rules and the rights of man are common to all nations, Christian and non-Christian, regardless of their religion, law, state, color and condition.

Las Casas's fate was exceptional; but his ideas were not unrelated to those of his contemporaries, whether religious or secular humanists. Even popes and emperors often professed similar creeds, although their behavior was not always in accord with their words. A few decades later, the humanist platform of universality and toleration would find an eloquent advocate in Montaigne, who also was not indifferent to the suffering of the Indians (nor to the suffering provoked by the religious wars in Europe) and who himself traveled, although on a smaller scale. "I believe all men to be my compatriots, I embrace a Polishman as I would a Frenchman, transferring this national liaison to the universal and the common," he wrote in his essay "Of Vanity." The implications of this position for the question of toleration are obvious: "The diversity of customs from one nation to another only moves me by the pleasure I derive from their variety. Each custom has its reason"; "It seems to me that I have never encountered customs that are not equal to our own." The vast field of customs for Montaigne is linked to the idea of toleration, which is itself based on the principle of universal equality.

The affirmation of humanist principles would reach its culmination in Enlightenment philosophy, where it would move into the policies of the American state and of the French Revolution; these, in turn, would have repercussions on all modern democratic states, since humanism was adopted by these democracies as their philosophical base. Already in the period that interests us, however, some particular problems emerge regarding both humanist theory itself, and its practical application in the form of toleration.

One relatively simple problem concerns the continually potential gap between theoretical declarations and actual behavior. In order to illustrate this, I have selected my examples from the very texts that elaborate and defend the creed of universal equality. Here is how La Bruyère, in his *Caractères,* presents humanist principles: "The predisposition of a country, joined to national pride, makes us forget that reason exists under all skies, and that one thinks correctly everywhere where there are men: we would not like to be treated like barbarians by those whom we call barbarians; and if there is, in us, a measure of barbarity, it consists of our being horrified at seeing other peoples reason in the way we do" ("Des jugements," 22). La Bruyère is one of the first to give this paradoxical turn to the egalitarian creed: barbarity consists of treating others as if they were barbarians. We must, however, ask ourselves the following: are the two expressions he uses in order to affirm universal equality — "reason exists under all skies," and "others reason in the way we do" — in fact, synonymous? The first is entirely impersonal and presupposes no "center" from where one judges the presence or absence of reason. The second, in contrast, introduces a point of view that is that of a "we": it presupposes, without saying so, that "we" have reason at our disposal: it problematizes only the reason of others, not our own. But if reason really exists "under all skies," why is it necessary to add that others are capable of reasoning as we do?

La Bruyère's statement can be pulled in two different directions: toward universality or toward ethnocentrism. If one reads the statement that follows, the choice is obvious: it gives us the exact measure of La Bruyère's toleration: "With a language so pure, with clothes so refined, with customs so cultivated, with such beautiful laws and white faces, we are barbarians to some" (ibid., 23). He is willing to recognize that the judgment of barbarity is often ill founded, since it is the excessive formulation of an acknowledgment of difference; but his arguments against this absolute judgment are themselves extremely questionable: La Bruyère believes once and for all that *our* customs are cultivated and that *our* laws are beautiful. He believes that our language is pure — a statement whose meaning escapes me; he believes that refined clothing, that is, the way one dresses, is relevant in judging barbarity. And finally, the ultimate barbarity, he believes that the color of one's skin attests to the degree of one's civilization.

La Bruyère's practice is not worthy of his theory; the same could be said of many other champions of humanist doctrine. Voltaire, in his own *Traité de la tolerance,* demonstrates his anti-Semitism and declares that the Egyptians are "at all times detestable people" (ix). But any statement of this kind that one could make does not affect the humanist principle itself precisely because that principle is not being applied in these instances; suffice it to say that overall intention does not shield one from specific errors, and that the humanists themselves must be judged by means of the criteria they have established.

A second problem concerns the humanist doctrine itself and must be examined more closely. The question is, does someone who claims to be tolerant forsake, for all that, all value judgments about a culture other than his own? By saying that all customs have their reason (historical, cultural, local), isn't one giving up one's ability to reason in order to approve or disapprove customs? Granted, this possibility to move from toleration to ethical relativism exists, but it does not correspond to the greatest tendency of humanist thought (and here Montaigne is not representative like Rousseau and Condorcet). Humanism in fact draws a line between what belongs to the domain of custom and what belongs to civilization; the latter is governed by a single hierarchy, whereas the former is not. The Enlightenment is an absolute good, whereas ways of dressing vary according to countries and times, and we are unable to judge them. Or, yet again, to take Montesquieu as an example, laws must be appropriate to circumstances; but tyranny is evil under all skies and its opposite, moderation, is an absolute good. Here again, practice may lag behind theory, but in any case the theory remains coherent by positing both the equality of human beings and the hierarchy of values.

The same cannot be said of some ideas often held by these same authors but which, in reality, contradict humanist doctrine. This is the case of the supposed relation between the moral and the physical that we only glimpsed in La Bruyère's words, but which is amply elaborated in the following century by Buffon. Buffon was not content to make no distinction between customs and civilizations (for him, all social life is subject to value judgment and he considered the fact that in a certain group in northern Japan the women painted their lips and eyebrows blue, rather than red or black, as a sign of barbarity). In addition, he established a causal link between customs and physical characteristics: skin color and body shape come from one's way of life; therefore he considered them as sure signs of the degree of evolution of the mind. But Buffon's racism — for it was indeed racism —

was not a result of Enlightenment principles; on the contrary. Although Buffon did share the idea of a hierarchy of civilizations with the humanists, he did not believe that every human being could attain civilization's heights, even under favorable circumstances, which in practice means that he or she accepts being educated. Consequently, Buffon reduced the principle of universal equality to its minimum: the possibility of mutual fecundation.

Others, on the contrary, strongly affirm equality, but to the detriment of the second great democratic principle (to which we shall return), freedom. Condorcet, for example, declares that "men [are] equal under all skies and brothers by nature's wish," but this is a principle and not a reality; it will therefore be necessary to undertake action that would lead to the "destruction of the inequality among nations" (*Esquisse d'un tableau historique*, viii, x). One must improve the condition of others, export the revolution from home; in Condorcet's terms, this is called "spreading the Enlightenment," and it constitutes the mission of enlightened peoples: "Must not the European population . . . civilize or eliminate the savage nations that still occupy vast areas of Europe?"

Here one recognizes the policy of nineteenth-century European colonialism, which is applied, with varying degrees of success, to civilizing or eliminating—as the case may be—the populations of other parts of the globe. But can one claim that this policy proceeds from the humanist creed itself? No, for it implies a minor premise that is absent, namely, one has the right, or even the obligation, to impose good on others (and therefore, for example, to "civilize" them). Condorcet returns to the intolerance of the evangelizers of the past, and, by refusing to give others the freedom of choice, he transgresses the very principle of equality he had wanted to impose, since it was he, Condorcet, who decided what meaning he would give to the word "civilization," without ever allowing others to take part in the debate.

To summarize: the principle of equality provides the basis of the practice of toleration; one must admit that men are equal in order to allow them to remain different. This principle lies at the foundation of humanist doctrine, which, in its turn, is implicitly or explicitly accepted by all democratic states. This does not mean that, in these states, de jure equality reigns (we know, for example, that until 1945 in France, "equality" was reserved for men; and that, for women, the obstacles to equality before the law have not been entirely removed); but it is possible to fight for this equality, by referring to a principle accepted by all. What may appear as internal contradictions in the humanist doctrine at first glance are in reality merely its incomplete application or its distortion, as in the case of racism or colonialism. Toleration based on equality must know no limits; reciprocally, all inegalitarian discrimination must be condemned.

## II

The acceptance of the equality of everyone is a necessary element of the modern doctrine of toleration; yet for all that it is insufficient. Equality is relevant in particular when it is a matter of affirming toleration toward foreigners; but one can also lack toleration within a society, if one does not accept the right of each individual to act freely. This is the case of religious intolerance, a burning problem during the sixteenth and seventeenth centuries; it is precisely one's co-citizens, one's equals, whom one forces to convert to Catholicism (or, in other countries, to Protestantism). Toleration requires not only equality but also freedom.

Now, if one could demand the absolute equality of each individual before the law, the same is not true for freedom: freedom is good only if it is limited. The ancient and the modern philosophers have struggled to distinguish between two meanings of the word freedom: on the one hand, the right to do what one wants, and, on the other, the right to benefit from what is permitted within a society. There exists therefore an inherent paradox in freedom (and, as a result, in toleration) since, in order to exist, it implies its own (partial) negation. If we all did what we wanted, our freedom would, in effect, quickly be reduced to nothing, since everyone else would be doing the same thing. In other words, the limit of freedom would be force; the weakest would enjoy no freedom. This is why Rousseau opposed civil liberty to natural independence, the right of benefiting from social protection to the right of harming others, that is, the right to force; he taught the preference of the former over the latter.

Civil liberty — the only desirable freedom — is a limited freedom. Within this limit, I have the right to do as I see fit; beyond it, I must submit to the rules and laws decreed by the society of which I am a member. A line therefore separates the *public* and the *private* domains; for freedom to prevail in the latter, it must be controlled in the former. The relevant opposition is not between a totalitarian state (in which the subjects have no freedom and nothing is tolerated) and a libertarian state (in which there exists no obstacle to freedom and everything is tolerated), but rather between these two extremes on the one hand and limited freedom on the other. This limited freedom is what constitutes the second great principle of democratic states, a principle that was also present in the humanism of the classical age, where it took the form of the fight for religious tolerance. Following the French Revolution, this principle would nevertheless be extended to the entire domain of politics and would become the linchpin of *liberalism,* illustrated by a series of thinkers from Benjamin Constant and Wilhelm von Humboldt to Tocqueville and John Stuart Mill. But the basic problems had already been set out in the debate on religious tolerance. And, among these problems, the first one is, where exactly does one place the boundary between the public and the private? How does one delimit the domain that society must regulate?

Spinoza's *Theological-political Treatise* provides one of the first formulations of the problem and its solution. Spinoza defends the right to freedom of opinion, in this case, religious opinion. He reasons thus: no one has either the right or the power to stop being a human being; and it is human nature to use reason and to make judgments. It would be entirely vain to attempt to restrict this freedom; the only thing to which a state may aspire is the suppression of exterior signs of these judgments, that is, the imposition of hypocrisy. Isn't it obvious, however, that a state is acting against its own interests if it forces its subjects to become hypocrites? Spinoza's thoughts on this subject in his *Treatise* have not lost their relevance. He wondered how one could imagine a worse condition for a state than that in which respectable men, because they have dissenting opinions that they are unable to hide, are sent into exile like criminals.

One cannot but share Spinoza's indignation at the repression of the free search for truth. Yet in order to truly appreciate the entire scope of the problem, we must acknowledge that we may be dealing not only with "respectable men" but also with their opposite. For perfectly understandable reasons, theoreticians of liberalism have always chosen to reflect on the useless repression of the best of men: should Socrates have been condemned or Jesus crucified because of the intolerance of others? Spinoza almost never makes exceptions to this rule. But everyone would agree that one must tolerate good: the victory, in short, is too easy. Yet just as in order to truly judge the usefulness of a prohibition, one must imagine that the best men were denied freedom, in order to justify a specific instance of toleration one must, on the contrary, imagine that it concerns the most loathsome opinion.

Spinoza is not in the least ignorant of the need for limiting freedom; on the contrary, the last chapters of his treatise are all devoted precisely to the search for and definition of the extent to which "this freedom can and must be granted without danger to the peace of the state and the right of the sovereign," and which at the same time would allow keeping religion in the private domain (and thus in the domain of free choice). In order to accomplish this task, Spinoza seems to have recourse to two criteria.

The first consists in interpreting the opposition private/public as that between thinking and acting: one must have total freedom to reason, while actions are only acceptable if they do not endanger the interests of the community. "In a democratic state . . . everyone agrees to act by common decree, but not to judge and to reason in common." A thought that is hostile to the state or a seditious opinion must not be punished unless it leads to an action.

But if the difference between thinking (in one's head) and acting (in the world) seems clear and simple, things become muddled as soon as we envision — as we inevitably must — the expression of thought, that is, speech. As expression, speech is indissolubly linked to thought; yet at the same time it is an act: saying is doing. Because speech is unavoidable, it makes the separation between thought and action much more difficult than it appears at first sight.

Spinoza resolves the problem by saying that speech is on the side of thought, not of action. "No one can, without endangering the right of the sovereign, act against his decree, but one can, with total freedom, opine and judge and consequently speak, provided that one does not go beyond mere speech or teaching. . . . The right of the sovereign is related to actions alone and for the rest each individual is allowed to think what he wants and say what he thinks." Spinoza is loath to reiterate, in the heart of speech, the separation between private and public, by restricting the former and by leaving the latter free; this is no doubt because such a separation would only further encourage hypocrisy.

Speech is thus not perceived as an action. If Spinoza can maintain this affirmation, it is because he implicitly imagines language in only one of its dimensions, that is, in its relation to the world. As long as one thinks of language as essentially an endeavor to grasp the world, whose horizon is the truth, the refusal to consider language as an action has few consequences. To express one's thought, to seek the truth: these are no doubt acts; but these acts are always the same and consequently can be placed, without too much damage, within parentheses. All verbal activity here is conceived in terms of science, which is ideally governed by the sole search for truth. But the speech of a scholar is obviously not the only speech possible, and with good reason: language is not only — in fact, it is hardly — a way of grasping the world; it is also and more so a way of establishing contact between two interlocutors, and thus a way of acting on another. Many discourses exist that do not seek truth but that act on the human community (and thus belong not to the sphere of science, but to that of rhetoric); others — the majority, no doubt — are a mixture of the two: both a discourse about the world and an appeal to the other. And from this standpoint, the acting nature of speech can no longer be put in parentheses.

Were I to read an article that insinuated that women like nothing more than the moral and physical pain they could be made to suffer, must I believe this article to be above all a search for truth (the truth of feminine essence) or a call to action (it is normal for men to beat their wives)? If a tract tells me that all the problems of the French come from the fact that there are too many foreigners on their soil, most of whom are North African, must I see in it primarily a thought, or an action? If I judge these to be actions, I can no longer demand unrestricted freedom for them, nor the toleration of opinion; but I do not yet know on what basis I should allow some of them and forbid others. In any event, it seems that a finer criterion must be introduced here: we cannot oppose speech and action, and it is not even sufficient to distinguish between public and private speech. We could imagine that the boundary would be placed between different kinds of public speech; the discriminating criterion would then be the nature of the publication (journal, newspaper, book, tract). There are scientific (and consequently limited-circulation) publications whose sole avowed goal is the search for truth: no restriction should be imposed on them, and research on the biological bases of racial or sexual equality should not be excluded on principle (they may, however, be rejected by the editor because of their scientific worthlessness — this would not be intolerance). There are other publications whose goal may be called communicative and nonreferential; in these, words are actions and must be judged as such.

The opposition between thinking and saying, on the one hand, and acting, on the other, does not get at the heart of the matter; this may be one reason why Spinoza was led to introduce a second criterion that allowed the drawing of a boundary between public and private, between the regulated and the free. Significantly, this criterion emerges when Spinoza imagines the possibility of allowing freedom of expression, not to "respectable men," but to some "hateful sect": its members, he says, also must benefit from freedom and security "provided they harm no one." This formulation was very successful, and for good reason. Rather than defining the task of the state as a positive good to be attained, it is described in a negative way:

the state is not required to assure the happiness of its citizens, but simply to prevent the evil that they could cause one another; individual happiness belongs only to the private domain. One does not have the right to impose good on another under any pretext; each individual is free to manage his life as he wants, provided that others do not suffer from it. Even if the community is convinced that a certain individual is in the wrong, it will abstain from intervening. One does not have the right to punish the drunkard because he is drunk, but only if he harms those around him or disturbs the peace; nor may one punish the drug addict, but only the dealer. Or, to take the extreme example: homicide is a crime, suicide is not. This restriction would never be forgotten by the great theoreticians of nineteenth-century liberalism: freedom in all areas, except if it harms others.

Nonetheless, it is permissible to question the effectiveness of this new criterion. If one were to take it literally, it is difficult to see where the scope of its action would end: one would be taking away with one hand all the freedoms that were generously granted by the other. One could say—without even mentioning all the previous examples—that any search for truth harms someone, that is, the person who was profiting from the former state of things. The person who fights for religious toleration, for example, obviously is harming the champions of fanaticism. The person who fights against a tyrant unquestionably causes that tyrant harm. Those who propose a materialist explanation of the world are harming creationists, and in a very direct way: their followers are becoming ever scarcer. The person who wins first place in a contest harms the person who comes in second. Or, in another domain, the one who leaves a former loved one precisely because he has stopped loving nevertheless causes the other great pain.

The drawbacks of this criterion are too conspicuous to be overlooked; but the efforts to complement it and to make it truly discriminating result in replacing it with another. For example, one would say that the winner of a contest does not illustrate the practice of intolerance because all the rivals competed under the same conditions; that the winner harmed a person, but not that person's rights. But this amounts to introducing the notion of right, which is not reducible to evil inflicted on another. Or again, one could say that the search for truth or progress is legitimate, whatever the consequences; but then one would be judging in the name of absolute values such as progress and truth, and not in the name of the suffering caused others. The criterion would thus have the drawback of being ambivalent.

In all the instances outlined here, "wrongdoing" has been proved, and yet one cannot find in it a sufficient reason for intolerance. One could consider things from the opposite point of view, and find even stronger reasons for rejecting the very principle of this criterion. An act is not reprehensible simply because it causes someone harm, but because it is, in itself, wrong. If today someone were to publish anti-Semitic propaganda, it would not necessarily inflict suffering on the Jews: the public consensus on the matter is such that, without even mentioning the lawsuits that threaten him, the anti-Semite would be ostracized by his compatriots, or would lose his job, or even some teeth in a brawl. He would thus be the one to suffer more than those he attacks. Yet this fact does not make his act any more excusable or acceptable: we condemn anti-Semitic propaganda because we judge it to be evil, and not because it harms someone.

Similar arguments could be leveled against a different interpretation of the principle of freedom, one that another great champion of tolerance — Pierre Bayle — proposed during Spinoza's time. In order to distinguish between the licit and the illicit, Bayle appeals to the judgment of conscience, that is, to profound conviction: "Everything that goes against the dictates of conscience is a sin, [for] it is obvious that conscience is a light that tells us if something is good or bad" (*Commentaire philosophique*, 2:8). But is it enough to be sincere in order to be just? Cannot racists or sexists pleading for their cause find a justification in their "profound conviction"? Isn't — as the proverb claims — the road to hell paved with good intentions? Judging an act by its effect, as Spinoza wanted, does not allow the judging of the act itself; but judging it according to the intentions of its agent, as Bayle would have it, does not allow it any more so, and in addition, it delegates the appreciation of social acts to purely individual judgment.

Here we find ourselves trapped in a paradox: we all agree with Spinoza (or Bayle) that one must practice toleration, for it alone guarantees the continued existence of the freedom that is our ideal; but, while we know that in order for it to exist, freedom must be limited, we do not know on what basis we should draw these limits. As a result, we are willing to grant our benign attention to the enemies of liberalism who would suppress freedom, or who base its restrictions either on national tradition or on religion: and here we can recognize a few of the dangers that threaten our own time.

## III

Liberal policy is unquestionably generous, but it is ill founded. Rather than abandoning it, however, isn't it possible to look for a better foundation? An interesting attempt to do so is proposed in the work of another of liberalism's founders, John Locke, the author of the celebrated *Letter concerning Toleration*.

Locke's program has many points in common with Spinoza's. Locke also wants to place a boundary between the public domain — constituted by community affairs — and the private domain, which comprises religious affairs as well as personal well-being. The laws and their agents, the magistrates, deal with the former, not with the latter: one has no right to impose good on others. "The Publick Good is the rule and measure of Law-making" (39); "The business of Laws is not to provide for the Truth of Opinions, but for the Safety and Security of the Commonwealth, and of every particular man's Goods and Person" (46); "Laws provide, as much as possible, that the Goods and Health of Subjects be not injured by the Fraud or Violence of others; they do not guard them from the Negligence or Ill-husbandry of the Possessors themselves. No man can be forced to be Rich or Healthful, whether he will or no" (35).

Freedom of conscience is total. But the boundary between interior and exterior is not airtight: profound convictions comprise modes of behavior that, in turn, belong to the realm of social life. Here again we find the problem of the boundary between licit and illicit; and it is here that Locke moves away from Spinoza's position (of which he was aware). Spinoza's first criterion concerned the very nature of facts: they were either thoughts or actions; but this distinction proved impracticable. His second criterion was related to effects; but it too proved to be unreliable, worthless even. Locke's solution is different: he establishes the common good as a criterion. What is contrary to the common good must be prosecuted by laws, whether or not someone has been done an injustice; what does not affect the common good must be left to the discretion of individuals. The common good is an absolute value that allows the properties of each action to be determined. Toleration is effective only if it is united with the idea of public good, the refusal of which constitutes the threshold of the intolerable. The common good is not directly produced by toleration, but neither is it its opposite; rather, the two necessarily complement one another. Liberalism can be internally coherent only if it is tempered by a concern for the community.

But, since this good is defined by each individual according to his own convenience, don't we run the risk of seeing it diverted from its true aims? No doubt this would be so if we are satisfied with a general formulation. Locke, however, does not hesitate to enter into detail, and in the end he enumerates a certain number of cases in which the magistrate must intervene.

Rather than evoking the historical circumstances to which these cases refer, I would like to attempt to see to what extent they may correspond to contemporary situations.

In the first place, a state has the right not to tolerate the rejection of what is called the social contract, that is, living in a community in which one forsakes independence in order to obtain protection. Locke believes that atheism leads to such an abdication, for if there is no God, everything is allowed. But an ethics may be based on reference to humanity and not to God, and maintaining the contract does not require theological justification. What must be added here is that the state is also bound to defend itself against attacks directed against it in the name of a principle other than the one it claims as its own but which may not be, for all that, any more consistent with reason. As Montesquieu would say, there is no harm in one moderate government replacing another, but the same is not true if tyranny replaces moderation. Within a democracy, it is necessary to tolerate those criticisms of the government that continue to conform to the democratic principle, but not those that reject the principle itself. In return, the democratic criticism of tyranny is morally licit, for it has recourse to a rational legitimation.

Obviously we are dealing here with a restriction of individual freedom, one that is practiced by the majority of modern democracies (in France, a 1936 law proscribes attacks on the republican form of government and the use of force in the propagation of one's convictions). The justification of this restriction is thus founded on democracy's best interests: democracy runs a greater risk of perishing if it rejects this restriction than if it practices it. By tolerating the freedom of speech and the freedom of assembly of the Nazi Party, the Weimar Republic facilitated the advent of fascism, which was not content to limit democracy, but simply suppressed it.

In the second place, a state has the right not to tolerate the actions of those who act according to the interests of another state: national duty replaces humanitarian duty here. If an individual living in State A "simultaneously recognizes owing a blind obedience" to the sovereign of State B, his attitude must be considered harmful to the affairs of the state. This is the problem of the "foreign party" and of the "fifth column." Such a demand requires some qualification. One does not judge behavior in the same way in time of war as in time of peace; when the very existence of State A is threatened by State B, and when it is not; when a dissident opinion can be expressed without needing material support from abroad, and when it cannot (from an ethical point of view, "treason" is, paradoxically, less tolerable in a democratic society that allows difference in political positions than in a totalitarian state, where it is often the only form of opposition possible). Here both extremes must be avoided: one is not obliged to believe that one's country is always right, nor to leave it if one does not love it; but one cannot claim impunity if one openly fights for the submission of one's country to another.

Finally, one must not tolerate those who, within a state, practice discrimination against some members and claim privileges for themselves (in other words, those who reject the principle of equality), for they found their own intolerance on this; and intolerance is intolerable. Of course, Locke is thinking of the different forms of Christianity; but for us today this third kind of necessary intolerance — probably more pertinent than all the others since it affects the majority of the population — concerns two inegalitarian practices: racism and sexism. The most active variant of racism today in Western democracies is that which affects immigrant workers (in France, Maghrebians in particular). It takes several forms: from religious intolerance (one forbids the building of a mosque, or claims that all Muslims are incorrigible fanatics), to the spread of psychological clichés (Arabs are dirty, lazy thieves), to the murder of victims chosen at random. The nature of the question asked has changed curiously since the sixteenth century. At that time the question was whether one should tolerate races (in their differences), and the answer was yes. Today, the question is whether one should tolerate racism, and the answer is no.

Racial discrimination affects a small segment of the population, but it relates to all aspects of that segment's life. Sexist discrimination, on the other hand, affects almost half the population, but concerns only some aspects of its existence. It is precisely because of sexism's omnipresence that it is less striking than racist practices; but its forms are, on the contrary, no less violent. For example, it is difficult for an unaccompanied woman to stroll in a large city without being harassed, especially after nightfall. If such a situation were transposed to the racial arena, it would correspond to a state of apartheid, where one part of the city is off-limits to certain segments of the population. One can imagine the cries of protest that would be raised by "Black" or "Asian" neighborhoods in which any white visitor could do as he pleased with the members of these two races who, in exchange for payment, would bow to his slightest whim. The existence of red-light districts, in return, shocks no one. The antiracism law has existed in France since 1939; the antisexism law still exists only in the planning stage. In addition, the victims of racism are often among those who are guilty of sexism, a situation that racist propaganda has not failed to exploit.

Voltaire claimed that "the right to intolerance is absurd and barbaric: it is the law of tigers" (*Traité de la tolerance,* vi). No doubt he was right for the particular cases he had in mind; but, if one were to apply his statement generally, it would become unacceptable. One could say, on the contrary, that the right to unlimited toleration favors the strong to the detriment of the weak. The toleration of rapists signifies intolerance toward women. If one tolerates tigers in the same enclosure as other animals, that means that one is ready to sacrifice the latter to the former, which is even more barbaric and absurd. The physically or materially weak are the victims of unlimited toleration; intolerance toward those who attack them is *their* right, not that of the strong.

The three types of intolerable acts thus concern the universal human society, the particular society that constitutes a state, and the individual members of that society. Whether this enumeration is sufficiently complete or whether this distribution of intolerable acts is justified — these things are open to debate. But one must at least give their creator credit for having posed the problem in its full complexity and for having understood that any solution to the problem of toleration that does not take into account the existence of the intolerable is a weak, or even misleading, solution. This fact does not prejudice the forms that the fight against the intolerable must take, nor can it be reduced to an appeal to censorship, as the champions of unlimited freedom pretend to believe.

This fight has both a positive side, which is education (even though the teaching in the schools is far from being able to fight racist and sexist prejudices effectively — to mention only those two), and a negative side — which is repression. In certain cases, repression can be carried out only by means of laws; in others, it occurs by means of the disapproval of public opinion (and this implies that public opinion must be educated in its turn). Lack of encouragement is at times a more effective means of fighting than censorship; intellectual and artistic activities need the material support of patrons. When the patron is the state, it can choose the beneficiaries of its generosity according to what it deems tolerable and what it deems intolerable.

One must not, of course, burn Sade; but for all that must one shower him with praise? The fact that Rousseau, in his *Lettre à d'Alembert,* demanded that there be no theater in Geneva in the name of the public good seems to us extremely anachronistic. Rousseau may have been wrong in this instance;

but doesn't our refusal to recognize any relation between politics and the arts come down, in the end, to the scorning of the one or the other, or both?

Censorship is undesirable; but total impunity of speech is no less so. The law punishes sexist crimes (rape) and racist crimes (discrimination). Must it be powerless before the incitement to these crimes? When faced with the degrading image of women one finds in the media, one often retorts: nothing proves that there is a cause-and-effect relationship between the sexism of words and the sexism of acts; perhaps the possibility of practicing the former even eliminates the necessity of falling into the latter. In this case preventive measures run the risk of turning against those who have requested them. On the one hand, however, this relation is unquestionable, even if it is difficult to measure and cannot be reduced to a mechanical determinism. Is there any serious doubt that there was a relation between anti-Semitic Nazi propaganda and the extermination of Jews? Between anti-Arab discourse and the increase in beatings, even executions, of North Africans? Between libertarian sexist discourse—exclusive to Western democracies—and the insecurity women suffer in the streets only in these same countries? On the other hand, to speak is to act: racist statements are not only an incitement to action, they are themselves an act; the same is true of sexism. One may enjoy unlimited freedom of expression; but one must be willing to assume responsibility for one's statements, particularly when they aim at acting on another rather than simply seeking the truth.

Recalling these few pages of European history of ideas leads me to affirm that one can defend toleration in the name of equality and in the name of freedom. In the first case, the demand for toleration must know no limits: everyone's human dignity must be acknowledged. In the second, the demand for toleration is limited by the concern for the common good. Our judgment in each individual case—our "prudence"—must take into account the role played by each of these principles.

This is why, although toleration is a universal concept, the form and the direction that the fight for toleration will take depend on the historical, cultural, and political context in which one lives. In a country that practices racial segregation or any other form of discrimination, the focus will necessarily be on toleration that stems from the principle of equality. In those countries that are military or totalitarian dictatorships, it is the fight for individual toleration and liberty that will take precedence. Finally, in liberal democracies where, in spite of isolated cases to the contrary, religious and racial tolerance, as well as freedom of speech, are acquired facts, but where the concern for individual prosperity leads to forgetting the common good, special efforts must be made to fight intolerance in all its guises.

In my eyes, contemporary Western European states belong to this last category. We know that others have claimed the opposite. For example, both Sartre in his preface to *The Wretched of the Earth* and Marcuse in his *Repressive Tolerance* maintained that we live in countries in which the governments and other groups that wield the power exercise a daily and legal violence on their inhabitants, and that this violence renders the common discourse of toleration a mere theatrical prop, a clever camouflage, which allows the powers to carry on with all impunity. This violence provokes another, opposite violence in reaction, such as the violence practiced by groups like Direct Action, the Red Brigade, and other factions of the red or black armies. Since I do not share this diagnosis, I have necessarily chosen another remedy. Yet it must be made clear that toleration is not a panacea: members of our society suffer from many other kinds of distress than those that can be cured by toleration, even well-tempered toleration.

# 12 / Freedom in Letters

The Restoration deserves better than its name implies: rather than the restoral of the Old Regime, it represents the creation of a public space in which beings and ideas could circulate more freely than during the Empire, the Terror, or the time of Louis XVI—more freely than ever before. It was under the Restoration that the French took their first timid steps toward democracy. This did not mean there were no conflicts—on the contrary; and these conflicts are illustrated by the positions taken specifically in relation to freedom. Freedom and letters: the question can be extended in two directions, according to whether one has in mind political freedom, the right to publish what one thinks; or philosophical freedom, the ability of the individual to act as an autonomous subject.

## I

The position of the public authorities specifically regarding the problem of freedom of speech is recorded in Article 8 of the Charter granted by Louis XVIII to the French people on June 4, 1814 (and not accepted by him, as the liberals had hoped). This article reads: "The French have the right to publish and have printed their opinions, in conformance with the laws that must repress the abuse of this freedom." The formulation satisfied the liberals and displeased the Ultras (the extreme right, in a sense): it did not provide for any preliminary censorship of books or the press, but placed them under the general jurisdiction of violations of press laws. Between 1814 and 1830 a ceaseless battle between the two extremes of Parliament would take place: at times the Ultras attacked the government's too liberal position, and thus the Charter itself; at other times, having succeeded in bending the royal policy, they managed to establish censorship, and it was then the liberals — the extreme left of the time (there were no longer any Jacobins in the public sphere) — who counterattacked, referring to the letter of the Charter. Louis de Bonald and Benjamin Constant — the ideologues and spokesmen of the two extreme groups — tirelessly devoted speeches, press articles, and brochures to the questions of censorship and freedom of the press. Only Bonald's retirement and Constant's death in 1830 interrupted this exchange, which was more like a duel. An analysis of these writings allows one to circumscribe the ideological space of this epoch, whose winding trails would later be followed by other authors. (Chateaubriand, for example, would manage a tour de force: he agreed with Bonald in 1814 and with Constant in 1827.)

Only a few months after the granting of the Charter, in the autumn of 1814, both Bonald and Constant reacted for the first time to the article on freedom of speech. Constant's text was entitled *De la liberté des brochures, des pamphlets et des journaux;* Bonald's text, which was in part a reply to Constant's, was called *Encore un mot sur la liberté de la presse.* In reality, however, the exchange had begun much earlier. In June of 1806, Bonald published, in the *Mercure de France,* an article entitled *Réflexions philosophiques sur la tolerance des opinions.* Constant, who was at this time putting the final touches on his great work of political philosophy, *Principes de politique,* which remained unpublished until 1980, devoted most of book VII — "On the Freedom of Thought" — to the question, and was already responding to Bonald. This text would form the heart of the chapter devoted to individual rights in Constant's *Réflexions sur les constitutions et les garanties,* published in 1814, a month before the granting of the Charter. It is in the two texts from 1806 that each author would find his main arguments for the future polemic. Once again, it was not entirely a first attempt: Bonald had already expressed his ideas on the matter in his very first text, dating from 1796, *Théorie du pouvoir politique et religieux dans la société civile,* and Constant had done so in a text signed by Mme. de Staël, but which he had coauthored, entitled *Des considérations actuelles qui peuvent terminer la Révolution et des principes qui doivent fonder la République en France,* in 1798. Thus, over the course of more than thirty years, the two ideologues returned obsessively to the same theme, repeating or refining their arguments, varying their formulations, but never really changing their points of view (for reasons that were purely tactical Bonald requested only the censorship of books, but not that of the press, from 1817 to 1821).

In 1814, Bonald led the attack against freedom of expression. His reasoning was as follows: in the first place, the problem had to be reformulated; it was not a question of an attack against freedom of thought, which in any case was impossible, since thought had at its disposal an impregnable shelter—the human mind (Bonald had not foreseen totalitarian techniques); nor was it an attack against freedom of expression—in speech or in writing—as long as one remained within the private domain. What Bonald *did* want to regulate was the freedom to *publish,* to act on others in the public domain. From this point on, his reasoning became a strict syllogism. The major premise was that public speech and writing are actions: to do is to say. The minor premise was that no government, no society, can grant its subjects or its members unrestricted freedom of action; to do so would be to return to the savage state of all-out war. The conclusion follows automatically: it is inconceivable for a reasonable government to exempt verbal actions—the most important ones in a civilized nation (think of the effects of a book such as the New Testament or Rousseau's *Contrat social,* and, we might add today, *The Communist Manifesto* or *Mein Kampf*)—from the laws it applies to the rest of public actions. It is therefore necessary to prohibit and to regulate.

The liberals want to defend freedom of thought. This, responds Bonald, is merely playing with words. It is not to think freely that they demand, but to publish freely. And it is really not a question of freedom but rather one of power, the power to direct and to judge. Unlike the other three powers (legislative, executive, and judicial), the fourth power—the press—escapes all control: journalists are not elected, and are not removable by nation or king; in order to publish, one need only have at one's disposal the material means to do so, or simply the personal sympathy of those who possess these means. What could be more unjust, regardless of whether the chosen rule of justice is monarchist or republican? (The governments of France have, to this day, remained sensitive to this problem: any change in the majority entails a change in the personnel of the main television stations.)

But Bonald does not stop at this argument; he adds another. What does it mean to accept that each person expresses his or her opinion freely? It means one of two things: either that the opinion in question concerns a subject that does not affect the public good, in which case there is nothing shocking in its publication, since it cannot harm anyone. But then how could one claim that questions of politics, morality, and religion are unrelated to the interests of society when they are precisely the questions about which society is most passionate? Or else — if one does not want to follow this route — one recognizes the gravity of these questions; but then, how can one dare to claim that all answers must be accepted indifferently? Isn't the best preferable to the worst? Christian values are, for Bonald, superior to all others. Aren't there ideologies whose harmfulness is established beyond all doubt and, as a result, whose circulation it is imprudent, to say the least, to encourage? Equal freedom for all opinions implies that all opinions are equal, in other words, that one has abandoned any hierarchy of values. Yet it is absurd to want to ignore the fact that certain things are better for a society than others; laws tell us what is allowed and what is forbidden, science prefers the true to the false. By what miracle would ideology alone escape the judgment that is carried out in all other domains?

As for the forms that the regulating of publications should take, Bonald prefers censorship to justice; he would rather prevent than repress; and he makes every effort to prove that this is the spirit, if not the letter, of the Charter. His arguments here are varied. First, one can reason by analogy: isn't it preferable to prevent an illness than to have to cure it? to prevent a crime rather than punish it? Isn't the police force a necessary complement of justice? It is true that in the case of other actions the law is content to repress; but, by specifying the nature of the offense, it acts in a dissuasive way: everyone knows that stealing is prohibited. Now, it is impossible to draw up laws regarding the press in such a precise manner: one cannot foresee all the forms an author's heresy could take; the censor is therefore the one who interprets the law in advance, obligingly letting the author know if the publication of his thoughts would or would not be an offense. In this way, one prevents the author from incurring heavy printing costs, and if one is discreet, one does not compromise one's good reputation. The possibility of a trial — which could provide publicity for a work to which one does not want to draw the readers' attention — is also avoided. "Censorship, strict censorship, universal censorship, is therefore necessary for all texts, periodical or other" ("Discours du 9 juillet 1821," 149). This is why Bonald, in accordance with his profound convictions, accepted, in 1827, the presidency of the Committee on Censorship.

Bonald's arguments carry weight, and his recommendations have been followed in every country ruled by tyranny; some of his recommendations can even be found in liberal democracies. What does Constant offer in opposition? It must immediately be said that his opposition is not as radical as one might think from certain formulations used in the course of these contests in eloquence. However, Constant, who often starts with the same statements as Bonald, does not arrive at the same conclusions; he demonstrates that the inevitable nature of Bonald's conclusions is an illusion, even if his starting observations are often correct. Thus, he accepts that speech and writing may be actions; as such, they must not be exempt from the law. In other words, even if he never formulates things in these terms, he accepts Bonald's initial syllogism. The differences come afterward.

Constant also acknowledges that "freedom of the press" is in reality a power; rather than regretting this, however, he rejoices in it. In the old republics, which were the size of a city, it was enough to go to the public square to inform one's co-citizens of everything they needed to know; and, by the same token, these citizens had the possibility of participating in the affairs of the city. At the present time, this "freedom of the ancients," the freedom to participate (*la liberté-participation*), has become impracticable, if only because of the size of contemporary states. It has been replaced, it is true, by a "freedom of the moderns," the freedom of autonomy (*la liberté-autonomie*), that is, the establishment of a private sphere in which neither the state nor society has the right of inspection; as a result, however, modern citizens have lost their means of participation. The press and books offer them a way to fill this lack; they inform the governing parties of the state of mind of their subjects and at the same time give these subjects a means of recourse against the arbitrariness of power: "Publicity is the resource of the oppressed against the oppressor" ("Discours du 7 juillet 1821," 1296). In a world in which the individual runs the risk of having only the private domain at his disposal, publication, as its name indicates, assures access to the public domain. The printing press is the indispensable tool of modern democracy; but, in order for everyone to have access to this tool, the press must be pluralistic, and thus its publications must not be controlled in advance. In this way, each individual has a good chance of finding a medium of expression: publicity is the guarantee of legality.

Like Bonald, Constant believes in a hierarchy of values; when he speaks of nihilism, it is to show its contemporary scope, not to glorify it. And like Bonald, he is sensitive to the necessary harmony between ends and means: Bonald placed a revealed truth (that of the New Testament) above everything, and consequently he wanted people's attitude toward that truth to be one of submission, not one of free discussion. But the truth and the values to which Constant aspires, unlike those of Bonald, must be the product of reason. It follows that the appropriate means to reach them is thus not a command given by the superior to the inferior, but free inquiry and debate with others, which in turn implies the freedom of the press; otherwise, Constant writes, "the means are not homogeneous" (*Principes de politique,* XIV, 3, 362). Not only does the use of inappropriate means run the risk of compromising the ends (a good value, as soon as it is promoted by the police, becomes unpopular), but, in addition, discussion has its own virtues: it leads to calm, since it forces the interlocutors to accept at least one thing in common, namely, the framework of the discussion itself. Good "social communications" lead to "the rectification of all ideas" (*Principes de politique,* VII, 3, 131). Profitable to the state, free discussion is obviously profitable to individuals also: truth accepted on someone's word (the truth of authority) deadens the mind; the necessity of seeking the truth fortifies it.

For these reasons Constant decides not on the necessity of unlimited freedom of the press and books, but on the necessity of their undergoing examination by justice (juries) rather than by censors. There is nothing of the anarchist about Constant, and he never fails to remind us that certain verbal actions (certain publications) seem reprehensible to him. He lists them regularly: attacks on the dignity of individuals or communities (defamation); incitement to violence to resolve individual or social conflicts (the call to murder or to civil war); "invitations addressed to a foreign enemy" (ibid., I, 126). But such offenses, like all offenses, are judicial matters, and therefore do not require the creation of any additional authority. Unlike what Bonald had suggested, publication is not, in itself, a "means to harm" (*Encore un mot sur la liberté,* 2), even if it can become one; one cannot prohibit its use under the pretext of abuse. "To impose silence upon citizens for fear they will commit these crimes is to forbid them to go out for fear they will disturb the peace of the small streets and great avenues; it is to prohibit them from speaking for fear they may insult someone" ("Projet de loi sur la liberté de la presse," in *Recueils d'articles,* 1:78).

Censorship, however, has its own drawbacks. In order to have firm control over everything that is being written in a country, there would need to be spies everywhere; in other words, it would be necessary to set up a police state, whose disadvantages would outweigh its advantages, and which would lead unnecessarily to extreme solutions. "In the matter of freedom of the press," Constant wrote, "one must permit or execute" ("De la liberté des brochurers," in *Cours de politique constitutionnelle,* 1:445). Since it is not possible to execute everyone, it is better to permit. In addition, all borders would have to be closed; otherwise forbidden writings would immediately be imported from abroad (totalitarian states were no innovators in this instance either). Another disadvantage lies in the fact that the government, since it would have to watch over everything, would find itself, in practice, responsible for everything that was published; yet there are opinions that, without being violations of the law, would be unacceptable as the expression of the government's will. Furthermore, if every public act of speech is guaranteed by the government, and therefore if the government is the only source of public speech, the latter would lose its credibility, since it is never exposed to the test of contradiction (in totalitarian countries, the people do not even believe weather reports). If censors control publications, power is still slightly more concentrated in government hands; if judges control them, the distribution of powers, and therefore their mutual control, are assured. Finally, freedom of speech is also a safety valve: revolutions explode where there is no other way of acting on society. In countries where participation in public life by means of the intermediary of publications is forbidden, subjects can choose between becoming insurgents or taking refuge in purely material pleasures; both solutions are as degrading for the subjects as they are harmful to the good of their country.

The July Monarchy that followed the Restoration in 1830 seems, on many counts, to prove Constant, rather than Bonald, to have been right. In reality, questions of censorship and freedom of publication continued to be asked for many years; today, the Fifth Republic has clearly chosen Constant's principles over those of Bonald. But the best comment on this controversy may be an anecdote that concerns Bonald himself. His 1806 article on (or rather, against) toleration attracted the ire of the famous Fouché, Napoléon's minister of police, who sent the following order to the prefect of the region: "Tell M. de Bonald that His Majesty the Emperor admires and compensates only useful talents and positive information, that he welcomes dissertations that spread light and severely represses discussions that could bring about discord within his Empire" (Moulinie, 35–36). It is not enough to prefer the useful, the positive, and "light"; one must also side with those who put content in this very conveniently vague notion. And the risk inherent in all censorship is that, one day, one may find oneself censored: whoever forswears equality must be able to imagine himself not only on the side of the masters, but also on that of the slaves.

# II

The freedom to publish is only one of the kinds of freedom with which writers must contend; there is another meaning of the word—less political and more philosophical, or more internal than external. One can ask one-self, in effect, to what degree a writer exercises his freedom in producing a literary work. Is it the writer who is expressing himself in this work, or rather, is it forces that he cannot control and for which he is simply the spokesman? The term opposed to freedom here is no longer repression, but determinism; it is primarily a matter of social and historical causality. The differences of opinion found in the work of Bonald and Constant are equally instructive in this matter.

Reflecting on the place of the poet in the city, one may say either how things are or how they should be. Bonald does not hesitate to take the sec-ond stance. Literature, from all evidence, is not a simple game of formal rules dealing with the classical unities, the plot, or the proportions of parts; just like religion, it is related to the inherent values of a society. "Poetry, considered in its essence and its primitive object, is the art of saying in an exalted way exalted things (and what is more exalted than morality?)" (*Mel-anges,* 1:448). Consequently, writers are called on to be the educators of so-ciety: "The literary profession is also a *militia* destined to combat false doc-trines" (ibid., 1:57). It is therefore useless, from this viewpoint, to valorize independence: writers must regulate their behavior in relation to good, not to freedom.

This choice of Bonald's is not surprising. What is surprising is that, ac-cording to him, even if a writer wanted to be independent, he could not be: freedom, in this sense of the word, is not only undesirable, it is also im-possible. The philosophers of the eighteenth century imagined that the hu-man being had been originally isolated, and that he only entered society afterward, through the intermediary of a kind of contract. According to Bonald, these doctrines are as harmful as they are false: "Man belongs to society by the necessity of his nature" (ibid., 2:23). Thus he is never "free" from the social relations into which he is born. What is true of all human beings is even truer, were that possible, of men of letters: not only are they subject to all the "general relations of humanity and the society that links them to their fellow men," but in addition, through their specific role as public educators, they are even more entangled in the network of social connections (ibid., 1:56). It is writers' pride that makes them think they are personally responsible for the quality of their works; or an even more subtle form of pride that makes them think, remorsefully, that they are responsible for their failure. In both cases, they are mistaken. The force of social determinism is such that their responsibility is not even involved: "The beauties found in the products of the arts belong, more than one thinks, to society; and . . . the errors are more often the fault of the century than of the man" (1:498).

This is because, according to one of Bonald's formulations that he repeats tirelessly from 1802 on (the date of his *Législation primitive*), "Literature is the expression of society." The writer can represent only what he knows; consequently, a certain society produces a certain literature. Hence the variety of literatures in time and space. Genres themselves reflect social distinctions, particularly the most important among them according to Bonald: the distinction between public and private, between political society and domestic society. It is this distinction that lies at the bottom of, and explains, the opposition between genres such as tragedy and comedy, epic and novel, ode and song. Style itself—regardless of what Buffon says—comes from society and not from man; for example, "in the works of Christian peoples, style is generally stronger in ideas and more sober in images" (1:289).

It is no coincidence that Bonald shares with Marxists this conception of literature as a "faithful satellite" of society (2:293): both Bonald's conservatism and Marxism presuppose that society is endowed with perfect unity and coherence, and that nothing escapes social determinism. But Bonald's position must not be confused with relativism, whether historical or geographical: facts are diverse, but judgments remain subject to unity. Unlike Herder, Bonald does not see any reason to consider each literature to be good in its genre, or to think that there are as many perfections as there are societies in this determination of literature by society. Societies themselves are in fact hierarchized (with, at the top, Christian theocracy), and literatures are correlative to societies; thus literatures also are hierarchized. For Bonald, all differences are inequalities: "If one were to object that the ideas of the *beau moral* are not the same for all peoples, I would point out that they are not different, but simply unequally developed" (2:53–54). The principles of taste are no less motivated than the principles of laws; the "public" is, in both cases, preferable to the "familiar," and the perfect style is that of truth. Simply put, knowledge of history and geography prevents us from committing anachronisms and from overestimating the individual responsibility of writers: one would not condemn the Greeks for the imperfections in their art if one acknowledged that they did as well as their society allowed. "Homer is perfect, even when he represents an imperfect society" (1:314); this in no way means that we should not prefer one art to another.

Once again, Constant's position on the same subject is not in perfect contrast to Bonald's; but again, starting from often analogous ideas, he arrives at entirely different conclusions. Like Bonald, Constant believes that the diversity of literatures is linked to the diversity of societies and historical moments (it was not by chance that he was the friend of Mme. de Staël, who developed these ideas at the same time as Bonald); like Bonald — even if he does not say so openly — Constant has very particular preferences and would like society to evolve in certain directions rather than others. His point of view is more nuanced when it comes to the relation between literature and morality. First, he affirms that didactic intent, such as Bonald recommends, is immaterial, or even contrary to poetic development: "The poetic painting of passions proves nothing in favor of a doctrine." Racine's *Phèdre,* "the most perfect of our tragedies . . . inculcates no precept that attempts to better the audience." Voltaire is proof to the contrary; in his work one always runs the risk of finding "the schoolteacher behind the hero." These are "effects foreign to the nature and harmful to the perfection [of tragedy]; for passion imbued with doctrine, serving philosophical developments, is a an error in relation to the arts" (Constant, "Reflexions sur la tragedie," in *Oeuvres* [1979], 907–8). For all that, Constant is not uninterested in the relation between literature and ethics, but he would like it to be indirect: the result would be all the better since "instruction would not be the goal, but the effect of the *tableau"* (ibid., 920).

Constant, no more than Bonald, does not imagine man as being originally or essentially alone. "Man is social because he is man, just as the wolf is unsocial because he is wolf," he writes ("Commentaire sur G. Filangieri," I, viii; vol. III, 213). This is also the lesson to be found in *Adolphe:* the character in the novel rejects Ellénore, thinking he is accommodating his need for independence; once he has done so, he discovers that it was an illusion. "How much my heart missed that dependence that had so often revolted me!" (*Oeuvres* [1979], 79). The human being cannot become "independent" of others.

Yet is this to say that the writer must not aspire to independence and freedom, as Bonald thinks? For Constant, this is merely playing with words, if not a sophism: one must not confuse the *social* dependence of the human being, the fact that he does not live in a vacuum, with his *political* dependence, with the obligation that his writing express the will of the prince (or, a fortiori, that of the pope!). One cannot "free" oneself from society, but one may preserve a space for individual activities, one's private sphere, from the interference of public force. Bonald offered the necessary political dependence of Latin poetry during Augustus's century as an example: Virgil and Horace took this poetry to its height at a time "when monarchic institutions were taking the place of democratic disorder" (*Mélanges,* 1:307); a "better ordered" society favors literary flowering (ibid., 1:317). Constant knows that, in his own language, "better ordered" translates as "more tyrannical"; and he contests Bonald's example. "It has been argued that nothing is more favorable to the progress and the improvement of literature than the unlimited authority of a single being" ("De la littérature dans ses rapports avec la liberté," in *Oeuvres* [1979], 853–54). What Constant will establish to the contrary is that great works are never produced in the absence of freedom: either they were conceived before this despotism, or the poets have chosen, under a despotic regime, a kind of internal emigration, precisely like Virgil and Horace did: "Both of them fled the court and aspired only to retreat" (ibid., 859).

Constant was certainly correct in affirming that political independence is compatible with social dependence; it is no less striking to see that, for him, the optimal relation between the writer and the group to which he belongs is a relation in which dependence is reduced to a minimum. Either, living in a democracy, the writer benefits from the freedom guaranteed to all; or, under despotism, he takes refuge in his own universe; but in both cases the ideal is autonomy. "Originality is always the result of independence. . . . Individuality is the only thing that can inspire interest" ("De la guerre de Trente Ans," in *Oeuvres* [1979], 862–63). One step further and we are dealing with the rebellious *poète maudit*. We find nothing of the sort in Bonald, who valorizes neither originality nor individuality, and for whom the ideal is more to be found in participation, in the harmonious fusion of the poet and his group: literature is at its best when it embodies the values of the society in which it is born. Where, for Constant, the norm is separation, even conflict, for Bonald, it is to be found in the indistinction between the individual and society.

Nothing illustrates this difference in position better than the predictions made by both men regarding the literature of the future. In his hours of melancholy (of which he has quite a few), Bonald imagines the total failure of the Restoration and the victory of new, subversive values: a lack of concern for the public good, the triumph of private pleasures, and the reduction of these pleasures to the purely sensual. Under these conditions, since writers have always been the faithful spokesmen of the society to which they belong, literature will no longer be able to represent anything more than daily life and, in particular, the erotic life of men. "Poets, dominated by their century and by customs will write — if I may speak thus — the epic of physical man" (*Mélanges,* 1:79). Literature will end up being pornography.

As for Constant, he obviously does not believe poets to be "dominated" to this extent; yet, for all that, he does not believe that the future of literature will be to describe the isolated individual. The only subject that seems appropriate to him for the tragedies to come is, precisely, the action of society on the character of the individual. And, more specifically, this "action" is immediately interpreted by Constant in terms of conflict: it is "the action of society in struggle with man, raising obstacles not only to his passions, but to his nature, or breaking not only his character, his personal inclinations, but the movements that are inherent to all human beings" ("Reflexions sur la tragedie," in *Oeuvres* [1979], 903). The human condition, according to Constant, is a stage on which a battle with unequal arms is being waged: "When man, weak, blind, without intelligence to guide him, without arms to defend himself, is, without his knowledge and without his consent, thrown into the labyrinth we call the world, this world surrounds him with an ensemble of circumstances, laws, institutions, and public and private relations. This ensemble places on him a yoke of which he is unaware, to which he has not consented, and which weighs on him like a preexisting weight" (ibid., 904). We are far from the tranquil fusion of individual and society that Bonald had envisioned.

For Constant, the individual is always a "victim" of society, which pits "a million against one" (ibid., 912–13). Social action replaces, for the moderns, providence in the tragedy of the ancients. The plots of future tragedies that he imagines all move in the same direction. One shows a black slave fighting for his freedom; his adversaries are "those institutions of iron, this regime of blood, these hanging judges, these pitiless masters, this entire arsenal of public force crushing a single miserable man, because his skin is a different color" (ibid., 914). Another tragedy evokes the persecution, torture, and extermination of the Huguenots. A third, an anecdote from the *Memoirs* of Saint-Simon, illustrates the arbitrariness and the violence of royal power, which punishes insubordination by death. Constant is himself impressed by the monotony of his examples, and denies that he always wants to paint society in a dark light. In the only other example that he offers, however, the conflict is no less violent; we simply find in this example a just society fighting against a tyrannical individual.

In all of his reflections on the future of literature, Constant draws together conclusions to which he had come, separately, in his private writings and in his political texts: according to the former, man is necessarily dependent on a social network; according to the latter, he must preserve his independence in relation to political pressures. Here, on the one hand, Constant acknowledges that "this action of society is what is the most important in human life" (ibid., 910); but, on the other, he always sees this relation as a subject for tragedy. Is he correct to view the relation between the individual and society as exclusively tragic? One may not share Bonald's dream of an organic society in which the individual merges with the All, and nevertheless still not adhere to this pessimistic vision. Constant himself, by finding in the freedom of the press a means for the citizen of contemporary states to participate in public life, allowed the perception of the existence of relations to society that are not necessarily tragic. His theory here seems to be lagging behind his practice. Nevertheless, his predictions have been shown to be more accurate than those of Bonald, even if he was mistaken in genre: the works he imagined have indeed been written, but they are novels rather than tragedies.

# 13 / Democracy and Theocracy

A popular magazine hastens to publish sensational photographs of a young woman cut up in pieces; the law intervenes. Is this intervention a concern for the public good or an unacceptable interference with freedom? The state wants to standardize education: is this guaranteeing equal opportunity for all or imposing the lowest common denominator? Is it taking a step toward a totalitarian state or eliminating a privilege of the rich? Should immigrants be granted all rights because they are individuals like everyone else, or should they be given incentives to go home so as to preserve the social and cultural identity of France? Is it acceptable to receive dictator-heads of state in France? Is it appropriate for moral judgment to intrude in relations between countries?

The answers to these questions—and thousands of similar questions—depend, in a democracy such as France, on the place accorded to shared values. Now, there is no consensus on this. Two trends in contemporary thought take diametrically opposed positions. According to some, this place is too great; for others, it is entirely insufficient; we are either too "modern" or not "modern" enough. Since the ideals to which one aspires are conflicting, two radically different solutions are advocated: according to the point of view of which nihilism is the extreme, one must work toward the greatest freedom from any trace of values; according to the "moralist" viewpoint, one must, on the contrary, make every effort to reestablish values that have been unduly shaken up. Both sides, however, criticize modern democracy for not having gone far enough: for some, it is only a police officer without a uniform, moralism in disguise; for others, it is masked nihilism, a hypocritical scoundrel. In each case we are dealing with the implacable logic of "either/or."

Having given an account of democracy's liberal boundary, I now turn to its conservative critics. And we may, in fact, speak of conservatism here, since this criticism always occurs with the praise of an older society, of a state prior to our own, or, especially, of values that at one time played a more important role. Within this very conservatism, several tendencies must be distinguished. These tendencies are often hostile to one another, depending on which models of society they valorize and, accordingly, which periods of the past they admire. One of these tendencies (that of the advocates of the "ancients") deems that it is the political philosophy of classical Greece — the philosophy of Plato and Aristotle — that has produced the most accurate analysis of society and formulated the highest ideal. Another tendency valorizes not antiquity, but the Middle Ages: in this instance it is religious thought, and particularly Christianity, that allows the ideal society to be imagined. It is this latter form of conservatism that I would like to address, using an analysis of the writings of three of its representatives — all "moderns" in the broad sense of the term — but who nonetheless belong to three different historical moments and three different countries. One is our contemporary and known to all: Solzhenitsyn. The second is more familiar to poetry lovers than to political theorists: T. S. Eliot, the well-known author of *The Waste Land*. The third — Bonald — is known today only to historians, but through him we will understand the others better. The portrait I sketch is deliberately limited to the major aspects of their thought.

## Bonald

Directly following the French Revolution, the survivors of the Terror turned a questioning glance on the previous centuries. This horror could not have come out of nowhere: something, in the past society, had paved the way for it. It was therefore deemed necessary to analyze the past in order to find in it the origin of the present evil, especially since the Restoration itself could not simply be a step backward; something of the revolutionary state was being maintained. The questions, then, were the following: must one accept it and, if so, what was its place? These questions preoccupied many authors, among whom one of the most important in France was Louis de Bonald. His position was one of the most extreme: he defended theocracy, or the religious state. There are two aspects of Bonald's thought—one critical, the other constructive—that I would like to address in succession.

According to Bonald, contemporary society—that is, the society that followed the "9 Thermidor," and the one that was outlined by the philosophers of the seventeenth and eighteenth centuries and of which France during the Terror was merely the paroxystic state—was a society that had lost its relation to values. Materialism was to blame, a materialism that encompassed both a preference for material values over spiritual ones and a philosophy that reduces man to a statue, a machine, or an animal and therefore leaves no room for a spiritual principle. Now, the aim of society should not be to "multiply human beings and to obtain for them riches and pleasures but, above all, to make them good and to make them happy" (*Mélanges,* 1:238). The overall deviation from these aims can be broken down into three major traits that characterize this society and to which we can accede through three essential notions that acquired a new status and a new meaning in this society: *individual, freedom,* and *equality.*

## Humanity as Minced Meat

The fact that material values had supplanted spiritual values was the inevitable result of an underlying transformation: individual values had taken the place of social values. For Bonald, it is the preference for "the well-being of the individual that passes, before the preservation of society that remains" (*Principe,* 102). This latter substitution had begun long ago, as the reflections of the philosophers of previous centuries demonstrate. Society is natural to man. The proof of this is the fact that no human being can come into the world outside a community; human offspring, unlike that of animals, is incapable of surviving without the help of others; there are no human beings without a language, and language implies society. Nonetheless philosophers have invented a "natural state" that predates society (thereby forgetting that prior to the state of society there can be no human beings); they have taken pleasure in inventing a social contract, which in turn implies that the parties to the contract—individuals—existed before the contract. In short, they imagined the invention of society by individuals, and conceived society as a voluntary association, which is absurd. The ethical choice in favor of the individual to the detriment of society thus rests on a judgment made about the very nature of man, and which is patently false.

Here is how Bonald expresses this idea (and I have selected one formulation among a hundred):

> The philosophy of the last century [that is, the eighteenth century] only saw man and the universe, and never society. On the one hand, it *made minced meat of*—if I dare use that familiar expression—states and families, seeing neither fathers, nor mothers, nor children, nor masters, nor servants, powers, ministers, or subjects [the last three terms form a classification of Bonald's to which we will return], but only men, that is, *individuals,* each with his own rights, and not *persons* linked to one another by relations [another of Bonald's fundamental oppositions: the person is a being perceived from the point of view of his social function]; it blended everything by trying to equalize everything, and dissolved everything, in wanting to free everything [here we recognize equality and liberty, the consequences of individualist choice]. On the other hand, it offered to our affections only the human race, humanity in its entirety, and it annihilated affections in attempting to extend them beyond the capacity of our hearts and the possibility of our relations. (*Mélanges,* 2:246–47)

Bonald provides no particular argument to support his affirmation of the interdependence of individualism and universalism other than their coexistence in the writings of the incriminated philosophers (in Rousseau's writings, for example).

Thus we find in Bonald's work the idea of human rights as a source of pride for the *"philosophes,"* whereas for him, they signify "desolation and death" (*Législation,* 1:185), since they are really no more than the rights of the individual. Human rights are the only kind of transcendence an atheistic society can offer itself; but this is an illusion, since, at the same time God was rejected, all reference to society was also rejected. If God is dead, then everything is allowed. Bonald expresses this idea as follows: "Men, if there is no God, can do nothing legitimately to one another, and all *duty* toward others ceases where *power* over all beings ceases" (*Législation,* 2:142). The only possible legitimation of social values is the one they secure from God; to obey God is the only way to (truly) respect man.

The individual is thus the common term in two oppositions, one between man and society, and one between man and God, and this guarantees the solidarity between social values and religious values. The Revolution is the end result of the doctrine of human rights. "The revolution began with the declaration of human rights and . . . it will only end by the declaration of the rights of God" (*Législation, 1:250*). It is the result of the "doctrine that substituted the reason of each one for the religion of everyone, and the selfish motives of personal interest for the love of the Supreme Being and the love of one's fellow human beings" *(Pouvoir, 1:494–95)*. The fault lies with Protestantism, which granted each person the right to speak with God in private, without having to account to anyone. The person who has taken one step in this direction can no longer stop himself: "Calvinism thus rejected any hierarchy, and each of its faithfuls is so much his own religious power that Calvinism in the end rejected all other power" *(Principe, 226)*.

Rationalism, or the elevation of reason to the rank of highest judge, is merely the result of individualism and must be condemned along with it; and the same is true for all of philosophy, which is, so to speak, the institutional framework of individualism, and to which one should prefer religion. Philosophy only teaches how to doubt (all evil begins with Descartes); it shakes up rather than consolidates; it raises questions rather than provides answers; and, above all, even when it does provide answers, it does not know how to impose them on mankind. It "only has advice to give, and it retreats if the advice is not followed" *(Lois, 28)*. Philosophy, therefore, and in the best of cases, is suitable only for a few superior minds; it lends itself to "use by a few Platonists," unlike religion, which is "a public form of worship and a popular doctrine" *(Principe, 338)*. Bonald often emphasizes that, because it appeals to individual reason, philosophy is always linked to individualism, both in its content and in its application; religion, on the other hand, is a way of thinking by everyone for everyone. And there is no doubt as to which one is more effective:

> [Reason] can be fixed in two ways, either by elucidating one's uncertainties, or by repressing one's curiosity. But the spirit of all men cannot be illuminated equally, and the spirit of no man can be illuminated entirely; instead, the curiosity of all men may be perfectly and equally repressed. Thus the repression of curiosity, and reason's submission to faith, is a more efficient and more comprehensive way of fixing the spirit of men and of all men. Thus it is more suitable to society, and thus it is *necessary*. This is the battlefield of philosophy and religion. (*Pouvoir, 2:300–301*)

What had begun as a critique of the individualistic presuppositions of contemporary society ends in obscurantism, or an appeal to repression and to the abandonment of the use of reason. How did we arrive at this? By a series of equivalencies whose logical rigor leaves much to be desired. Universalism and individualism are professed by the same authors: but does their concomitance mean the two are identical? Society is the opposite of the individual and God is the opposite of man; but does it follow that every social value is necessarily religious? Protestant individualism favors rationalism. But does this effect have but one cause and this cause but one effect? For, until proof is offered to the contrary, one can criticize individualism without condemning the use of reason. The same is true for the relation between the Revolution and individualism, and, even more so, between the Revolution and philosophy. In each case, is it a matter of an inevitable consequence? In a short allegory, Bonald has the Revolution being born of a union between philosophy and atheism: "This final relationship, which had already been dubious for a long time, became scandalous in the end and was *philosophy's* downfall. . . . Finally, the fatal day arrived, and *philosophy* gave birth to . . . the *Revolution*" (*Mélanges*, 2:278–79). But what if social facts are not born in the same way as children?

## Praise of Intolerance

The second great source of the modern upheaval of values is the ideal of individual freedom, one of the fundamental principles of democracies. The liberals divide human life into two domains, private and public; society, or the state, has the right of inspection in the latter, but not in the former. Now, the entire field of opinion comes under the private domain: the freedom to think, to say what one thinks, to believe or not to believe, and finally to choose certain values or to reject them all. The separation of church and state sanctified this state of affairs; liberalism is thus only one of the consequences of individualism.

It is an unacceptable consequence for Bonald, however, who was already not lenient toward its cause. One of two things is possible: either one judges a matter to be important for the life of the community, in which case it is aberrant to leave it up to individual decision; or one leaves a matter to individual choice, in which case it is something unimportant. Toleration, or the respect for individual choices, is acceptable regarding the color of one's socks, but not in the matter of truth and good. For toleration means indifference: "Absolute toleration, or indifference, is not suited to truth or error, both of which can never be indifferent to the intelligent person. . . . Absolute toleration . . . would only be suited, therefore, to what would be neither true nor false, to what would be of no importance in itself" (*Mélanges,* 1:208). What is more intolerant than the sciences, whose ideal is truth? Should they, in the name of freedom of opinion, forsake trying to discover which among all opinions is the correct one? For Bonald, the same also holds true for religious freedom: it is acceptable only if one has decided beforehand that God is a matter of no importance. "What could be more absurd than to claim that all ways of honoring God are indifferent, even those that are most opposed?" (*Principe,* 343). If one accepts both the Bible and the Koran, isn't it because one is, at bottom, indifferent to the message of truth that both of them claim to contain? One hundred and fifty years later, this idea would be formulated by Simone de Beauvoir in this way: "Truth is unique, error is multiple. It is not by chance if the right-wing professes pluralism." Although de Beauvoir was wrong here, Bonald was not a leftist. The opposite of pluralism is dogmatism, and we may find dogmatism—of this we have ample proof—on both the left and the right.

Bonald concludes that it is not toleration that must be cultivated, but intolerance; not the freedom of opinion, but the search for the truth. The progress of a society consists in eliminating zones of doubt: "Thus, as a society becomes ever more enlightened, there must be in it less absolute toleration or indifference regarding opinions. The most enlightened man would therefore be a man who is the least indifferent toward or the least tolerant *of opinions*" (*Mélanges,* 1:209). "Man is, and even must be, intolerant of all things, of all kinds, which lead him away from the true, the beautiful, and the good" (ibid., 1:215).

There is no room for toleration when it comes to error; this is what Stalin—a distant emulator of Bonald (whom Stalin had surely never read)— would also say: "Calumny and fraudulent maneuvers must be stigmatized, and not transformed into subjects of discussion."

The liberals call for an unlimited freedom of opinion. Would they also accept the promotion of total freedom of action? Most likely they would not, for that would mean the freedom to carry out any crime. Is it, however, possible to separate the two? Is it sheer coincidence that it is precisely the most liberal countries—France and England—in which we find "an overabundance of crimes about which other countries do not complain? Could it be that the license to act is the result of the license to speak and to write?" (*Principe,* 154). We have already seen the illustration of these ideas regarding freedom of the press.

Democracies want to avoid crimes, but they can no longer act on the causes of crimes (freedom of action stems from the sacrosanct freedom of opinion), for they have declared the separation of public and private and, thus, the separation of action and opinion. Their sole recourse is to act directly on consequences, and in order to do so they have been obliged to increase and reinforce laws. *Legalism* is the answer (a desperate one, in Bonald's eyes) to the problem posed by the disappearance of public morality. This answer is insufficient for two reasons. First of all, it replaces moral law, to which one may adhere with one's conscience, with a purely formal law, which one must obey simply because it is the law, and not because it is just. Second, since legislation puts all of its weight behind the regimenting of society, laws necessarily become ever more numerous and ever more restrictive. "Civil law must be extended to all acts when moral or religious law can no longer direct the will" (*Législation,* 1:263). Thinking he is freeing himself, man is in reality devising new chains for himself: despotism is not the opposite of liberalism; it is the logical result of it, as in fact the Terror has proved.

Bonald thus accepts the separation between interior and exterior (between thinking and acting), but not the separation between private and public: he replaces it with a distinction between important and unimportant things; from then on, there are no grounds for claiming individual freedom, except for those unimportant things.

## The Return to the Savage State

The final trait of modern societies that leads to the effacement of values is their egalitarianism. Everyone has the same rights, everyone belongs to the same social body, there is no longer any distinction made among different social *persons.* The same is true for the family where, under the influence of Protestantism, one tends to acknowledge that women and men have the same rights (the right to divorce). Values therefore no longer have any social existence.

Now, true equality is obviously impossible both because human beings are not all equally gifted and because all places in society are not equivalent, nor can they be. In a democratic society there are also those who give orders and those who obey: "Out of so many who are admissible, there can only be very few who are admitted" (*Principe,* 135). Democracy is a society that has banished the inequality, not of customs, but of discourses. The result of this situation is the cult of ambition and envy: those who could have lived happily in their role as private citizens now knock each other down at the gates of public function, and harbor hatred toward their rivals. Democracy therefore brings men closer to the condition of animals, which, in Bonald's terms, is not their natural state but their native state. "Pure democracy is precisely a savage state in which every will, every *power,* every force clashes and fights with all the others" (*Pouvoir,* 1:148). Democracy is a return to a state of the war of everyone against everyone else.

In addition, the truth of egalitarianism — like that of individualism and liberalism — is despotism, revolutionary terror. "Despotism and democracy are, at bottom, the same government" (ibid., 382–83). Their shared characteristic is "the relentlessness with which the people in their revolutions and the despot in his conquests seek to annihilate hereditary distinctions by means of the death or the exile of those who display them" (ibid., 383). The proof of their sameness is also the ease with which one is transformed into the other. If one does not want hierarchical distinctions, one accepts the war of everyone against everyone else, which in turn can only be stopped by tyranny. Today, Louis Dumont expresses the alternative in these terms: "There are two ways to acknowledge . . . the Other: hierarchy and conflict" (*Essais sur l'individualisme,* 261). This is what Bonald called his own "political axiom": "Wherever men necessarily want to dominate with equal will and unequal force, it is necessary for one single man to dominate or for everyone to destroy each other" (*Pouvoir,* 1:160).

## Toward the New Society

Democracy is a *negative* society; it defines itself by the rejection of what had guaranteed the good working order of the old society. "What essentially constitutes the democracy of the moderns is (1) no public religion; (2) no single power; (3) no permanent social distinctions" (*Pouvoir,* 1:213). It is this absence of characteristics to which the terms *liberalism, individualism,* and *egalitarianism* refer. Bonald's constructive program therefore consists in the restoration of three things: hierarchy, unity, and public morals.

First, hierarchy: for Bonald, society is not a collection of individuals, but a system of necessary relations, an order, and one could compare it to a vault, where each stone has a different place — superior or inferior — with a key to the vault at the top, which ensures the stability of all the elements. This allows Bonald to make this rather pompous statement: "Society is a bridge erected across the river of human passions, on which man must pass in order to arrive at eternity" (ibid., 176). Of what does this hierarchy consist? It is the same everywhere, in the natural world as well as the social world, and it is composed of three elements: cause, means, and effect. This results in three social persons (the three functions?) called power, minister, and subject, which translate, in public society, as king, functionaries, and people and, in the family, as father, mother, and child. Woman, in fact, is not man's equal, neither in mind nor in physical strength, but she must nevertheless give orders to and instruct the child; one could therefore call her a "man-child." "Man is to woman as woman is to child" (*Principe*, 104). Woman is the middle term both in her role as instrument and in her nature as intermediary power. The ideal society, the "most perfect model of society" (*Législation*, 3:64), nonetheless remains the army, with its strict hierarchization of general, officers, and soldiers.

Next, public morality: the law must not be separate from morality, as we have seen, nor from politics: "Good politics is great morality, public morality, as opposed to morality in the strict sense, which is private morality" (*Mélanges*, 1:151). The government's obligation is to promote moral principles that must then be in every manifestation of social life. The sciences are not excluded, and Montesquieu's error was to have thought they could be: "It is time to provide or to recall the *reason* laws exist, and to seek not so much the spirit of what is, but the reason for what should be" (*Législation*, 1:248). Now, there is no morality other than religious morality, and the best religion is Christianity. The proof of this last assertion may be found, for Bonald, in the fact that Christian societies are the most powerful: "Christianity, taken as a whole, is the strongest, and even the only strong, political society, because Christianity is the truest, or even the only true, religious society" (*Principe*, 321). "Where there is strength, there is right [*raison*]." No doubt without realizing it, Bonald begins to deduce what must be from what is, thereby contravening his own principles.

Finally, unity: this is one of Bonald's veritable obsessions. Monocracy — that is, unity of power, or monarchy — must be preferred to democracy. "There is no truth for man nor salvation for society outside of religious and political unity" (*Lois*, 40). And since there is only one law that is good, it must be the same for all countries: "The principle of one society cannot be different from that of another, since man is the same in every society" (*Pouvoir*, 1:151). Unity must prevail everywhere, even in the arts. Bonald's own method is the faithful reflection of this imperative. This is why he attempts to unify all hierarchies, which, moreover, he equates with the three grammatical persons, or any other tripartition; he values "vertical" distinctions as much as he refuses those that are merely "horizontal." "Unity, unity, unity," he exclaims (ibid., 3:11). It obviously follows that one must abandon the separation between church and state. "This impossible separation is the great error of the Age of Enlightenment" (*Principe,* 343). On the contrary, "the most perfect society is the one in which the constitution is the most religious" (*Législation,* 2:133). Such is the ideal of theocracy.

One can see this procedure applied to education. One must first distinguish between *education,* which instills values, and simple *instruction,* which is content to transmit knowledge: "Instruction forms scholars; education forms men" (*Mélanges,* 2:163). This opposition is carried over into the one between civility and civilization; their opposites are ignorance and barbarity, which also must not be confused. Only theocracy is capable of education; democracy is content with instruction. This is why, seeing only instruction around him, Bonald cannot stifle his regrets. True education does not necessarily include a large dose of instruction. "One must not think that it is absolutely necessary for the happiness and well-being of the people to know how to read and write. . . . Good laws, and a firm and vigilant government, that is what all men need" (*Législation,* 2:133). One would also refrain from a too-intensive teaching of the natural sciences, which are not very useful for the running of society, and which unfortunately teach others how to seek and question the truth by individual means: "One does not send a child to school so that he will doubt, one sends him so that he will know" (ibid., 3:78). And even that is saying too much, for the only thing that he must know is how to obey: "Obedience above all . . . for that is an advantage to which no other can be compared" (ibid., 3:100). Another restriction has to do with women: because they are destined to family life, they must not receive public education. The little girl loves her dolls, the little boy, his toy soldiers; one need only follow this inclination, and all will be well.

Public education must be total: "Society wants to form man, all of man, so that he may serve it" (ibid., 57). It must not leave room for any individual variation. For this reason, schools should be situated outside the cities, thereby removing them from any possible influences of their environment; all of the children will be boarders, and the parents will be able to visit them only at regular intervals, and never for long. Bonald's ideas here are not far from the image of public education that one finds in Rousseau's

*Considérations sur la Pologne* (Considerations on Poland), and which we could easily label as totalitarian. Bonald's other imperative requirement is—as one can surmise—uniformity, which he demands absolutely in everything, as one can see from these pitiful words, where the accents of his incensed voice may still be heard:

> There must be, in public education, perpetuity, universality, uniformity, the same clothing, the same food, the same instruction, the same distribution of work time and rest time, the same schoolteachers, the same books, the same exercises, uniformity in everything for everyone, in all times and in all places, from Brest to Strasbourg, from Dunkirk to Perpignan. (*Pouvoir*, 2:23–24)

## T. S. Eliot: From Protestantism to Fascism

An Englishman of American origin, Eliot was neither a philosopher nor a scholar, but a poet and an essayist. His contribution to the debate in question, however, deserves attention for several reasons. First of all, his precise and laconic prose is in pleasant contrast to Bonald's prolixity; and one can imagine—even if it is slightly unjust to do so—that this prose will still be read when the names of more profound philosophers and more rigorous scholars have long been forgotten. Also, Eliot enjoyed immense prestige during the second quarter of the twentieth century, especially in the English-speaking world; his reputation as a poet assured him a large audience for his nonpoetic writings. Finally, the essay I would like to comment upon, *The Idea of a Christian Society,* was written in a significant context, and it bears the mark of that context. It was begun right after the Munich Accords, and was published a few days after the declaration of war between Germany and England. Thus this context has a name: the confrontation with fascism.

The following question underlies Eliot's reflections: given that fascism is evil, what type of society is most radically opposed to it? The answer, reduced to the basics, would be, not democracy, but theocracy. Rather than a critique of totalitarian society (a critique Eliot considers to be more or less self-evident), his book represents an attack on democracy.

His grievances against states such as England are familiar by now. The idea of liberty, the cornerstone of democracies, is a purely negative idea: it signifies that the individual is liberated from a certain number of social constraints. From this viewpoint, democracy has no positive content; it is characterized by an absence of characteristics and could be qualified as a

"Neutral Society" (44). This is why everyone—even the champions of totalitarianism—can appeal to democracy without running the risk of being contradicted. In addition, democracy is subject to a materialistic ideal: the desire for wealth and personal prosperity is the only one we know, and our world is dominated by money and economic values; so-called democracies are, in fact, "financial oligarch[ies]" (48).

This liberalism and this materialism have their common origin in Western individualism, in the destruction of the "traditional social habits of the people," and the dissolution of "their natural collective consciousness into individual constituents" (49); in the flattening out of all the intermediary entities, founded on family ties, common origin, milieu, or religion—an action that results in the production of a "race of spiritual nomads" (146), of atomized individuals. The trouble with individualism, as Bonald had already said, was that it had "made minced meat" of society. Unity was renounced in favor of (individual) diversity, even in matters as important as faith; and Eliot bitterly notes the progression around him of those who "maintain that unity is a matter of indifference" and that "a diversity in theological views is a good thing to an indefinite degree" (71). When such individuals assemble, the result is no longer a community, but a mob, that is, the ideal prey for demagoguery.

Another undesirable consequence of individualism is, according to Eliot, the demand for equality, extended to each member of society. Because they are so carried away by their condemnation of fascism, English democrats even criticize its positive aspects, for example the restricting of women to the "three Ks": "Küche, Kinder, Kirche." "Might one suggest that the kitchen, the children, and the church could be considered to have a claim upon the attention of married women? Or that no normal married woman would prefer to be a wage earner if she could help it?" (85). It is not that all those who defend democracy publicly also do so in private: liberal sexists are just as numerous as the others. But one can criticize them for their inconsistencies, whereas Eliot himself remains consistent. In the same way—even though he claims to be hostile to the Vichy regime—he must maintain the superiority of the Pétainist ideal over the ideal of the Third Republic: "The device *Liberté, Egalité, Fraternité* is only the memorial of the time of revolution: Famille, Travail, Patrie has more permanent value" (139).

All of these critiques of democracy share a common goal: to demonstrate the close relation between democracy and totalitarianism. The English democrats content themselves with denigrating foreigners (in this case, Germans and Russians), without bothering to question their own faults.

"Instead of merely condemning Fascism and Communism, we might do well to consider that we also live in a mass-civilization following many wrong ambitions and wrong desires" (102). "The difference between the Idea of a Neutral Society" like our own and a "Pagan Society" like a totalitarian society "is, in the long run, of minor importance" (44).

The truth is that, in both cases, we are dealing with a materialistic and petty-bourgeois society. The liberalism of the former *seems* to be opposed to the dictatorship that characterizes the latter; in reality, however, one leads to the other: "Liberalism can prepare the way for that which is its own negation: the artificial, mechanised or brutalised control which is a desperate remedy for its chaos" (49). The liberalism of the former *seems* to be opposed to the collectivism that characterizes the latter; in fact, it is another desperate attempt—and an all the more violent one—to introduce social and even religious elements within a society that has lost them and that is suffering from this loss. The differences that remain, including the one between violence and moderation, are superficial and secondary, because they concern the means and not the ends. Fascism is the distant but certain end result of the initial attack against the Christian church that individualistic and liberal Protestantism represents.

It is impossible to condemn the essence of fascism from a democratic standpoint: we must content ourselves with expressing our aversion to it, without being able to justify this aversion. What, in fact, do we object to in fascism? "The fundamental objection to fascist doctrine, the one which we conceal from ourselves because it might condemn ourselves as well, is that it is pagan" (52). "Both Fascism and Communism have fundamental ideas which are incompatible with Christianity" (102). They can therefore not really be condemned from the position of a neutral society, such as democracy, but only from that of a Christian society.

If it does not evolve as a Christian state, democracy will inevitably slide toward totalitarianism. "If you will not have a God (and He is a jealous God), you should pay your respects to Hitler or Stalin" (82). Eliot's thinking here evolves in constant agreement with the law of the excluded middle. "The only alternative to a progressive and insidious adaptation to totalitarian worldliness for which the pace is already set, is to aim at a Christian Society" (52–53). This route will not be easy to follow, "but here as hereafter, the alternative to hell is purgatory" (55). In other words, in order to escape totalitarianism once and for all, democracy must be replaced by theocracy, and the disastrous separation of church and state must be abolished. The religious and the secular, the sacred and the profane must no longer constitute two autonomous domains; religion is something much too important to be left to individuals to decide. "The task of the Church is to Christianize the State and society" (158).

Let us again take the familiar example of education in order to illustrate this transformation. Eliot follows Bonald in opposing instruction to education, the pure acquisition of knowledge to the gaining of wisdom, which includes ethical values. Instruction begins from the principle that one must "adapt school to life," without asking whether this life deserves being adapted to; instruction wants to avoid any reference to values, and this can lead to monstrous results: a fascist state, for example, attempts to prepare its children to lead a fascist life, and, without reference to values, we have no means to condemn this choice. Education, on the other hand, places its principles and its values above the demands of adaptation; it is based on judgments about good and evil, it rests on "a dogmatic view" (152). One must therefore also criticize the trend that calls for "equal opportunity," without having first asked: the opportunity to do what? Must one be overjoyed if all children have the same opportunity of becoming good SS? The kind of instruction that allows young people to "follow false lights" must be condemned, because teachers "have the responsibility of inculcating the right values" (146). A "quantitative" restriction is added to this "qualitative" advice: because it is not certain that unlimited acquisition of knowledge is good, it may be better to ensure that there is a certain "availability" in the mind of man, so that we can then devote ourselves to more important things than the natural sciences — to religion, for example. Our society is suffering not from a lack of education, but from too much education, or rather, from too much instruction.

## Solzhenitsyn

Solzhenitsyn does not claim to be a philosopher or a scholar, anymore than did Eliot. His writings on democracy have nonetheless had real impact because of the extraordinary moral prestige of their author. They (in particular his commencement address delivered at Harvard University) represent a very small part of his work, but the positions he defends in them are clearly related to the ideas he develops in his other works.

After having analyzed and stigmatized Soviet totalitarianism, and after having spent a few years in the West, Solzhenitsyn formulated several criticisms of Western democracies. He presents a rather pessimistic discovery as his starting point: the decline of the West, which is no longer a model for the peoples of the other parts of the world. But, on further consideration, there is no reason to regret this state of affairs: the Western ideal in itself was not worthy of much respect.

The criticism Solzhenitsyn levels against Western society could appear somewhat banal today. Western egalitarianism leads only to a situation in which "mediocrity triumphs" (*The World Split Apart,* 19), but that is not the worst; the damage caused by liberalism is even worse. The most striking characteristic of democracy is "an almost unlimited freedom in the choice of pleasures" (15), "a boundless liberty... for the satisfying of one's passions," and, thus, a way of relieving the individual of any social constraint. Yet such an interpretation of freedom is purely negative and cannot resolve any social problems. On the contrary, it creates others: Solzhenitsyn comments, as Bonald had previously, that there is more crime in democratic states than in others; he adds that freedom creates favorable conditions for violence, pornography, and drug dealing.

And just as Bonald did not accept opposition unless it was opposition to evil, Solzhenitsyn recommends distinguishing between "the freedom for good deeds and the freedom for evil deeds" (19), and the granting of the former only; in other words, he subordinates the idea of liberty to the idea of good. In the same way, one must prefer truth, which is single and unique, to diversity and pluralism.

> If diversity becomes a supreme principle, one can no longer speak of universal values.... If there are neither true judgments nor false judgments, man is no longer bound by anything. Without universal foundations, there can be no morals. "Pluralism" as a principle sinks into indifference. (*Nos pluralistes,* 10)

Isn't the goal of science truth, rather than the diversity of opinions? The enlightened person is intolerant.

Western society is an amoral society. Nonetheless, it must defend itself from evil. Its solution to the problem, as Bonald had already remarked, is the recourse to legalism, that is, the constant reference to formal and positive law, without any thought for natural law: "A society based on the letter of the law and never reaching any higher fails to take advantage of the full range of possibilities. The letter of the law is too cold and formal to have a beneficial influence on society" (*The World Split Apart,* 17). This does not mean that we must renounce positive law, but nor must we be content with "soulless" legalism (35), particularly since this law protects the good and the bad indifferently; and Solzhenitsyn is not at all convinced that we must have so much regard for "terrorists' civil rights" (21). To this one could object that, once the terrorists have been sentenced, they lose their civil rights; but as long as they have not been found guilty, we cannot know if they are terrorists or innocent people.

Like Bonald, Solzhenitsyn uses the "freedom of the press" as his main example of the abuse of freedom. "Freedom" of the press is, in fact, as we have already learned, an abuse of the term: one claims to be asking for freedom of expression; in reality one gets the right to impose one's point of view, thereby depriving others of their freedom. "The press can act the role of public opinion or miseducate it" (25). There is no control over the choice of journalists, who enjoy their privileges thanks solely to the financial power of their newspaper; they were neither elected nor appointed. The state, once again, is powerless.

The other major reason for which Western democracies must be condemned, according to Solzhenitsyn, is that they obey the logic of individualism and materialism, which are inseparable. The Western ideal reduces society to a mere commodity for the individual: "Man lives in order to be free and pursue happiness" (13). Under these conditions, it comes as no surprise that no individual wants to give up the least part of his personal well-being in order to better defend the common good. But this state of affairs is equal to a return to the savage state, to natural independence, and to the rule of "every man for himself." Solzhenitsyn sees the proof of this in the numerous crimes that occurred after the great New York blackout: once fear of the police disappears (because they cannot see), everyone follows his passions and desires without restraint, plundering and raping. "The smooth surface film must be very thin!" (37).

Replacing good with individual happiness is merely the first step; and the second—the reduction of this happiness to the mere satisfaction of material desires—follows quickly in its wake: "the possession of material goods, money, and leisure" (15). Today, "state systems [have become] ever more materialistic" (51).

According to Solzhenitsyn, if the Middle Ages suffered from excessive contempt for man's physical nature, modern times are suffering from a comparable excess, but in the opposite direction: the trampling of "our integral spiritual life" (59). It is therefore necessary to return to a "new Middle Ages" (to use the title of a book by Berdiaev) that, without going to the extremes of the preceding one, would recapture its lofty ambitions.

These diverse characteristics of Western democracies have a common origin. At the "very root" of modern evils we find the philosophical concept that holds a dominant position: it could be called "rationalist humanism" or "humanist autonomy," which proclaims and carries out human autonomy in relation to any power placed above it; or it could even be called "anthropocentricity — with man seen as the center of all" (49). The initial error was to have wanted to imagine the world without God and to make man the standard for everything. It is Western humanism, born with Descartes and developed to its apogee during the Age of Enlightenment, that is the main cause of our current decline. The moment has come to reject the Enlightenment's legacy and to recognize in God the guide to our actions on earth.

If we do not do this, we will be heading straight for totalitarianism. Just as Bonald saw the truth of individualism in the Terror, and Eliot saw this same truth in fascism, Solzhenitsyn sees the West and the East as afflicted by a similar disease (57). The related symptoms are numerous: in both East and West there is the same absence of freedom, even if it is the result of censorship in the East and of the tyranny of fashion in the West. In both East and West, spiritual life is crushed: "It is trampled by the party mob in the East, by the commercial one in the West" (57). It is no accident that Western intellectuals are all more or less champions of the Soviet model. What is the cause of these visible symptoms? Materialism, rationalism, humanism. "These two worlds are atheist and not so foreign as that to one another" (*Message d'exil*, 29).

There is only one true alternative to totalitarianism: a return to a Christian state, to theocracy. Solzhenitsyn calls for the reestablishment of public morals: if the West is weak today, it is because it is lacking these morals, and because it has accepted the separation of law and morals, and especially the separation of politics and morals. This is what is making "space for the absolute triumph of absolute evil in the world" (*The World Split Apart*, 39). And morals can only come from religion. The West has "finally achieved the rights of man, and even to excess," and has demonstrated by this the impossibility of a purely human ethics; instead, it should have maintained its "sense of responsibility to God and society" (51), terms that, as in Bonald's thinking, go hand in hand. "The truth in the universal flow is single and unique; it comes from God. . . . To seek the just point of view, to approach the truth of God" (*Nos pluralistes*, 11): the two expressions are perfectly synonymous.

As for the practical side of the theocratic state, Solzhenitsyn does not bother with it. Nevertheless, one can get an idea of how he perceives it by the way he presents what he calls the "reasonable wishes formulated by the new emigration" (*Nos pluralistes,* 44) (the Russian Jews who emigrated to the United States). Here are some of these wishes: "To limit the interference of public opinion in government affairs; to reinforce administrative power at the expense of parliamentarianism; . . . to rid the police of the obstacles of excessive legislation; to ease the judicial proceedings of the Homerica/formalism of defense, once the guilt of the criminal has been established; to stop insisting so much on human rights, and to put the emphasis on the duties of man."

Why, one wonders, did these critics of democracy feel the need to leave their own countries, when their governments seem to satisfy their demands so well?

## A Critique of Moderation: A Middle Ground?

I am overcome by a strange feeling on reading these theocratic critiques of democracy. I often find their critical starting point most convincing, since I also disapprove of a number of aspects of the society in which I live. And yet, as I arrive at the end of their arguments, I disagree with them entirely, and the remedies they propose seem to me much worse that the evil they are meant to combat. Is it at all possible to retain a part of their teachings without being led to the extremes to which they go? Or are their arguments perfectly logical, and am I the one lacking the courage to draw the same conclusions from the same premises?

It may be interesting in this context to take a look at the attitude of theocrats toward what could be called "intermediary" solutions—those solutions that attempt to maintain the democratic ideal while accepting a critical diagnosis of the state of society. There is not much to be found on this subject in Solzhenitsyn who, speaking of the West in general, offers little in the way of detail or nuance: Western intellectuals are "massively" pro-Soviet, and all life in democratic states is characterized by the "revolting invasion of commercial advertising, by TV stupor, and by intolerable music" (*The World Split Apart,* 36–37), all of which are the inevitable consequences of the humanism of the Enlightenment. But this "intermediary" category is definitely present in the thinking of Eliot and Bonald, both of whom unequivocally reject it.

Eliot calls the writers in this category "humanists," thus using the term not, as Solzhenitsyn did, to designate the anthropocentrism of Western philosophy, but rather to refer to a kind of secular morality, the search for transcendence without recourse to divinity; he is thinking here in particular of

the early-twentieth-century American critic and philosopher Irving Babbitt. What Eliot criticizes in humanism is the same thing that Bonald dis-
approved of in reason and rationalism: proposing without imposing. "To
those who mock his advice, he can only say 'do as you like and you will
see'; after which he has the cold consolation of remarking: 'I told you so' "
(*Christian Society*, 153). Humanism helps to raise questions, but offers no
answers. It simply says: seek! rather than: here is what I have found. Humanists have too many solutions to be able to choose firmly between them;
the result is necessarily eclectic. In one respect, therefore, it is identical to
the materialism of which it wanted to cure us, but this is essential and it results in the confusion of the two: "You can not make humanism itself into
religion" ("The Humanism of Irving Babbit," 280). The attempt at media-
tion has failed.

Such an attitude of doubt, of questioning, and of moderation could
perhaps suit some superior minds, but it is a "state of mind of a few persons in a few places at a few times" (278–79), and it has no role to play in
history. For what matters to the "masses" is not the ability to question but
the security of answers. The masses cannot tolerate the state of doubt. Therefore one must instead opt for "the power of influencing the mass of humanity and of leading it to what is just"; one must "change the will of those
who worship false gods" (*Christian Society*, 153). And now I myself begin
to see similarities behind the oppositions, and to hear in this voice the
tone, if not of the totalitarian master, at least of the Grand Inquisitor.

As for Bonald, he is on principle opposed to any effort to mediate between choices that seem to him to be absolutely contradictory. Moderation
or neutrality, he finds, are more dangerous than the opposite pole of truth,
since they do not announce themselves openly. Truth "fears outright enemies less than neutral parties" (*Mélanges*, 2:345), and one can console oneself by thinking that "this neutrality is no more in the French spirit than
the neutral gender in the French language" (ibid., 2:111). Bonald's thought
proceeds in strict oppositions, from which a third alternative is always excluded. "Truth is always absolute, is always only in one extreme or the
other" (1:91). The New Testament is also on his side: whosoever is not
with me is against me. Nevertheless, there still exist moderate people, or
rather, intermediate, average people — that is to say, mediocre people — who
attempt to reconcile opposites. In religion, this tendency to unite fire and
water, theism and atheism, is called deism: an absurd idea because it is impossible to find the middle term between the presence and the absence
of God, just as it is impossible for "thought to conceive of a middle term

between *yes* and *no,* between being and nothingness" (ibid., 1:92). In philosophy, the middle ground gave birth to a new philosophical school in the early nineteenth century: eclecticism (for example, that of Victor Cousin), an attempt to retain the positive aspects of both materialism and spiritualism. The flaw Bonald finds in eclecticism is the same one that Eliot saw in humanism: eclectic ideas, if followed, "would create only a population of scientists, who would have nothing fixed in their dogmas, nothing certain in their beliefs" (*Principe,* 21). Yet this is not what people want, nor what the noble spirit appreciates: "It is to a school that knows, or that thinks it knows, and not to a school that is seeking and that will always seek, that a superior mind can attach his name and his flag" (ibid., 8). But is the man with the flag, in fact, a superior man?

Finally, in terms of political regimes, the search for a compromise leads to democracy, which lies halfway between monarchy and anarchy. It is therefore not surprising to discover that the instigators of democracy were deists (Voltaire and Rousseau) and that its defenders, in Bonald's days, were eclectics. The main thing, however, lies elsewhere, and that is that the truth of the middle term is negative. Democracy inevitably leads to anarchy, just as eclecticism leads to materialism and deism to atheism; the extreme and the moderate already have in common the capacity to do without God and to put in his place the individual person, endowed with reason alone.

## Living on the Second Floor

Thus, the middle ground does not exist, at least if one takes the theocrats at their word. Yet when one reads their writings, it seems that they arrive at this conclusion by means of deduction that is less than rigorous. We have already seen some of their methods, all of which work in unison toward the same goal: a maximalization of every position and a flattening out of plurality into binary choices. Sometimes it is the law of the excluded middle that is applied indiscriminately: to use the terms of logic, they confuse "contrary" and "contradictory"; they constantly impose the necessity of thinking in alternatives. At times the presence of a common trait leads to identification, as in the case of metaphor or "transduction" (reasoning by analogy). You say A, your adversary immediately concludes from this that you think B, C, and so forth, up to Z. Everything is already caught up in the mechanism. Yes and no, being and nothingness, are perfectly opposed in language; in the world, as everyone knows, countless transitions between the two extremes exist. It is therefore possible to go through the theocrats' reasoning with the fine-tooth comb of logic and from the same premises arrive at different conclusions.

Nothing is gained, except perhaps elegance of expression, by reducing all the "isms" to a single one. It is regrettable for material values to be the only ones at work within a society, but this does not mean that the whole body must be cursed (this is not, in fact, what Solzhenitsyn calls for). It is not true that individual values are necessarily materialistic: the ascetic is also an individualist. And individualism is not the same thing as universalism, the love of humanity cannot be reduced to the concern for the self, and generosity is not the same thing as egotism, just as social values are not necessarily religious: there exists a kind of transcendence that is purely human, that can make me prefer the concerns of my neighbors, my community, and even humanity to my own. The exercising of rational thought cannot be reduced to individualism either, even if the former led to the flowering of the latter: through the use of reason, the individual partakes of humanity. Egalitarianism does not signify equality at the start (human beings are not all gifted equally), nor equality at the point of arrival (the highest reward goes to the most deserving), but the possibility of an equal *route,* so to speak, that is, an equality of rights. Children will not have the same rights as adults, of course, but women are completely developed beings and not intermediary beings; they should be able to choose for themselves between the three Ks and a paying career. Liberalism does not signify anarchy because it assumes the existence of private and public zones, the former free, the other regulated.

Reducing "all that" to totalitarianism is even more untenable. Totalitarianism denies the unity of the human race and the equality of all beings by positing that the discontinuities of "race," class, and ideology are irreducible. Despite appearances, totalitarianism is not a monstrous product of rationalism: rationalism implies that one arrives at a consensus by means of rational arguments, by means of dialogue; totalitarianism places scientific discussion beneath authority and demands faith. One does not convince dissidents, one deprives them of their work, puts them in an asylum, or throws them into prison. In Western Europe, those who still believe in this continuity are being taken in by superficial propaganda that attempts to persuade the "masses" that official policy is scientific. On the other hand, the man in the street, in Paris or in London, may think that he is free when in fact his behavior is dictated by fashion in its different forms; it is good to remind him of this, but nevertheless one would not confuse this lack of freedom with the one that exists in a police state; to do so would be to act as if consciousness and will were nothing, and to take from man that which makes him a subject. There is no natural road leading from democracy to totalitarianism.

One must not, however, go to the other extreme and equate theocracy with totalitarianism, even if in places we cannot help but find similarities between the two. Nothing is gained by transforming terms such as fascism, Stalinism, or totalitarianism into mere insults. Today no one escapes the totalitarian label: theocrats accuse democrats of totalitarianism, while Popper (a democrat and an atheist) and Shafarevich (who is orthodox) find Plato at its origin. For Eliot, it is Protestantism; for (prophetic!) Dostoevsky, it is Catholicism. Yet the existence of common traits does not imply identity. The Christian church separates the profane and the sacred from the start, the kingdom of Caesar and the kingdom of God; while it is intransigent about the latter, it has no direct control over the former. This is the boundary that theocracy transgresses by attempting to unite church and state. In modern times, it is an opposition of legal origin—the one between private and public—that has become dominant, partially overtaking the opposition between religious and secular powers. By claiming to govern everything (by eliminating the private domain), totalitarianism upsets this division. There exists therefore a structural similarity between totalitarianism and theocracy, but the comparison must stop there. Christianity regulates consciences and leaves society free; democracy does the contrary. As a result, their opposites cannot be identical either.

It becomes clear, then, that political regimes—not to mention their historical actualizations—are resistant to elegant binary oppositions. Here one must go beyond the problem of logical rigor. Eliot assures us that we only have the choice between hell and purgatory; perhaps this is so: the Terrestrial Paradise is not for us. But then, there is more than one purgatory, and one can legitimately prefer certain purgatories to others. Theocracy cannot be confused with democracy, which cannot be reduced to socialism (let's use this name for the project that has been caricatured in totalitarian states: the two are no more alike than individualism and nihilism, or theocracy and the Inquisition). Each model of society privileges certain elements of social life over others; each model can therefore serve as the starting point for a critique of the others. Conservative criticism of a society dominated by liberalism can be refreshing, for it allows attention to be drawn to the need for transcendent values, just as "socialist" criticism of an individualistic society leads to a little more social justice. Both remind us that there are no human beings who exist prior to society, and that society is not a hypothesis that can easily be bypassed.

The fact that this criticism is salutary is one thing; that it must lead to the replacing of one model by another is something entirely different: instead of the present defects, others — often more serious — suddenly appear. One can, for example, criticize the media's abuse of power. But must one wish for their complete control by the state in order to escape this abuse of power? In addition, the monopoly Solzhenitsyn denounces is an illusion; contradictory opinions may be expressed, as his own example proves. In the end, self-regulation, resulting from various diverse and unforeseeable actions, seems more efficient here, just as it is in the case of the exchange of goods. We can use the example of Solzhenitsyn in another area: moral demands can exist and act within a society, without being taken over by the state and transformed into public morals. Solzhenitsyn himself, who is a mere individual, managed to have an effect on millions of people. One could even wonder if this is not one of the main functions of intellectuals in a democracy: not to serve either power or the revolution, but to keep the ideal of a society alive. And this ideal would make it possible for the negative effects of legalism to be neutralized: Solzhenitsyn is right to remind us that we need a standard by which to judge whether the law is iniquitous or not; those who do not have this standard run the risk of having to reply in the same way as the concentration camp executioners: "I was following orders."

There are both positive and negative elements in theocracy, just as there are in democracy; in individualism, just as in socialism (not necessarily in the same proportion). But is saying this the same as embracing an eclectic ideal, as making constant compromises, as finding advantages wherever one can? Eclecticism may be preferable to dogmatism; but if it lacks coherence, it is not convincing. In order to go beyond, one must first delimit the spheres of application of each principle: this is why the separation of the private and the public is essential, wherein freedom in relation to social constraints corresponds to the former, and the concern for the common good to the latter. And then one must utilize notions such as values, freedom, or equality not as fixed substances, but as regulating principles of behavior that allow us to envision, in each particular case, the hierarchy of their articulation.

The humanist doctrine (and not one particular author or another) already constitutes such an attempt at mediating between various demands; it is therefore inadmissible to reduce it to one of its components alone. Both Bonald's and Eliot's descriptions of this doctrine are sound in many respects. Humanism does not define the content of values; rather it affirms the need to aspire to them. It keeps us aware of them without giving precise instructions; it does not offer answers but teaches one how to look for them. It secures neither dogma nor belief: it indicates a direction, not a point of arrival. Both Eliot's and Bonald's descriptions of humanism are faulty in that they associate it with opportunism or nihilism. Bonald offers us but one alternative: to choose between a society that contents itself with allowing each individual to become rich and to live as he or she pleases, and a society that endeavors to make individuals better in relation to a preestablished ideal. We are not, however, obligated to accept this alternative. We may refuse the idea of a dogmatic good (defined by the church) and nevertheless make the search for good into a regulating principle of life within society.

The same is true of education. Eliot is right to criticize a school whose sole slogan is: adapt more quickly to life. He is wrong, however, to see only one response to this choice: the instillment of good values. One is capable of learning not only knowledge or obedience; one may also learn to think, to examine in a critical way. From this standpoint, one should not bemoan the "overdevelopment" of reason, or "overeducation." Humanist education offers nothing other than "chances," possibilities, and means without a fixed content; but it cannot form future SSs: that possibility has been eliminated by humanism's universalism (from which equal rights for all ensue) and by its rationalism, which favors dialogue and excludes the recourse to force. And here, universalism and rationalism are merely the rules of a method of inquiry, and not hypotheses regarding human nature or the nature of the world.

If we turn a critical eye on society, it is difficult to have a discussion with those who think that everything is perfect in it: the debate calls for a certain shared intuition about the realities around us. This is not sufficient, however: monistic answers (let's go back to theocracy; let's free ourselves of all reference to values) do not facilitate matters either; they reduce an individual to a single one of his or her possible profiles. It is only once one has acknowledged the multiplicity and the diversity of the demands to which we are submitted that the true debate can begin. Yet this does not mean that a conclusion can be reached: the real difficulties begin here, and the problems are never resolved; at most they are elucidated.

All is not for the best in our democracies. They are linked from the start to individualism and do not govern the relations between the individual and society perfectly. They are doubly threatened: on the one hand, the private sphere is whittling away at and finally swallowing up the public sphere, leaving no space for the search for a common good. Second, social norms are progressively penetrating personal life: each individual believes he or she is different, but in reality has the same motives and refers to the same models as everyone else. Distinctions among social roles are diminishing: young and old, rich and poor, women and men are all wearing jeans. In short, social and individual values are not clearly divided; the public space is empty, whereas the individual is nothing more than a member of the crowd. The causes of these transformations are distant, manifold, and difficult to pin down. This does not mean that they cannot be acted on: nothing is socially inevitable.

Montesquieu called this effort to take into account the contradictory demands of the world "moderation," and he believed it to be the greatest of public virtues. In *L'Esprit des lois* he stated, "Political good and moral good are located between two boundaries" (29:1). But he also knew that it was a difficult road that few of his contemporaries had accepted to follow: "I had the fate of all moderate people," he wrote in a letter to the Marquis de Stainville on May 27, 1750, "and I find myself in the position of neutral people, whom the great Cosmo de Medici compared to those who live on the second floor of a house, and who are bothered by the noise from above and the smoke from below."

# 14 / The Debate on Values

I

The second chapter of Leo Strauss's *Natural Right and History* (1953) represents a questioning of Max Weber's ideas on values, especially the role they play in the social sciences. The debate is important, not only because of its subject, but also because of the eminence of its protagonists. Strauss chooses Weber as the most remarkable representative of the social sciences and, through Weber, questions their very project. As for Strauss himself, he is powerfully eloquent and shows great conviction, and one cannot remain indifferent to his arguments. In the following analysis, however, I shall attempt to disregard the exceptional qualities of style and the appeal of these two great men, and concentrate only on the substance of their ideas.

In the first chapter of his book, Strauss takes issue with another failing of the social sciences, what he calls their historicism, and which he sees as the renouncing of transcendent (universal and eternal) categories. According to Strauss, however, Weber commits no historicist sin, since he maintains the difference between historically determined categories and transhistorical categories. The criticism that Strauss levels at him is of a different type: it concerns the status of values. Strauss criticizes two things. The first is linked to social theory: Strauss criticizes the fact that Weber separates

197

facts and values—which Strauss finds inadmissible—and the subsequent attempt to eliminate values from the field of science. The second has less to do with knowledge than with ethics: Weber claims that it is impossible to choose between different value systems, and this, according to Strauss, leads to the worst kind of nihilism. Let us look more closely at the arguments advanced by each of them.

First of all, we must specify that Weber, as presented and interpreted by Strauss, is not calling for the pure and simple exclusion of any reference to values from the field of the social sciences; rather, he admits certain references and brushes others aside. He is careful to distinguish between "reference to values" and "value judgments": the first is a characteristic of the object of the social sciences, which it would be absurd to attempt to eliminate; political acts, psychological behavior, and aesthetic works are all constituted in reference to values, which are part of their identity. Value judgment, on the other hand, belongs to the work of the scholar himself (to the subject, and no longer to the object, of knowledge); and it is this that must be prohibited. The exclusion of value judgment must be further qualified: these judgments are to be suspended during the main and specifically cognitive stage of knowledge; but they will intervene both before and after this stage. In effect, at one extreme, the very questions that the scholar asks of his material are dictated by the interests inherent to society and thus, in the final analysis, by his own value judgments. At the other extreme, this work also leads to values: only on rare occasions does the scholar refrain from making these judgments, even if he is not always aware of it. According to Strauss, this is the case of Weber himself. Finally, in the case of specifically cognitive activity, one must be prepared to turn to value judgments if, for example, it becomes necessary to choose between a norm and a deviation from that norm. "But, Weber argued, the construction of the model and the ensuing value judgment on the deviation from the model are merely a transitional stage in the process of causal explanation" (54).

Weber's thesis can be summarized by saying that he demands not the radical exclusion of values from the social sciences, but rather, a distinction between factual judgment and value judgement, and a nuanced regulation of their relations.

Strauss, for his part, refused to separate fact from value in the field of what is specifically human. Any effort to eliminate value judgments is illusory. "As for the question whether the inevitable and unobjectionable value judgments should be expressed or suppressed, it is really the question of how they should be expressed, 'where, when, by whom, and toward whom'" (54). Up until this point, the disagreement between Strauss and Weber is not substantial: as we have seen, Weber also believes that value judgments are inseparable from scientific activity. It is from this point on, however, that their positions diverge. According to Weber, these judgments are necessary at a certain stage or in relation to a certain aspect of this activity, and they must be suspended at other moments. Strauss's position, however, is more radical. Such a suspension, even if temporary and partial, seems impossible to him, since it is the very distinction between fact and value that is untenable.

In order to form an opinion of the scope of these contradictory theses, let us look at the counterexamples Strauss uses to refute Weber. Weber himself, says Strauss, saw two possible directions for the evolution of humanity: spiritual renewal and mechanical petrifaction; but he refused to make a value judgment about them. This seems absurd to Strauss: "How can we give a causal explanation of a social phenomenon if we do not first see it as what it is? Do we not know petrifaction or spiritual emptiness when we see it? And if someone is incapable of seeing phenomena of this kind, is he not disqualified by this very fact from being a social scientist, just as much as a blind man is disqualified from being an analyst of painting?" (50).

Nevertheless, one could respond to Strauss that he is implicitly, yet constantly, confusing necessary conditions with sufficient conditions. In order to appreciate and understand visual art, one must be able to see, of course; but everyone who is able to see is not, alas, an authority on art. The critic can see like all normal beings; but what distinguishes him from them (and not from the blind person) is a knowledge, a competence, that cannot simply be reduced to vision. The same is true for the sociologist: he has a moral sense, like all other normal human beings; but what makes him an expert is not this shared characteristic, but something more, which we call, rightly or wrongly, his science. The qualities invoked by Strauss are therefore very necessary to the scholar, but they do not constitute him as such (which Strauss implies rather than states outright).

One might also wonder whether the practices of the two antagonists are not in fact closer than their declared intentions. Strauss refuses to subdivide scientific activity into stages, some of which could do without value judgments; nevertheless, he doesn't seem far from admitting such a distinction when he states that one must "first of all" recognize valorized facts in order then to search for a "causal explanation" of them. Weber claims to stop himself before making a value judgment; but can one trust this claim, when the two situations he places in opposition to one another are described as "spiritual renewal" and "mechanical petrifaction"? In such an instance, to say that one is not making a judgment is to use the rhetorical figure of preterition. It must be admitted that Weber, in calling these two possibilities by these names, is not acting scientifically.

The other counterexamples that Strauss uses call for the same kind of remarks. He imagines the following situation: "We are permitted to give a strictly factual description of the overt acts that can be observed in concentration camps, and perhaps an equally factual analysis of the motivation of the actors concerned: we would not be permitted to speak of cruelty. Every reader of such a description who is not completely stupid would, of course, see that the actions described are cruel" (52). This does not mean, however, that by ceaselessly pronouncing the word *cruelty,* one would have proceeded in a scientific manner. Here again, Strauss's position suffers from his extremism: it is true that one cannot get around value judgments in the social sciences, but it is not true that the social sciences may be reduced to value judgments. After having recalled Weber's demand to distinguish between several stages of scientific activity, Strauss ironically states: "As good children, we are then to forget as soon as possible what, in passing by, we could not help noticing but were not supposed to notice" (54). Yet Weber does not want to omit this part of the process of knowledge; he simply does not want to stop there.

From this perspective, Strauss's position seems even more open to criticism than Weber's. Weber, in short, is at fault because he is too hasty, not explicit (or conscious) enough regarding his own practices: his distinction between relation to values and value judgments is too lax, and he does not always abide by his own principles. But he has the merit of having explicitly questioned the relations between facts and values; one can imagine better answers to what would, in the end, remain the same question. Strauss hits the nail on the head when he shows the inconsistencies in Weber's thought; but his position of principle (refusing all distinction between factual judgment and value judgment) leaves us with the impossibility of distinguishing between science and sermon (upon seeing concentration camps, we are satisfied with crying out: cruelty!) or between science and propaganda. This—and it almost goes without saying—is contradicted by Strauss's interpretative practice. In his analyses, he knows perfectly well how to separate the establishing of facts from the value judgments made about them.

# II

The second part of the debate, as I have said, leaves behind the theory of science in order to address the theory of ethics. Weber's thesis, summarized by Strauss, is the following: "There is a variety of values which are of the same rank, whose demands conflict with one another, and whose conflict cannot be solved by human reason" (42). Weber does not deny the existence of transhistorical values; on the contrary, in a certain sense he notes a profusion of them. There are so many that it is impossible to integrate them into a single system; there exists more than one value system, and it is impossible to choose between them: this is what he calls the "war of the gods."

Faced with this impossibility, one cannot demand that human beings conform to true values (these do not exist), but simply that they remain as faithful as possible to a system that has been arbitrarily chosen: "The dignity of man consists in his autonomy, i.e., in the individual's freely choosing his own values or his own ideals or in obeying the injunction: 'Become what thou art'" (44). "Weber's own formulation of his categoric imperative was 'Follow thy demon' or 'Follow thy god or demon'" (45). Human beings will therefore no longer be judged according to the *conformity* of their behavior to an outside and absolute ideal, but only according to its *coherence* with other, equally subjective choices. In defending this thesis, Weber joins a good number of thinkers of the late nineteenth century, representatives of one variation of nihilism or another (in Weber's case, one can easily see Nietzsche's influence).

Nonetheless, the demand of coherence is not sufficient to allow us to choose between two modes of behavior: in effect, individual lives—just like value systems—may be coherent and in the end impossible to compare. Weber goes beyond this atomist notion of humanity; after having refused classical transcendence, he finally introduces another kind of transcendence, which is that of vital forces. It is no longer a question of values in the strict sense of the term, but rather another dimension: the intensity of experience. "At the moment when the 'vitalistic' values are recognized as of equal rank with cultural values, the categoric imperative 'Thou shalt have ideals' is being transformed into the command 'Thou shalt live passionately'" (47). When choosing between two actions that are in equal accord with the chosen value system, one will therefore prefer the action that produces the greatest *frisson*.

Faced with a choice between various value systems, Weber seems to take a neutral position; but this merely appears to be so on the surface; it is, in fact, inconceivable: to claim neutrality in this instance is to take a strong position. For example, he presents the conflict between what he calls the ethics of reponsibility and the ethics of conviction as insoluble. These "two" ethics correspond, at least in their main points, to politics and actual ethics, respectively. In the first case, one acts according to real possibilities, circumstances, and tactical objectives; in the second, one refers only to the ideal of justice in which one believes. But to call each of these two types of behavior "ethics" implies that one presents politics as being an ethics like any other; the two have been placed on equal footing even before comparison begins. One could answer Weber, and justifiably so, that from a moral standpoint there is nothing insoluble about this conflict: a just act is preferable to a useful act. The fact that an individual might hesitate between two different paths—for example, between love of humankind and the defense of the interests of the French—in no way implies that the two value systems are equally respectable; to believe this suggests that one has chosen politics over morals, since morality is no more than one "politics" among others.

The same may be said for the nature of the truth to which we may have access and on which we base our judgments. By refusing to choose between different systems, and, for example, between the system of philosophy and the system of science on one hand, and the system of a religion, on the other, Weber no longer differentiates between truth by reason (*la verité de raison*) and truth by revelation (*la verité de revelation*), or even truth by authority (*la verité d'autorité*). "He contended that science or philosophy rests, in the last analysis, not on evident premises that are at the disposal of man as man but on faith" (71). As Strauss comments, "The mere fact that philosophy and revelation cannot refute each other would constitute the refutation of philosophy by revelation" (75). Symmetry here is once again misleading: if the two are declared equivalent, it is because truth by reason has been reduced beforehand to truth by revelation.

Weber offers two main justifications of this impossibility to choose between different systems. The first is epistemological: he states that reason itself is powerless to resolve such conflicts. But this argument, as we can see, is merely a reformulation of Weber's thesis that leads one to believe that reason and faith are not distinct. The second justification is ontological: Weber believes that "human life is essentially an inescapable conflict" (65). Here we are dealing with a hypothesis about human nature that is not far from the one that teaches us this is a man-eat-man world.

Confronted with this variant of modern nihilism, Strauss's attitude is close to the one he attributes to the ancients, that is, to the classical philosophy of Plato and Aristotle. He believes in the trandscendence of values and in their absolute hierarchy. He does not fail to call to mind that the motto "Become what you are" leads to putting the assassin and the saint on the same level, and that vital forces are, precisely, forces and not rights. As for abdicating before the choice of a system of values, this is like adjusting what should be to what is, and it is unacceptable. "Lest there be peace anywhere, peace must not be simply rejected.... There must be an absolute duty directing us toward universal peace or brotherhood" (65). Here Strauss assumes a distinction between fact and value that he had previously refused.

If Weber's thesis—and, in fact, the ideas of nihilisim in general—is taken to the extreme, it leads to unacceptable consequences, consequences that its partisans do not, in fact, accept, preferring inconsistency to giving up their assumptions. Strauss's thesis is undeniably more accurate; this time, his position is superior to Weber's. And yet the arguments he sets out to support his choice are few: it is as if he could not tell us clearly why we should prefer his point of view to Weber's or, more generally, how we could legitimate the choice of a value.

Already we can see a certain reticence on Strauss's part when he argues against Weber's theses, in particular that of the helplessness of reason: he seems to content himself with stating that Weber did not manage to support it sufficiently. Weber, he writes, "never proved that the unassisted human mind is incapable of arriving at objective norms or that the conflict between different this-worldly ethical doctrines is insoluble by human reason" (70). Strauss, however, does not indicate by what means one may reach these "objective norms." Must we take his word as if it were truth by revelation or by authority? Rather than refuting this thesis, he contents himself with offering a biographical explanation: Weber must have confused religion and ideals; having lost the former, he ceased to believe in the latter. However, even if we were to suppose that this hypothesis were correct, it still does not tell us why Strauss's position is preferable to Weber's.

Strauss speaks favorably of "objective norms." But how do we arrive at this objectivity? He doesn't tell us here, and elsewhere he seems to condemn certain paths that could lead us to it. When he describes the task of the historian, he states that it consists of one stage, and one alone, from which value judgment is absent: this is because before being able to appreciate a human being one must attempt to understand him on his own terms, as that human being has understood himself. However, in the process of such understanding through identification with the other, one suspends as much as possible one's own preferences and even one's own mental categories: "Within the limits of this purely historical and hence merely preparatory or ancillary work, that kind of objectivity which implies the foregoing of evaluations is legitimate and even indispensable from every point of view" (57). First let us note that Strauss agrees with Weber here in the demand to distinguish between several stages in the work of knowledge (*le travail de connaissance*). But if the only truly objective stage of this work is the preliminary accumulation of information, of what can the objectivity of norms — obviously not reducible to historical reconstruction — consist?

One must conclude from this that the establishment of norms is foreign to the work of the scholar; norms must be given to him in advance and from the outside. Thus we can see that, beyond their differences, there is a certain consensus between Weber and Strauss: for both of them, the elaboration of norms is a very different activity from the work of knowledge, and there can be no legitimate debate about the hierarchy of values. It is true that their justifications of this refusal are not at all the same: Weber does not believe that one can ever have access to values; Strauss from the outset positions himself on the side of values and of truth.

## III

Raymond Aron is among those who have contributed the most to introducing Weber's work in France; but he is also one of the directors of the collection in which Strauss's *Natural Right and History* appeared in translation in 1954; the translators thank Aron for his help in their preface. Aron is thus very familiar with the ideas of both Weber and Strauss, and he is aware of their conflict. When in 1959 two essays of Weber's ("Wissenschaft als Beruf" and "Politik als Beruf") appear in the same collection, Aron seizes the opportunity to give his opinion on the debate, adding twenty pages of commentary to his introduction.

The commentary is very dense; I will only mention those aspects of it that touch on the ideas already discussed here. On the first point of disagreement between Weber and Strauss (the distinction between fact and value), Aron is succinct: he notes the imprecision of Weber's vocabulary, but remains sympathetic to his methodology; it is possible to improve his words without betraying his thought, and to overcome thereby Strauss's objections. It is the second point that interests him in particular, that of the possibility or impossibility of choosing between several value systems. He adopts Strauss's thesis—the affirmation of an absolute hierarchy of values—all the while bringing to it an additional kind of legitimation; this is also Aron's principal contribution to the debate. He arrives at this legitimation by reexamining the question from the ground up. Weber, as we have seen, justified his refusal to choose between systems with two arguments: the powerlessness of reason and the conflictual nature of life. Aron then applies himself to refuting these two explanations but from a perspective different from Strauss's, whom he criticizes for not demonstrating clearly "what is in itself the best regime, nor how reason manages to make explicit its traits and to base universal validity upon it" (*Le Savant et le politique,* Introduction, 31).

If Weber could affirm the powerlessness of reason, this is because he had given it too narrow, and too "strong," a definition from the start; it was easy afterward for him to claim its absence here and there, and especially from the choice between different value systems. In fact, he interprets reason and the truths it can establish in a way appropriate to the natural sciences. Since ethical choices do not belong to these sciences, they are relegated to the realm of the arbitrary, of personal preference; after that one can hierarchize them in a new way, according to the intensity of the experience or the vigor of vital forces. One must, therefore, begin by rehabilitating reason outside the domain of logicomathematical argumentation, and refusing the Manichaean division between "scientific rationality" versus "personal arbitrariness."

In order to get out of this impasse, Aron raises the following question: of what does the strength, the superiority, of scientific reasoning consist? His answer is, it aspires to universality, to autonomy in relation to surrounding circumstances. On this, more abstract level of the analysis, a bridge can be extended between science and ethics, since ethics, in its turn, is founded on universality:

> Even if we admit that logically the truth of "$2 \times 2 = 4$" is not of the same kind as "thou shalt not kill," it remains that the final meaning of mathematical equality is addressed to all mankind, a universality that the forbidding of killing gains in another way. The formal rules of rationalist ethics ... are the logical development of the idea of humanity, of a universal society of man, an idea that is inseparable from the profound meaning of scientific truth. (ibid., 40)

The same is not true when one chooses to abide by the principle "live passionately." "The cult of vital values, the affirmation of the will to power
leads to a refusal of universality: rivalry, not community, of individuals would
be the essence of humanity" (ibid.).

Contrary to what Weber believed, values cannot all be put on the
same level: one cannot say that faith in the equality of men "is equal to"
the cult of force. This was also Strauss's position. Where Aron differs
from Strauss, however, is in the way he legitimizes this choice: superior
values are not given as an absolute but are discovered through reason,
which is thereby based—and here we find again the Weberian respect
for science—on the idea of universality. These values therefore are open
to a debate in which certain arguments are admissible and others are not;
rather than finding their justification in the very nature of things, they
are justified by a human consensus that ultimately encompasses all of
humanity.

We arrive now at the second reason Weber advanced in order to justify his refusal to choose: conflict is the truth of life. Aron would agree
with Strauss's argument that one cannot regulate what should be according to what is. But he attacks another aspect of Weber's reasoning: the
establishing of facts itself. One cannot deny the existence of war among
human beings, in various guises and on differing scales. But just how
broad the sense of this word is meant to be must be specified. If one understands politics to be the defense of the interests of a particular group (party,
social class, nation), one could say that conflict is in the very nature of
political activity: the interest that I have in one group is correlative to the
absence of such an interest in rival groups, or even to an action directed
against the interests of these other groups. Up until this point, Weber is
correct. Things become less clear when he identifies human life in its entirety with politics understood in this way. Human beings do not devote
all their energies to the defense of their group's interests. In addition to,
and sometimes instead of, this concern, they are also involved, on the
one hand, in an interior, private life; and, on the other, in a life where
they judge others, not according to whether they belong to the same
group, but in light of their shared belonging to humanity; such is the
basis of moral life. And so, if "politics is war, universal ethics—that of
Christ or of Kant—...is peace" (Aron, 43). It is therefore not true
that the war of everyone against everyone else is the truth of human
society.

Contrary to politics, which is the defense of the interests of a group, even to the detriment of all other groups, true ethics are universalist and egalitarian. To be in politics means that one accepts — not all the time but at least in extreme cases — putting local interest before the search for truth and justice. "All men of a party are by that alone an enemy of truth," wrote Rousseau (*Rousseau juge de Jean-Jacques,* 965). It follows that the perspective of the scholar (or of the philosopher) is, in its principle, incompatible with that of political man, even if in practice one can successively follow one path or the other. By enlisting in a political cause — whether in the apparatus of the ruling power or in the service of one revolution or another — one can no longer claim to be acting as a scholar or a philosopher: if someone is a great physician or a great thinker, this does not make his political acts either more or less just. This is why "wisdom teaches philosophers not to enter into war" (*Le Savant et le politique,* Introduction, 43).

Because war is not the truth of life, one can reconcile Strauss's aspiration to the absolute and Weber's sensitivity to diversity, without for all that falling into eclecticism. But in order to do so one must reinterpret the two terms of the relation. On the one hand, this absolute must not be understood as a material identity; it only exists on the level of meaning, as an ensemble of categories allowing observable diversity to be made intelligible. "It is not necessary for humanity to subscribe to a single idea of itself in order for it to have unity: it is sufficient that the various ideas it has had of itself are organized in such a way that they do not appear without links or without reason" (ibid., 36).

Having thus modified the status of the essential and the general, we must also revise common ideas on diversity. Pluralism does not mean that all choices are equal, nor that each option has a place within the democratic state: destructive elements or — and it comes down to the same thing — people who want to impose their own model on society as a whole, would be removed. From there, the peaceful coexistence of different conceptions of the world and different interests becomes possible: we do not give up the search for truth, but we do give up imposing on others, by means of force, what we believe to be the truth. The life of human societies cannot be reduced to war on the outside and class struggle on the inside. Weber was wrong to transform phenomenal diversity into a "war of the gods" — all the more so since this philosophy, which is inadequate as a vision of the world, can become in its turn an incitement to conflict.

Aron thus removes, one after the other, the illusory obstacles Weber raised on the path to knowledge of mankind, without, however, giving up Weber's scientific project. Without ever confusing science and sermon, he shows the way to maintain the link between science and ethics, and to resist the unceasing attacks of nihilism.

# Modern Gadflies

Subjects such as conquests, colonialism, racism, democracy, and even truth carry considerable emotional weight. What must one do when studying them? We have gotten in the habit of opposing, in this regard, the man of science and the man of action. The attitude of the former is well known: he observes and comments, avoiding making any judgments; the "emotional weight" in question is thus unknown. The attitude of the latter is completely different: I know on what side of the barricade I place myself; I participate in demonstrations and I sign petitions; or, if my temperament is less bellicose, I devote part of my time to literacy classes for foreign workers. But this is precisely where the problem lies: I only tend to these things during my free time, along with and outside of my main activity. Like everyone else, I can take part in actions to benefit one mistreated group or another, but what I do the rest of the time is unrelated to this: it is not because I am, in my so-called private life, a historian or a sociologist, that my militancy is in any way different from anyone else's.

These two activities — scholarly and political — of one and the same person, suffer equally as a result of being isolated from each other. But is it possible to imagine a relationship between the two other than alternation (scholar from nine to five, militant from five to nine)? It is, provided that we accept in addition the existence of a third role, which I call by an ambiguous if not devalorized term: that of the intellectual. I would like the word, this time, to resound with the necessity — for the specialist of the human spirit and its creations — of making the values underlying his or her work, and their relation to the values of society, explicit. The intellectual is not, as such, a man (or woman) of action: even if he "acts" elsewhere, it is not because of his work for the government or his underground battle that he is an intellectual. The man of action starts with values that, for him, go without saying; the intellectual, on the contrary, makes these values the very object of his reflection. His function is basically a critical one, but in the constructive sense of the word: he compares the particular that each of us experiences to the universal, and creates a space in which we are able to debate the legitimacy of our values. He refuses to see truth reduced either to

209

the pure adequation of facts that the scholar demands or to truth-revelation (*verité de revelation*), the faith of the militant; rather, he aims for truth-disclosure (*la verité de dévoilement*) and a consensus toward which one moves by accepting self-examination and dialogue.

I therefore perceive a goal shared by the arts and the human sciences (or, if my reader has stayed with me until now, by the moral and political sciences), which usually practice such different forms and dicourses: to reveal and, eventually, to modify the network of values that act as regulating principles in the life of a cultural group. Artists, like other specialists of what is human, do not really have the choice of whether or not to situate themselves in relation to this network, inasmuch as it is in the very nature of their project to bring to light an unknown side of human existence, which in turn could not be conceived outside of the relation to values. But, once they have become aware of this inevitable relation, they can assume it with more responsibility than if they remained unaware of its existence. In his book *The Captive Mind,* Czeslaw Milosz writes that many Polish nationalists discovered with horror how the anti-Semitic stance they had adopted out of bravado before the war was transformed, during the Nazi occupation, into material facts, that is, into human graves. It is in order to avoid this belated awareness and the horror that may accompany it that artists and scholars should immediately take on their role as intellectuals, their relation to values: they should accept their social role.

This image must be made somewhat more specific; and for questions about the role of intellectuals to be worthwhile, one must first eliminate some of those responses that immediately come to mind, but which all tend to end the debate before it has begun.

First of all, one must eliminate the purely determinist idea of intellectuals, according to which this social group, like all other groups, can have but a single function, that of the defending its own interests or, more generally, the interests of the class to which it belongs. If, for example, one claims that intellectuals are necessarily bourgeois and that, as such, they can only express bourgeois ideology, the question is quickly resolved; yet for all that, no light is shed on it. In reality, such a conception of humanity is itself unacceptable, since it denies the fact that, above and beyond the various determinisms to which human beings are subject, they are characterized by the possibility of exercising free will, and of making choices for which they take responsibility; in short, human beings are moral beings. If this is true of all human beings, it is even truer of intellectuals whose nature it is to tear themselves from their specific condition and to judge the world with criteria that are other than self-seeking. In a book one is bound to encounter if one takes an interest in this question, Paul Bénichou writes: "Man is made in such a way that he puts himself at a distance in order to reflect on his behavior in light of absolute values: there would be no intellectuals were it otherwise. . . . Their autonomy within society is the very one from which thinking benefits in life" (*Le Sacre de l'écrivain,* 19) — that is to say, that autonomy is incomplete, yet irrepressible.

In addition to this causal reduction (whose Marxist variant is the one most often practiced), there is another, symmetrical, one that reduces the function of the intellectual to one of immediate utility; in this view, the end dictates behavior with the same rigor that causes did in the other conception. Here, it is not a matter of excessive determinism, but of hyperfunctionalism. If one must refuse this second reduction, it is not because such situations of direct utility do not exist; but they are marginal rather than central, and therefore do not advance us a great deal. Two cases must be distinguished here. In the first, it is the intellectual himself who uses his mental skill for his own advantage, in order to increase his wealth and his power. This figure has been familiar to us since Plato's caricature of the Sophists, according to which they used their eloquence first to win their trials, whatever the actual responsibilities, and then to secure political power, or at least the benefits it entails, because of their ability to work the crowd during public meetings. We can all easily supply contemporary counterparts to these figures.

In the second case, it is society, or one of its outgrowths, that puts intellectuals directly in the service of its goals. Thus thinkers, scholars, and artists may undertake to contribute to the victory of the revolution, that is, the victory of an ideology that at the moment is not in a position of power but aspires to one (variant: Pol Pot enrolling in the Sorbonne). Or, if it is the state itself that employs the intellectuals, it can turn them into well-paid, official poets of the authoritarian regime that it sets up, of the doctrine it follows, or of the dictator who leads it. In other circumstances, intellectuals become specialists, ministers, or advisers to the president. Yet in so doing, they forsake their identity as intellectuals, since their actions can no longer be said to be guided solely by the search for truth and good. This is what Bénichou calls "the cross of the Man of Letters": "Inclined to dream of a society constituted and governed by an Idea, he is never in such a miserable position as when his dream comes true. The free exercise of thought — in other words, its exercise *tout court* — and its incarnation in power, these two natural demands of modern intellectuals are cruelly contradictory" (*Le Sacre de l'écrivain*, 63). During the French Revolution, had philosophers been solidly entrenched in power, a paradoxical situation would have arisen: there would no longer have been any philosophers, for they would all have been exterminated for heterodoxy.

One can, therefore, concede that intellectuals at times express the interests of their professional group or of their class; that, in certain circumstances, they put their abilities in the direct service of their own interests, of the revolution, or of the state. Yet we may also concede that these reasons are not sufficient to allow us to grasp the role of intellectuals, for in each of these cases, freedom — which nonetheless serves to define them — is limited. In order to take one further step, we should cast a quick glance at the recent history of our society and see what it has to teach us in this regard.

It seems that all European societies (and most likely those of other continents as well) recognize the distinction between temporal power and spiritual power. On one side we find the warrior-chief, and on the other the priest. The interrelation between these two powers varies, but it is always great: the emperor secures his legitimacy from the pope, who in turn can be deposed by this same emperor. Spiritual power itself is, in our tradition, either secular or religious, the passage from one to the other coinciding with the advent of Christianity. This state of things existed up until approximately the mid-eighteenth century. Although it is true that during the Renaissance the poets of the Pléiade dreamed of exercising spiritual power themselves, this aspiration had not the least result, and the episode was quickly forgotten. Thus when, in the next century, Malherbe considered "a good poet [to be] no more useful to the state than a good skittle player," he was in no way denigrating spiritual power in general; he was merely acknowledging that this power was in fact reserved for priests rather than for poets.

Things began to change as of the mid-eighteenth century, since the priests were deprived of their role and the position they occupied was left vacant. We have the great good fortune of having at our disposal the exemplary work of Bénichou on the period that began at that time, which he studies in *Le Sacre de l'écrivain* (1973), *Le Temps des prophètes* (1977), and *Les Mages romantiques* (1988). The excellence of this work derives from the fact that Bénichou first formulated the problem and delimited the field, and then explored it in minute detail, without, however, losing a clear view of the whole and, in fact, gaining a certain philosophical loftiness. The "consecration of the writer," anticipated by Enlightenment philosophy, would be achieved by the writers of the Romantic period; one could even say that the minimal definition of Romanticism as a doctrine is the extolling of art as the highest of human activities and the attributing of the role of prophet and spiritual guide to the poet. In order to develop their doctrine, the Romantics drew on the most varied sources: they needed what the liberals had to offer just as much as what the counterrevolutionaries could provide; they needed the illuminists as well as rationalist philosophers. In regard to these latter, one change is particularly remarkable: the philosopher was replaced by the poet.

Unfortunately, Bénichou's inquiry stops in the mid-1800s; yet we also need to recall the more recent past in order to reflect on the role of intellectuals. While awaiting the patient research of other historians, I shall content myself here with a quick sketch of the hundred or so years that have elapsed since.

It must be stated first of all that the taking on of the same priestly role by another actor was a project that was destined to fail; the scenario had changed in the meantime. The poets had hoped to become the priests of modern times; Bénichou remarks that they "were promoted only precisely because there was no longer room for authority in the spiritual domain." This is "the sacerdoce of a time that no longer believes in priests, which only accepts the divine under the benefit of doubt and critical freedom" (*Le Sacre de l'écrivain*, 473–74). It is not surprising that, under these conditions and with some rare exceptions, the Romantics did not concretely achieve their ambition. The bourgeoisie — that is, the readers of the Romantic poets — had its own worries and its own priorities. The events of 1848 and the disappointments they carried with them in particular destroyed many hopes.

At this point, a new phase in the history of this "consecration" began: since no one was listening to the prophet, he transformed himself into an avenger. The emblematic figure of this new attitude was not Victor Hugo, but Flaubert, whose favorite word was "to execrate." Society did not embody the ideals of the writer and did not respond to his appeals. Taking offense, he decided either to stigmatize it, to condemn it *en bloc*, and reject its very essence (nothing but Philistines!); or to pay it no mind and to cultivate the garden of art for art's sake, the disinterested search for the Beautiful. This second phase ·was the reverse of the first, and its bitterness was equal to the hopes that were expressed by the previous generations. The writer saw himself just as much as before at the top of the

214 / *Modern Gadflies*

human hierarchy, but he now rejected society, whereas previously he had wanted to be its guide.

Things changed once again at the end of the nineteenth century with the Dreyfus affair, and it was in fact at this moment that the noun "intellectual" appeared, replacing "men of letters" (since the concept of "letters" or "literature" had in the meantime been reduced to mean writings aspiring to beauty). Writers and artists returned to the "city," passionately taking sides; and, even once the Dreyfus affair was closed, their involvement remained, so that they were at times transformed into simple militants, rather than getting their prestige from their spiritual preeminence. It is at this moment that the phase described by Julien Benda as "la trahison des clercs" occurs. [Richard Aldington, who translated Benda's *La Trahison des clercs* into English as *The Betrayal of the Intellectuals,* nonetheless uses the word "clerk," always in quotation marks, in the body of his translation. I have retained his title, as well as his use of the word "clerk" here. — Trans.] Benda criticizes the contemporary "clerks," not because they have given up their role (the exercising of spiritual power), but because they have radically modified the content of their ideal, substituting specific demands (of nation, race, class) for universal demands, material appetites for spiritual values, intuitive approximations for the rigorous methods of reason. In other words, they have betrayed their identity, which is to oppose the "laymen" (non-"clerks"), and they wind up confusing themselves with them, in claiming a "realistic ideal" — an impossible thing if ever there was one.

Several parts of Benda's 1927 work have retained their power and their relevance today; nonetheless, his selective use of history, as well as certain ideological biases, falsifies his analysis, and most of his predictions never came true. Barrès is the typical "clerk" for Benda, yet he was hardly imitated by the generations who followed (and whom one could not, in point of fact, criticize for their excessive realism). In a certain sense, however, there was indeed a "betrayal of the intellectuals": a betrayal not in relation to a transhistorical ideal (the rejection of practical considerations), but in relation to their society, which was an embodiment, however imperfect, of the democratic and humanist principles that evolved from the French Revolution. This betrayal, which did not occur in the Romantic phase, was anticipated by the generation of "avengers." It consists of the involvement (*engagement*) of intellectuals in different kinds of nationalist, fascist, or communist ideology, all of which are incompatible with democratic principles; Sartre is emblematic in this regard. In this sense the "clerks" — or at least most of them — are opposed to the masses (to the "laymen") in the majority of European countries, rather than being their passive spokespeople, as Benda thought they should be.

Once again, things have changed. One result of World War II was a weakening of European states and their relative marginalization; consequently, nationalism (French, German, Italian) has suffered, and now reappears only in certain specific forms: as, for example, cultural demands, conflicts with non–European countries (colonies), or finally as the ideology of a relatively marginal extreme right. Fascist ideology was definitively discredited following the revelations of the "final solution." It took much longer for the communist dream to be relinquished: despite the millions of victims of the 1930s in the Soviet Union, communism's prestige was enhanced after the war; and neither the macabre trials of 1948–49, nor the repression in Berlin in 1953, nor the crushing of Hungary in 1956, nor even the occupation of Czechoslovakia in 1968, was sufficient to shake this ideal of Western intellectuals (even if the Stalinist model was forced to give way to other variants, whether Trotskyite, Maoist, or Castroite). And yet, 1968 marked the beginning of the end of communism's long reign. The "events" that occurred in May and June in Paris and in other French cities were not, as the protagonists of the time believed, the beginning of a new era but, on the contrary, the swan song of a period that was ending, a farewell: they prepared the end of the hold that "utopianisms" (of the "right" or the "left") had on the minds of intellectuals. With the help of the translation of Solzhenitsyn's writings, the communist ideal has become, in Europe (in France?) an intellectual anachronism, just like fascism and nationalism.

And what about today? It seems that, even before being able to discuss the different roles of intellectuals today, one must defend this role as such. The intellectual is the one who judges the real in comparison to an ideal; if he relinquishes values, if he is no longer interested in the real, he abdicates his very function. This is not a new temptation: it is somewhat like choosing the *vita contemplativa* over the *vita activa*. Tacitus's *Dialogue of the Orators,* to use an example from the ancients, already opposed the orator engaged in the affairs of the city to the poet who "retires to pure and innocent places and tastes the delight of a sacred stay" (*Dialogue des orateurs,* xii). Thus Tacitus's sympathies can be said to lie with the poet. Good reasons for this choice can easily be found: in times of tyranny, retreat is preferable, for the dictator makes his decisions alone in any event; in times of democracy, mediocrity and vulgarity predominate, for such is the taste of the common lot. Isn't it therefore better to retire to some secret tower and devote oneself to the cult of art or of the senses? In our own times, and especially since 1968, individualist principles dominate, and contemplative retreat wears a new mask: up until very recently, writers and thinkers renounced judging others, and preferred to devote themselves to exploring their own experience. The only politics they knew was the politics of desire; the only revolt, the revolt of bodies. This renunciation, however, has been neutralized by the prestige that our consumer society grants to creators. Even when these creators tell us, "I have nothing to teach you," we take it as a precept, and we want to imitate them.

Thus, if we want intellectuals to have a role, we must fight to maintain, to reestablish a public life that is something other than the juxtaposition and the protection of countless private lives. The situation of modern intellectuals is, in this regard, very different from that of Bossuet's contemporaries. The latter made themselves the interpreters of the divine word; the former, the interpreters, of public opinion. The former become directly involved in politics; the latter—with an effect that was less immediate, but can last longer—remained essentially within an ideological debate. The old "clerk" acted on the wielders of power themselves; today, the typical intellectual is not an adviser to the prince, but addresses all of society, which he would rather represent than the state (when such a choice presents itself). The media thus have a vital role to play in establishing contact between the intellectual and his society—books and the press, radio and television: their diversity is indispensable to free expression. Contrary to what Benda thought (but he had elitist tastes), the daily paper favors, rather than impedes, democracy.

What then becomes of the different functions of the intellectual that we have identified over the last two centuries? The role of guide and prophet seems to have fallen into disuse (assuming that this role was ever anything other than a poet's dream). Democracy mistrusts inspired guides; it elects its own prosaically, by means of universal suffrage. Rather than praising its poets as prophets, our society lowers prophets to the level of poets. And if, on a particular question, we seek a competent opinion, we ask the poet or the scholar—considered then as a "pure expert," rather than as an intellectual.

The role of "avenger" and of "naysayer" has also been compromised, although for different reasons. By rejecting today's society as a whole, by execrating it and denying it in its very principle, we become the defenders of a radically different society. Efforts to replace the democratic principle with another principle—fascist or communist utopianisms—have ended in failure: the cure has been revealed to be worse than the disease. The possibility of a rejection remains, now not in the name of a radiant future, but in the name of a return to the past; conservatives replace revolutionaries in their attacks against democracy, rationalism, and humanism ("blame it on Descartes, blame it on Condorcet"). And we must admit that the conservative position is often adopted, under various guises, by modern intellectuals—whether as a certain nostalgia for the Old Regime, or even for ancient Greece, or ecology and third worldism—but it still implies adhering to what Louis Dumont has called "holistic values": an attachment to the hierarchy, a privileging of the social over the economic, a tightening of community ties, and the idea of harmony with nature.

A third and final possibility does exist, which one could call the critical function, and which seems particularly appropriate to the contemporary era (even if each of these functions—prophet, avenger, and critic—exists throughout our history). The difference between a critical attitude and the attitude of the "naysayers" is that the latter turn to either the future or the past to judge and condemn the present, whereas the former refer to the constitutive principles of present society—in this instance, democratic principles—in order to criticize their imperfect realization in everyday life. Our world is far from homogeneous; it is constantly being affected by a variety of movements, all of which claim these constitutive principles as their own. The fight for women's rights, for example, has led to half the population's acquiring the same legal status as the other half. Another example is the integration of immigrants, independent of their religious beliefs, their language, or their skin color. In a somewhat similar fashion, critical intellectuals are not content to belong to society; rather they act on it, by attempting to make it closer to the ideal in which they already believe. They judge present society not from without, but by reviving the intensity of its principles; they call not for a radical revolution, nor for a return to the past, but for the reanimation of an ideal that has been extinguished. To act in such a way is more than a right: it is a duty imposed on them by the very position they occupy in the heart of democratic society.

Clearly, there is nothing new in this portrait of the critical intellectual, since it is the same as that of the first intellectual celebrated by Western tradition: Socrates himself. According to the *Apologia* of his disciple Plato, Socrates refused two alternatives. On the one hand, he did not want to participate directly in the government of his city, and he refused political duties when offered to, or even imposed on, him. Nor, however, did he accept to be completely disinterested in the affairs of the city, and to withdraw into an entirely contemplative life. It is impossible for me to keep still, he claimed; and even if I had been forbidden to do so, I would have continued to philosophize. For Socrates, this did not mean commenting on the philosophers of the past, but rather criticizing public life as it existed around him, and devising recommendations. It is, in fact, precisely because Socrates never wanted to forsake the possibility of criticizing and fighting for justice that he refused to enter into active political life. If I were to do so, he said, I would die quickly; opposition with other political men would be unavoidable and merciless. Criticism and struggle nevertheless had a limit for Socrates; even when he was unjustly condemned, he refused to flee and preferred obeying the laws of his city.

Socrates, who neither participated in political power nor scorned public life, found a strange metaphor with which to describe his function. He saw himself as if he were

> something stuck on the state by the god . . . ; for the state is like a big thoroughbred horse, so big that he is a bit slow and heavy, and wants a gadfly to wake him up. I think the god put me on the state something like that, to wake you up and persuade you each and every one, as I keep settling on you everywhere all day long. (*Apology*, 30e, 436–37)

To play the role of the gadfly, to be the goad in society: this is what the role of modern intellectuals could be, if they are not too afraid of suffering Socrates' fate.

# Works Cited

Aguilar, F. de. *Relacion breve de la conquista de la Nueva España.* Mexico, 1954.

Aristotle. *On Rhetoric.* Trans. George A. Kennedy. New York: Oxford University Press, 1991.

Aron, Raymond. *Introduction à la philosophie de l'histoire.* Paris: Gallimard, 1981.

———. Introduction. In Max Weber, *Le Savant et le politique.* Paris: 10/18, 1982, 5–52.

Augé, Marc. *La Traversée du Luxembourg.* Paris: Hachette, 1985.

Barrès, Maurice. *Scènes et doctrines du nationalisme.* 2 vols. l985. Paris: Juver, 1902.

Bayle, Pierre. *Commentaire philosophique.* In *Oeuvres diverses,* vol. 2. The Hague, 1725.

Beauvoir, Simone de. "La Pensée de droite aujourd'hui." *Les Temps modernes,* 1955.

Benda, Julien. *La Trahison des clercs.* Paris: Jean-Jacques Pauvert, [1927] 1965. [*The Betrayal of the Intellectuals,* trans. Richard Aldington. Boston: Beacon, 1955.]

Bénichou, Paul. *Les Mages romantiques.* Paris: Gallimard, 1988.

———. *Le Sacre de l'écrivain.* Paris: Jose Corti, 1973.

———. *Le Temps des prophètes.* Paris: Gallimard, 1977.

Berdiaev, N. *Un nouveau Moyen Age.* Paris: Plon, 1927.

Bloch, Marc. *Apologie pour l'histoire, ou Métier d'historien.* Paris: A. Colion, 1949.

Bonald, Louis de. *De la chretienté et du christianisme.* In *Oeuvres,* vol. 12. 1830.

———. *Démonstration philosophique du principe constitutif de la societé.* 1830.

———. "Discours du 9 juillet 1821." In *De l'opposition dans le gouvernement et de la liberté de la presse.* 1827.

———. "Discours du 7 juillet 1821." In *Oeuvres.* 1830.

———. *Encore un mot sur la liberté de la presse.* 1814.

———. *Essai analytique sur les lois naturelles.* 1840.

———. *Législation primitive.* 3 vols. 1829.

———. *Mélanges littéraires, politiques et philosophiques.* 2 vols. 1838.

———. *Pensées sur divers sujets et discours politiques.* 2 vols. 1817.

———. *Théorie du pouvoir politique et religieux.* 3 vols. 1854.

Cabeza de Vaca, Albar Nuñez. *Naufragios y comemtarios.* Madrid: Taurus, 1969. [French translation: *Naufrages et commentaires.* Paris: Fayard, 1980. English translation: *Adventures in the Unknown Interior of America.* New York: Collier Books, 1961.]

Césaire, Aimé. *Discourse on Colonialism.* Trans. Joan Pinkham. New York: Monthly Review Press, [1955] 1972.

Charton, E. (ed). *Voyageurs anciens et modernes.* Vol. 3. 1863.

Chateaubriand, François-René de. *Mémoires d'outre-tombe.* 2 vols. Paris: Ministère de l'Education Nationale, 1972.

Cicero, Marcus Tullius. *De l'orateur.* 3 vols. Paris: Les Belles Lettres, 1966.

Columbus, Christopher. *Oeuvres.* Paris: Gallimard, 1961.

Condorcet, Marie-Jean-Antoine-Nicolas de Caritat, Marquis de. "Discours de réception à l'Académie française." In *Oeuvres.* 12 vols. Paris: F. Didot Frères, 1847–49, vol. 1.

———. *Esquisse d'un tableau historique des progrès de l'esprit humain.* Paris: Editions sociales, 1971.

———. "Vie de Turgot." In *Oeuvres*. 12 vols. Paris: F. Didot Frères, 1847–49, vol. 5.

Constant, Benjamin. "Commentaire sur G. Filangieri." In *Oeuvres*. 3 vols. 1840, vol. 3.

———. *Cours de politique constitutionnelle*. 2 vols. 1861.

———. *Oeuvres*. Paris: Gallimard, 1979.

———. *Principes de politique*. 2 vols. Geneva: Droz, 1980.

———. *Recueil d'articles. Le Mercure, la Minerve et la Renommée*. 2 vols. Geneva: Droz, 1972.

Dante Alighieri. *Divina Commedia*. Trans. Charles S. Singleton. 3 vols. Princeton, N.J.: Princeton University Press, 1970–75.

Diderot, Denis. "Supplement to Bougainville's 'Voyage.'" In *Rameau's Nephew and Other Works*. Trans. Jacques Barzun and Ralph H. Bowen. Garden City, N.Y.: Doubleday, 1956.

*D'une culture à l'autre. Le Français dans le monde,* 181 (1983).

Dumont, Louis. *Essais sur l'individualisme*. Paris: Seuil, 1983.

Eliot, T. S. *The Idea of a Christian Society*. New York: Harcourt, Brace, 1940.

———. "The Humanism of Irving Babbitt." In *Selected Prose*. London: Faber & Faber, 1975.

Emerson, Ralph Waldo. *English Traits*. Boston: J. R. Osgood, 1876.

Fanon, Frantz. *The Wretched of the Earth*. Preface by Jean-Paul Sartre. Trans. Constance Farrington. New York: Grove, 1968.

Fénelon, François de Salignac de la Mothe de. *Les Aventures de Télémaque*. Paris: Garnier, 1987.

Foley, Frederic J. *The Great Formosan Impostor*. Taipei: Mei Ya, 1968.

Frye, Northrop. *Anatomy of Criticism*. Princeton, N.J.: Princeton University Press, 1957.

Gérando, Joseph Marie de. *The Observation of Savage Peoples*. Trans. F. C. T. Moore. Berkeley: University of California Press, 1969.

Gobineau, Joseph-Arthur de. *Essai sur l'inégalité des races humaines*. Vol. 1 of *Oeuvres*. Paris: Gallimard (Pléiade), 1983.

Goethe, Johann Wolfgang von. *Ecrits sur l'art*. Selected, annotated, and translated by Jean-Marie Schaeffer with an introduction by Tzvetan Todorov. Paris: Klincksieck, 1983.

*Goethes Briefwechsel mit W. und A. von Humboldt*. Berlin, 1909.

Goldschmidt, Victor. *Ecrits*. 2 vols. Paris: Vrin, 1984.

Gunnard, A. *Trois ans d'esclavage chez les Patagons*. Paris: Aubier-Montaigne, 1979.

Helvétius, Claude-Arien. *De l'esprit; or, Essays on the Mind and Its Several Faculties*. London: Dodsley, 1759.

Herodotus. *Herodotus*. Trans. A. D. Godley. 4 vols. Cambridge, Mass.: Harvard University Press (Loeb Classical Library), 1920.

*Histoire des ouvrages des savans*. November 1704.

Jennings, Francis. *The Invasion of America*. New York: Norton, 1976.

Julien, Charles-André. *Les Voyages de découverte et les premiers établissements (XVe–XVIe s.)*. Paris: PUF, 1948.

Kant, Emmanuel. *Critique of Pure Reason*. Trans. Norman Kemp Smith. New York: St. Martin's Press, 1965.

La Bruyère, J. de. *Oeuvres complètes*. Paris: Gallimard, 1951.

Lamartine, Alphonse de. *A Pilgrimage to the Holy Land*. Vols. 1 and 2. Philadelphia: Carey, Lea & Blanchard, 1835.

Lanson, Gustave. *Méthodes de l'histoire littéraire*. Paris: Société d'édition "Les Belles Lettres," 1925.

———. "L'Unité de la pensée de Jean-Jacques Rousseau." In *Annales de la Societé Jean-Jacques Rousseau,* 8 (1912): 1–31.

Las Casas, Bartolomé de. *Historia de las Indias*. Ed. Augustín Millares Carlo. Mexico City: Fondo de Cultura Económica, 1951.

———. "Lettre au prince Philippe." In *Las Casas et la défense des Indiens*. Paris: Julliard, coll. "Archives," 1971.

Leroy-Beaulieu, Paul. *De la colonisation chez les peuples modernes*. 2 vols. Paris: Alcan, 1902.

Lessing, Gotthold Ephraim. *Hamburg Dramaturgy*. Trans. Hellen Zimmern. New York: Dover, 1962.

Levillier, Roberto. *America la Bien Llamada*. Buenos Aires: Kraft, 1948.

Locke, John. *An Essay concerning Human Understanding*. New York: Dover, 1959.

———. *A Letter concerning Toleration*. Ed. and intro. James H. Tully. Indianapolis: Hackett, 1983.

Machiavelli, Niccolo. *The Prince*. Trans. Luigi Ricci, rev. E. R. P. Vincent. New York: New American Library, 1952.

Magnaghi, Alberto. *Amerigo Vespucci. Studio critico*. Rome, 1948.

Marcuse, Herbert. "Repressive Tolerance." In *A Critique of Pure Tolerance*. Ed. Robert Paul Wolff. Boston: Beacon, 1965.

Marrou, Henri-Irenée. *De la connaissance historique*. Paris: Seuil, 1960.

Martyr D'Anghiera, Peter. *De orbe novo. Les huits decades*. Paris, 1907. [*The Decade of the Newe Worlde or West India*. Ann Arbor, Mich.: University Microfilms, 1966.]

Marx, Karl. *The Eighteenth Brumaire of Louis Bonaparte*. New York: International Publishers, 1963.

Michaux, Henri. *Ecuador: A Travel Journal*. Trans. Robin Magowan. London: Peter Owen, 1970.

———. *Un Barbare en Asie*. Paris: Gallimard, 1982.

Mikhov, N. *La Bulgarie et son peuple d'après les temoignages étrangers, I. Extraits des publications françaises*. Lausanne: Libraire centrale des nationalités, 1918.

Milosz, Czeslaw. *The Captive Mind*. Trans. Jane Zielonko. New York: Vintage, 1990.

Montaigne, Michel de. *The Complete Essays of Montaigne*. Trans. Donald Frame. Stanford, Calif.: Stanford University Press, 1958.

Montesquieu, C. de. *Considérations sur les causes de la grandeur des Romains et de leur décadence; De l'esprit des lois; Mes pensées*. In *Oeuvres complètes*. Paris: Seuil, 1964.

———. *Lettres*. In *Oeuvres complètes*. Vol. 3. Paris: Nagel, 1955.

Moulinie, Henri. *De Bonald*. 1915.

Novalis. *Oeuvres complètes*. 2 vols. Paris: Gallimard, 1975.

O'Gorman, Edmundo. *La invencion de America*. Mexico, 1958. [*The Invention of America: An Inquiry into the Historical Nature of the New World and the Meaning of Its History*. Bloomington: Indiana University Press, 1961.]

Pascal, Blaise. *Pensées*. Paris: Garnier, 1964.

Plato. *Apology* and *The Republic*. In *The Great Dialogues of Plato*. Trans. W. H. D. Rouse, ed. Eric H. Warmington and Philip G. Rouse. New York: A Mentor Book, New American Library, 1956.

———. *Gorgias*. In *The Dialogues of Plato*. Trans. B. Jowett. Vol. 1. New York: Random House, 1920.

———. *Phaedrus*. Trans. with an introduction and commentary by R. Hackworth. New York: Cambridge University Press, 1990.

Popper, Karl Raimond. *The Open Society and Its Enemies: The High Tide of Prophecy*. Princeton, N.J.: Princeton University Press, 1966.

Psalmanazar, George. *An Historical and Geographical Description of Formosa*. London: "Printed for Dan. Brown, at the Black Swan without Temple-Bar; G. Strahn, and W. Davis, in Cornhill; and Fran. Coggan, in the Inner-Temple-Lane," 1704.

———. *Memoirs*. London: Printed for the executrix. Sold by R. Davis, in Picadilly; J. Newbery, in St. Paul's Church-Yard; L. Davis and C. Reymers in Holborn; 1764.

Quintilian. *The Institutio Oratoria of Quintilian.* 4 vols. Trans. H. E. Butler. New York: G. P. Putnam's Sons, 1933.

*Récits aztèques de la conquête.* Texts selected and presented by G. Baudot and T. Todorov. Paris: Seuil, 1983.

Renan, Ernest. *The Future of Science.* Boston: Roberts Brothers, 1891.

———. *Philosophical Dialogues and Fragments.* Trans. Râs Bihârî Mukharjî. London: Trübner, 1883.

———. "Lettre à Gobineau" (June 26, 1856). In *Oeuvres complètes,* vol. 10, 203–5.

Rousseau, Jean-Jacques. *Emile.* In *Oeuvres complètes.* Vol. 4. Paris: Gallimard, 1969.

———. *Lettre à M. D'Alembert sur les spectacles.* Geneva: Droz, 1948.

———. *On the Origin of Language.* Trans. John H. Moran and Alexander Gode. New York: Frederick Ungar, 1966.

———. *Rousseau juge de Jean-Jacques.* In *Oeuvres complètes.* Vol. 1.

Sade, Donatien-Alphonse-François, Marquis de. *The Complete Justine, Philosophy in the Bedroom, and Other Writings.* Trans. Richard Seaver and Austyn Wainhouse. New York: Grove Press, [1795] 1965.

Sahagun, Fray Bernardino de. *Florentine Codex.* Trans. Charles E. Dibble and Arthur J. O. Anderson. Santa Fe: Monographs of the School of American Research and Museum of New Mexico, 1979.

Sergheraert, G. *Présence de la Bulgarie dans les lettres françaises expliquée par l'histoire.* 3 vols. 1963–71.

Shafarevich, Igor. *The Socialist Phenomenon.* Trans. William Tjalsma. New York: Harper & Row, 1980.

Solzhenitsyn, A. I. *The World Split Apart: Commencement Address Delivered at Harvard University, June 8, 1978.* New York: Harper & Row, 1978.

———. *Message d'exil.* Paris: Seuil, 1979.

———. *Nos pluralistes.* Paris: Fayard, 1983.

Soyinka, Wole. "Discours à Stockholm." In *Lettre internationale* 12 (1987).

Spinoza, Benedictus de. *Ethics.* Trans. Andrew Boyle, rev. G. H. R. Parkinson. London: J. M. Dent & Sons, 1989.

———. *Traité theologico-politique.* Paris: Garnier-Flammarion, 1965.

Staden, Hans. *Nus, féroces et anthropophages.* Paris: A.-M. Metailie, 1979.

Stalin, Joseph. In Patrick Seriot, *Analyse du discours politique sovietique.* Paris: Institut d'etudes slaves, 1985.

Stanley, Henry Morton. *How I Found Livingstone.* New York: Scribner, Armstrong, 1872.

———. *Through the Dark Continent.* London: George Newnes, 1899.

Stendhal. *On Love.* Garden City, N.Y.: Doubleday, 1957.

Strauss, Leo. *Natural Right and History.* Chicago: University of Chicago Press, 1953.

Tacitus, Cornelius. *Dialogue des orateurs.* Paris: Les Belles Lettres, 1967.

Taguieff, Pierre-André. *La Force du préjugé. Essai sur le racisme et ses doubles.* Paris: La Decouverte, 1988.

Taine, Hippolyte. *Derniers essais de critique et d'histoire.* Paris: Hachette, 1894.

———. *Essais de critique et d'histoire.* Paris: Hachette, 1923.

———. *Histoire de la littérature anglaise.* 12th ed. 5 vols. Paris: Hachette, [1864] 1905–6.

Thucydides. *History of the Peloponnesian War.* Trans. Rex Warner. Baltimore: Penguin Books, 1972.

Tocqueville, Alexis de. *Oeuvres complètes.* 16 vols. Paris: Gallimard, 1951–89.

Todorov, Tzvetan. *La Conquête de l'Amerique: La Question de l'autre.* Paris: Seuil, 1982. [*The Conquest of America: The Question of the Other.* Trans. Richard Howard. New York: Harper & Row, 1984.]

————. *Mikhail Bakhtin: The Dialogical Principle*. Trans. Wlad Godzich. Minneapolis: University of Minnesota Press, 1984.

————. *Nous et les autres: La réflexion française sur la diversité humaine*. Paris: Seuil, 1989. [*On Human Diversity: Nationalism, Racism, and Exoticism in French Thought*. Trans. Catherine Porter. Cambridge, Mass.: Harvard University Press, 1993.]

Valéry, Paul. *Regards sur le monde actuel*. Paris: Gallimard, 1962.

Vespucci, Amerigo. *El Nuevo Mundo*. Buenos Aires, 1951.

Vigand, H. *Americ Vespuce*. 1917.

Voltaire. *Candide*. Trans. Robert M. Adams. Norton Critical Edition.

————. *Dictionnaire philosophique, Traité de la tolerance*. In *Oeuvres complètes*. 1878–79. Vols. 18 and 25.

Waley, Arthur. *Three Ways of Thought in Ancient China*. Garden City, N.Y.: Doubleday, 1956.

# Index

Compiled by Robin Jackson

**Tzvetan Todorov** is Maître de Recherches at the Centre National de la Recherche Scientifique in Paris and has been visiting professor at various North American universities. He is also the author of numerous books on literary theory, the history of thought, and analyses of culture. The University of Minnesota Press has published his *Introduction to Poetics* (1981) and *Mikhail Bakhtin: The Dialogical Principle* (1984).

**Alyson Waters** has a Ph.D. in comparative literature from the Graduate School of the City University of New York and is currently on the faculty of the Department of French at Yale University and is managing editor of *Yale French Studies*. She has translated numerous articles and essays for a variety of publications, including *Zone* and *Art in America*. Her translation of Louis Aragon's *Treatise on Style* appeared in 1991.